Jane T. van Gelder

The Storehouses of the King

Or, The pyramids of Egypt, what they are and who built them

Jane T. van Gelder

The Storehouses of the King
Or, The pyramids of Egypt, what they are and who built them

ISBN/EAN: 9783743407381

Manufactured in Europe, USA, Canada, Australia, Japa

Cover: Foto ©ninafisch / pixelio.de

Manufactured and distributed by brebook publishing software (www.brebook.com)

Jane T. van Gelder

The Storehouses of the King

THE
STOREHOUSES OF THE KING.

THE
STOREHOUSES OF THE KING

OR

THE PYRAMIDS OF EGYPT

WHAT THEY ARE AND WHO BUILT THEM

BY

JANE VAN GELDER

(*née* TRILL)

And I heard a voice in the midst of the four beasts say, A measure of wheat for a penny, and three measures of barley for a penny; and see thou hurt not the oil and the wine.—*Revelation* vi. 6.

LONDON: W. H. ALLEN & CO., 13 WATERLOO PLACE.
1885.

(*All Rights reserved.*)

LONDON:
PRINTED BY W. H. ALLEN AND CO., 13 WATERLOO PLACE, S.W.

THIS VOLUME

IS RESPECTFULLY INSCRIBED

TO

EGYPTOLOGISTS AND FREEMASONS
OF ALL NATIONS,

BY

THE DISCOVERER OF WHAT THE STONE PYRAMIDS OF EGYPT ARE,

AND WHO BUILT THEM,

THE AUTHOR.

PREFACE.

The Pyramids have been reckoned among the wonders of the world, and every effort has been made to discover for what purpose they were constructed, and by whom they were built.

Their immense size, their solid construction, the lonely positions in which they are placed, add to the amazement of the spectator.

Many conjectures and assertions have been made regarding them. Some assert they were the tombs of the kings of Egypt, and others differ, and say they were built for astronomical purposes; and those who give up guessing or speculating regarding them, consider they were the tokens of the folly and tyranny of the rulers of Egypt.

All travellers, and learned men and women who have visited these gigantic monuments, admit their grandeur, and admire their sublimity.

Many expeditions have been sent to Egypt for the purpose of gaining information regarding these Pyramids; and many public and private individuals have spent princely fortunes in exploring them ; and on almost every occasion a book has been written, and given to the world, showing the result of each expedition. Everything that could possibly be said and written regarding these relics of antiquity has been given forth to the world in all languages, from the remotest times till the present day.

It is now the pleasant task of the author to state that the vexed question may be set at rest, as the solution to the mystery has been found. The discovery was made whilst reading the latest works on the Pyramids; she recognised some features in the interior of the Great Pyramid, and recalled to mind for what purpose such passages have been used, and followed up the incident by reading more carefully every book, and examining all the illustrations showing the interior and the exterior of the noble buildings, till ultimately there remained not the shadow of a doubt that the discovery was real. The sensation after the removal of doubt was painful. When this sensation of amazement and wonder had passed away, a feeling of gratitude took possession of the mind.

This memorable discovery was made in August 1880. Began writing this work on the 20th August and finished it on the 30th November.* The entire work has been begun and brought to a conclusion without the assistance of any person.

* It was revised, and two-thirds rewritten by the author in October and November 1884.

The narrative connected with the Pyramids is most touching; on that account the writer proposes giving the life of the builder as she describes these wonderful monuments of antiquity. She has never attempted writing for publication before, therefore she humbly prays the reader to be indulgent and to overlook all errors and shortcomings, and to believe that this volume is brought before the world simply to uphold the truth of the Holy Bible which has recorded the narrative; and the appositeness of St. Paul's assertion, that God hath chosen the foolish things of the world to confound the wise; and God hath chosen the weak things of the world to confound the things which are mighty; and base things of the world, and things which are despised, hath God chosen, yea, and things which are not, to bring to nought the things that are.

CONTENTS.

Chap.		Page.
I.	Joseph—the Builder	1
II.	Moses—the Recorder	16
III.	Tower of Babel—the Model	38
IV.	The Pyramids as Granaries	49
V.	The Hebrews in Egypt	58
VI.	The Sphinx—the Entrance	75
VII.	Mission of Moses in the East	86
VIII.	Mission of Moses in the West	123
IX.	Granaries of the Ancient World	162
X.	Death of Moses	189
XI.	Record of Famines	198
XII.	Apotheosis of Moses	237

APPENDICES—

I.	The Great Famine in Egypt	247
II.	The Translation of the Septuagint	273
III.	Herodotus on the Pyramids of Egypt	296
IV.	On the Hebrew and Grecian Feast of First-Fruits	298
V.	Predictions concerning Egypt	308

THE STOREHOUSES OF THE KING.

CHAPTER I.

JOSEPH—THE BUILDER.

JOSEPH was the son of Jacob's old age, and consequently he loved him more than any of his other sons, by which Joseph incurred the envy and hatred of his brothers, and they, knowing that the lad carried evil reports of their conduct to their father, determined to do him some harm. Besides, Joseph was always having strange dreams, which he related to his father in the presence of his brothers, which dreams were interpreted to mean some great advancement in the life of the dreamer. The brothers watched for an opportunity to get rid of this favourite child. The opportunity presented itself, and they availed themselves of it. Jacob sent Joseph to see the state of affairs in the field where the flocks were fed, and to bring him word; so Joseph, in obedience to his father's command, went, and when the brothers who were guarding the flocks saw him approaching, they agreed to kill him. But one of the elder ones said that it would be a great sin to shed the blood of their relative, and that it would be better to throw him into a pit and leave him there to die; to which suggestion the rest consented. When Joseph came up to them, they insulted him, and stripped him of the coat which his father, in his fondness for him, had made for him, and, unheeding the lad's cries and remonstrances, they threw him into a pit. After this cruel deed, the men went to their meal; and whilst eating it they saw a caravan of Ishmaelites, and to them they sold Joseph, who was taken out of the pit and given to them. The Ishmaelites, fearing that Joseph was not a slave, judging from his handsome face and noble carriage, sold him to a company of Midianites, merchants going down to Egypt. When these merchants arrived in Egypt, they sold him as a slave to an Egyptian nobleman. Here he was kindly treated by his master, who had confidence in his integrity, and was made an overseer of his master's property. Joseph was seventeen years old when he was taken away from his home and country, and his father mourned for him as dead. This took place in the year 1728 B.C.

The ways of the Almighty God are mysterious, and far above human comprehension. God blessed Joseph, and he grew into man's estate goodly and well-favoured.

His master's wife noticed him and became madly enamoured; losing all self-control, she made criminal advances to him, which he repelled, and entreated her to remember that he was her husband's trusted servant, and that she should not induce him to commit such wickedness against his master and sin in the sight of God. She still persisted, till at last she used force, and he fled from her presence, leaving a piece of his coat by which she held him. Seeing that he was not to be overcome, she hated him, and, to revenge herself on him, she reversed the story and told it to her husband, who, believing her tale, became very angry with Joseph and prosecuted him. Though the Court wherein he was tried found him innocent, yet the nobleman persuaded the judge to place Joseph in confinement, that his wife's conduct might not be made public; and, as Joseph had neither friends nor means, he was helpless, and consequently was sent to prison, where he remained many years.

In his solitude, the mind of the captive must have often recalled scenes of home, and all the lessons that he had learnt orally—as was the custom in the East—and remembered the great deeds and renown of his ancestors, and the marvellous acts of God towards Noah and Abraham and Isaac, and his own father Jacob, who was surnamed by God Israel. In regarding his miserable condition he must have thought of the visit to Egypt of his great-grandfather, Abraham, who came as a prince, and was treated by the king as his friend; and how the king, when he found he was misinformed by Abraham regarding his wife, made honourable amends, and gave him flocks and herds as presents; and when the famine in Canaan was over, he and his wife and their nephew left Egypt in state (the Egyptian historians call these visitors "Shepherd Kings"); and how when there was another famine in Canaan, in the lifetime of

Isaac, there was corn in Egypt, and Isaac would have visited Egypt as did his father, but that he was forbidden by God.

Thus time sped till Joseph was thirty years old, when Pharaoh, King of Egypt, was warned in dreams of the approach of the great and memorable famine, which was to last seven long years, during which time the earth would make its sabbath, and produce no food for man or beast. It was then that the unhappy captive was remembered by a fellow-prisoner, whose dream Joseph had interpreted, and which was realised as he predicted ; so that, when all the wise men of Egypt could not tell the King the meaning of his dreams, and when the King in his disappointed rage was about to condemn them to death, Joseph was called.

He was taken from the prison and brought before the King, who, seeing in him a superior deportment and a stately person, came down from his throne and addressed him as an equal; he told him his dreams, and said there was none who could interpret them, and that he had heard that he understood dreams and could interpret them. Joseph answered the King with humility, and told him what was the will of God regarding the land of Egypt ; that there would be seven years of great plenty throughout all the land of Egypt, and after them seven years of famine; that all the plenty would be forgotten in the land of Egypt, and the famine would consume the land. Joseph advised Pharaoh to look out for a man discreet and wise, and set him over the land of Egypt; to appoint officers over the land, and to take up the fifth part of the produce of the land of

Egypt in the seven plenteous years; to let them gather all the food of those good years that were to come, and lay up corn under the hand of Pharaoh, and let them keep food in the cities, that it might be for store to the land against the seven years of famine which should be in the land of Egypt, that the land might not perish through the famine.

Pharaoh was greatly pleased, both at the interpretation and the advice; and, as there was none like him, in whom was the spirit of God, Pharaoh made Joseph the Viceroy of Egypt; and Pharaoh took off his ring from his hand and put it upon Joseph's hand, and arrayed him in vestures of fine linen, and put a gold chain about his neck; and he made him ride in the second chariot which he had, and the people cried before him, "Bow the knee!" or "Bend the knee!" and Pharaoh made him ruler of all the land of Egypt.

And Pharaoh said unto Joseph, "I am Pharaoh, and without thee shall no man lift up his hand or foot in all the land of Egypt." And Pharaoh called Joseph's name Zaphnath-paaneah, or "Preserver of the Age."

Consequently Joseph had absolute power vested in him. The King also gave him to wife Asenath, the daughter of Potipherah, priest of On. And Joseph went throughout all the land of Egypt. And in the seven plenteous years the earth brought forth by handfuls. And he gathered up all the food of the seven years, which were in the land of Egypt, and laid up the food in the cities; the food of the field, which was round about every city, laid he up in the same. And Joseph gathered corn as the sand of the sea, very much, until he left off numbering; for it was without number.

The land of Egypt is six hundred miles long, and is bounded by two ranges of naked limestone hills which sometimes approach, and sometimes retire from each other, leaving between them an average breadth of seven miles. Northwards they part and finally disappear, giving place to a marshy meadow plain which extends to the Mediterranean coast. To the south they are no longer of limestone, but of granite; they narrow to a point; they close till they almost touch; and through the mountain gate thus formed the river Nile leaps with a roar into the valley, and runs due north towards the sea. This land and its neighbourhood was first inhabited by the descendants of Ham, the third son of Noah; Mizraim, the second son of Ham, occupied Egypt. The noble river Nile is recorded in the Scriptures as the second river which parted from the main stream which went out of Eden to water the garden where Adam and Eve were placed by their Creator.

In the winter and spring it rolls a languid stream through a dry and dusty plain; but in the summer an extraordinary thing happens. The river grows troubled and swift, it turns red and then green; it rises, it swells, till at length, overflowing its banks, it covers the adjoining lands to the base of the hills on either side. The whole valley becomes a lake, from which the villages rise like islands, for they are built on artificial mounds. The land of Egypt is by nature a rainless desert, which the Nile, the mysterious Nile only, converts into a fruitful garden every year.

The task that Joseph had been entrusted with was stupendous. He had to build storehouses that would contain all the fifth part of the produce of the plenteous years of the fertile land of Egypt that were gathered up during the seven years. Before he set himself to the building of these vast receptacles he must have searched for models, and whilst doing this the building of the Tower of Babel must have come to his recollection, for the father of Abraham was the chief officer of King Nimrod who built it. This was a grand model, and that he followed it is evident from what we see in the Pyramids, or Storehouses of the King, in this, the nineteenth century of our Lord.

When the Temple at Jerusalem was about to be built by Solomon, he must have read how the storehouses were built, and he must have been aware for what use they were intended, as well as by whom they were built. Solomon married the daughter of Pharaoh, King of Egypt, and as son-in-law of the King he must have had free access to all the secret buildings and records of the land of Egypt.

This is the account of the building of the Temple: Solomon laid the foundations of the Temple very deep in the rock of Moriah, and the materials were strong stones, and such as would resist the force of time; these were to unite themselves with the rock, and become a basis and a sure foundation for that superstructure which was to be erected over it. They were to be so strong in order to sustain with ease those vast superstructures and precious ornaments, whose own weight was to be not less than the weight of those other high and heavy buildings which the King designed to be very ornamental and magnificent. He erected its entire body, quite up to the roof, of white stone; its height was sixty cubits, its length was the same, and its breadth was twenty. There was another building erected over it, equal to it in its measures, so that the entire altitude of the Temple was a hundred and twenty cubits. Its front was to the east.

Now the whole structure of the Temple was made, with great skill, of polished stones, laid together so very harmoniously and smoothly that there appeared to the spectators no signs of any hammer, or other instrument of architecture, but as if, without any use of them, the materials had naturally united themselves together, the agreement of one part with another seeming rather to be natural, than to have arisen from the force of tools upon them. The King also had a fine contrivance for an ascent to the upper room over the Temple, and that was by steps in the thickness of its wall ; for it had no large door on the east end, as the lower house had, but the entrances were by the sides, through very small doors. He also overlaid the Temple, both within and without, with boards of cedar, that were kept close together by thick chains, so that this contrivance was in the nature of a support and strength to the building.|

The Temple was built on the crown of Moriah, "the threshing floor of Ornan the Jebusite" (2 Chr. iii. 1), with a surrounding platform six hundred and twelve feet square. The building called the Naos would seem to have stood on the summit of the rock, in which graduated platforms were cut, forming the courts of the Jews and women. The Naos was small (sixty by twenty cubits), and was divided into the Holy of Holies and Holy Place, the former used once a year, the latter occupied only by the priests performing daily service. In the former was the Ark; in the latter the altar of incense, with the table of Shewbread on its one side, and golden candlestick on the other. These two parts were separated by a veil, which was rent at the crucifixion (Matt. xxvii. 51). The court of the Gentiles surrounded the Naos, but was on a lower platform, separated by a trellis fence. The Naos was, like Mount Sinai, the sanctuary of Jehovah, fenced off from the Gentiles' court, the plain below.

Solomon must have referred to the discovery that he had made regarding these buildings (the Pyramids) and to the builder of them, when he said: "Better is a poor and a wise child than an old and foolish king, who will no more be admonished. For out of prison he cometh to reign; whereas also he that is born in his kingdom becometh poor" (Eccl. iv. 13, 14).

Joseph built these storehouses near the fields of every city, according to the size of the city and the number of its inhabitants. In the north, near the Delta, he built many and large, according to the amount of corn the fields there yielded. He was occupied seven years in building them, and during the time thus occupied, he must often have recalled the fond memories of home, and of his aged father, and his youngest brother, the son of his deceased mother; and doubtless the three largest Pyramids of Jeezeh he dedicated to the memory of his ancestors, Abraham, Isaac, and Jacob.

So Joseph laid the foundations of each storehouse very deep in the rock on which it was built, and the materials were strong stones, such as would resist the force of time ; these were to unite themselves with the rock, and become a basis and a sure foundation for that superstructure which was to be erected over it. They were to be so strong in order to sustain with ease those vast superstructures whose own weight was to be not less than the weight of the casing stones which he designed to be used. He erected its entire body, quite up to the roof, of stone. Its base was square, the sides rising up slantwise, till there was only a small square aperture left unfinished; these sides were in steps, so that the labourers could ascend to the aperture.

The interior had chambers for the officers to reckon the quantity of corn stored, and for the measure a stone coffer or box to measure the corn with. There were vast chasms and receptacles with passages like tubes leading to them, all the length from the walls, with their mouths outside the walls, which Egyptologists call air passages, so that the men could get to them from the exterior by the steps. The corn was thrown into these vast spaces from outside, from the apertures in the sides, and the aperture at the summit. When the whole receptacle was well filled with the corn, which was as plentiful as the sand of the sea, then all the apertures were stopped with stones, like stoppers of bottles, made for the purpose. The side steps were then encased, from the base to the summit, with large casing stones, so that the sides became level, and, with the coatings of cement, the entire building outside became level and smooth, and the top in a peak.

The corn within this grand storehouse was hermetically sealed, utterly impervious to the sun, rain, and wind. The doors of it, as in Solomon's temple, were small, and in the sides. Now the whole of this structure was made, with great skill, of stones, and those laid together so very harmoniously and smoothly that there appeared to the spectators no signs of any hammer or other instrument of architecture, but as if, without any use of them, the materials had naturally united themselves together, the agreement of one part with another seeming rather to be natural than to have arisen from the force of tools upon them.

The foresight and discretion of Joseph were rewarded by Pharaoh, who gave him the powers of a king and the attributes of a god.

And the seven years of plenteousness that was in the land of Egypt were ended, according as Joseph had said, and the dearth was in all lands; but in all the land of Egypt there was bread. And the famine was over all the face of the earth. Joseph opened all the storehouses, and sold corn unto the Egyptians; and all countries came into Egypt to Joseph to buy corn, because the famine was sore in all lands. Now Joseph's thoughts reverted to his father's home, and he knew that his brothers would be obliged to come to Egypt to purchase food, for the famine was very grievous in the land of Canaan. He gave orders that no man desiring corn should send his servant to purchase it, but that the head of each family should personally appear as a purchaser; he also proclaimed that no man should be allowed to purchase corn in

Egypt to sell it again in other countries, but only such as he required for the support of his immediate family; neither should any purchaser be allowed to buy more corn than one animal could carry. He put guards at all the gates of Egypt, and every man who passed through the gates was obliged to record his name and the name of his father in a book, which was brought by the guards every night for Joseph's inspection. By doing this he ascertained when his brethren entered Egypt. When they came and stood before him, they wondered at his magnificence, the handsome appearance and the majestic presence of the powerful man, but they did not recognise in him their brother. He sold them corn, but contrived to entrap them, so that they should bring down with them his own brother Benjamin, who did not come with them this time; they departed, leaving an hostage with Joseph, and on their next visit to buy corn they brought with them his brother Benjamin, and a letter and presents from Jacob. When Joseph recognised his father's hand, his feelings grew too strong for him; the recollections of his youth overpowered him, and, retiring into a side apartment, he wept bitterly. He entertained all his brothers, and sold them corn, but the price thereof he returned without their knowledge into the sacks of each of his brothers. Before they left Egypt he made himself known to them, and, after greetings and explanations, he presented his brothers to Pharaoh; and Pharaoh, seeing they were goodly men, was much pleased and very gracious towards them. Then it was arranged that Jacob should come with all his family into Egypt; and Pharaoh gave his chariots for their accommodation. In due time Jacob and all his family came into Egypt. Joseph went to meet his father, dressed in royal robes, with the crown of state upon his head; and when he came within fifty cubits of his father's company, he descended from his chariot and walked to meet his father. Now when the nobles and princes of Egypt saw this, they too descended from their steeds and chariots and walked with him. And when Jacob saw all this great procession he wondered exceedingly, and he was much pleased thereat, and, turning to Judah, he asked, "Who is the man who marcheth at the head of this great array in royal robes?" Judah answered, "This is thy son." And when Joseph drew nigh to his father he bowed down before him, and his officers also bowed low to Jacob. And Jacob ran towards his son and fell upon his neck and kissed him, and they wept and shed tears of joy and gratitude. Joseph greeted his brethren with affection. And Joseph brought his father and presented him to Pharaoh; and Jacob blessed Pharaoh. And the King said unto Jacob, "How old art thou?" And Jacob answered him, and said, "The days of the years of my pilgrimage are an hundred and thirty years: few and evil have the days of the years of my life been, and have not attained unto the days of the years of the life of my fathers in the days of their pilgrimage."

And Joseph placed his father and his brethren, and gave them a possession in the land of Egypt, in the best of the land, in the land of Rameses, as Pharaoh had commanded. And Joseph nourished his father, and his brethren, and all his father's household, with bread according to their families (1706 B.C.).

And there was no bread in all the land; for the famine was very sore, so that the land of Egypt and all the land of Canaan fainted by reason of the famine. And Joseph gathered up all the money that was found in the land of Egypt, and in the land of Canaan, for the corn which they bought: and Joseph brought the money into Pharaoh's house. When all their money was spent they brought their cattle unto Joseph, and he gave them bread in exchange for horses, and for the flocks, and for the cattle of the herds, and for the asses: and he fed them with bread for all their cattle for that year. After this, Joseph bought all the land of Egypt for Pharaoh; for the Egyptians sold every man his field, because the famine prevailed over them: so the land became Pharaoh's. And as for the people, he removed them to cities from one end of the borders of Egypt, even to the other end thereof. Only the land of the priests bought he not; for the priests had a portion assigned them of Pharaoh, and did eat their portion which Pharaoh gave them: wherefore they sold not their lands.

During these seven years of famine the Egyptians sold all they had, and that being insufficient they sold themselves, so that from subjects they became servants to Pharaoh. Joseph again showed his forethought and discretion, and called the people and said to them, Behold, I have bought you this day and your land for Pharaoh: lo, here is seed for you, and you shall sow the land. And it shall come to pass in the increase, that ye shall give the fifth part unto Pharaoh, and four parts shall be your own, for seed of the field, and for your food, and for them of your households, and for food for your little ones. Thus they became serfs. The wretchedness and poverty of the people was complete; as if the curse of Noah on his son Ham was accomplished to the letter.

After this Jacob died, and his sons buried him in great state in the cave of the field of Machpelah, which Abraham bought with the field for a possession of a burying-place, in the land of Canaan (1689 B.C.).

Joseph had two sons by his wife Asenath. At the age of one hundred and ten years this remarkable man died, and they embalmed him, and he was put in a coffin in Egypt, and afterwards laid in the ground near the banks of the Nile. And all Egypt wept for Joseph seventy days, and his brethren mourned for him seven days, as they did for Jacob his father.

Then Pharaoh took the dominion in his own hands, and governed the people wisely and in good faith.

CHAPTER II.

MOSES—THE RECORDER.

The narrative in connection with the Storehouses of the King would be incomplete without a brief survey of the life of the inspired writer who recorded all the particulars regarding them; and as almost every existing religion is derived from his writings, it will not be deemed superfluous. Moses was born in 1571 B.C. At this time a proclamation was issued throughout the land of Egypt, dooming every male born to the Hebrews to immediate destruction. The elders and wise men advised the King to do this, because they feared that a war might come upon them, and they feared that the Israelites might so increase and spread in the land that they might drive them away from their own country. At first they gave the Israelites hard work to reduce their numbers, but, as that was unavailing, they advised the King, who did not know Joseph, nor remember all the good that he had done for the Egyptians, to adopt this barbarous method of reducing the numbers of the Israelitish inhabitants of Goshen.

It was foretold to Amram, a descendant of Levi, the son of Jacob, that the child, out of dread of whose nativity the Egyptians had doomed the Israelite children to destruction, should be his, and be concealed from those who watched to destroy him; and having been brought up in a surprising way, he should deliver the Hebrew nation from the distress they were under from the Egyptians. His memory should be famous while the world lasts; and this not only among the Hebrews, but foreigners also; and that this child should also have such a brother that he would himself obtain God's Priesthood, and his posterity should have it after him to the end of the world. Amram and his wife Jochebed were in great perplexity, and fear increased upon them on account of this prediction. And when the child was born they nourished him at home privately for three months. But after that time Amram—fearing he would be discovered, and, by falling under the King's displeasure, both he and his child would perish, and so he should make the promise of God of none effect —determined rather to entrust the safety and care of the child to God, than to depend on his own concealment of him, which he looked upon as a thing uncertain, and whereby both the child, so privately to be nourished, and himself should be in imminent danger; but he believed that God would in some way procure the safety of the child, in order to realise the truth of his own predictions. When they had thus determined, they made an ark of bulrushes, after the manner of a cradle, and of a size sufficiently large for an infant to be laid in without being too straitened. They then daubed it over with slime, which would naturally keep the water from entering between the bulrushes, and put the infant into it, and setting it afloat upon the river, they left its preservation to God; so the river received the child, and carried him along. Now Thermuthis, the daughter of Pharaoh, was diverting herself by the banks of the river; and seeing a cradle borne along by the current, she sent some that could swim, and bade them bring the cradle to her. When those that were sent on this errand came to her with the cradle, and she saw the little child, she was greatly in love with it, on account of its largeness and beauty. Thermuthis bade them bring her a woman that might afford her breast to the child. Now Miriam, the sister of Moses, was standing near when this happened, and, when she had this order given her, she went and brought the mother, and the child gladly took her breast, and seemed to stick close to it; and so it was that, at the Queen's desire, the nursing of the child was entirely entrusted to its mother.

The following names were given to Moses by the different persons interested in him:—

 Moses, "I have drawn him from out the water," by Thermuthis, Pharaoh's daughter.

 Heber, "Because he was reunited to his family," by his father Amram.

 Yekuthiel, "I hoped in God," by his mother Jochebed.

 Yarah, "I went down to the river to watch him," by his sister Miriam.

 Abigedore, "For God had repaired the breach in the house of Jacob, and the Egyptians ceased from that time to cast the infants into the water," by his brother Aaron.

Abi Socho, "For three months he was hidden," by his grandfather Caath.

Shermaiah Ben Nethaniel, "Because in his day God heard their groaning and delivered them from their oppressors," by the children of Israel.

Moses became as a son to Thermuthis, the daughter of Pharaoh, as a child belonging rightly to the palace of the King.

The first exploit of Moses was as a general of the Egyptian army, which he led into Ethiopia; he marched by land, and on the way gave a wonderful demonstration of his sagacity. The ground was difficult to be passed over, because of the multitude of serpents; these it produces in vast numbers, and, indeed, is singular in some of those species, which other countries do not breed, and yet such as are worse than others in power and mischief, possessing unusual keenness of sight. Some of these serpents ascend from the ground unseen, and also fly in the air, and so come upon men unawares, and do them mischief. Moses invented a wonderful stratagem to preserve the army safe and without hurt; for he made baskets, like unto arks, of sedge, and filled them with ibises, Egyptian birds, and carried them along with them. These birds are the greatest enemies to serpents imaginable, for they fly from them when they come near them, and as they fly they are caught and devoured by them. As soon, therefore, as Moses came to the land which bred these serpents, he let loose the ibes, and by their means repelled the serpentine kind; using them as his assistants before the army came upon that ground. When, therefore, he proceeded thus on his journey he came upon the Ethiopians before they expected him; and, joining battle with them, he beat them and overthrew their cities, and, indeed, made a great slaughter of the Ethiopians. Moses laid siege to Saba, afterwards called Meroë, the capital of Ethiopia, a strong city encompassed by the Nile and by two other rivers, Astapus and Astaboras, and strongly fortified with great ramparts, insomuch that when the waters come with the greatest violence it can never be overthrown; these ramparts also make it next to impossible for even such as have crossed over the rivers to take the city. However, while Moses was uneasy at the army's lying idle (for the enemies durst not come to battle), this accident or incident occurred: Tharbis, the daughter of the King of Ethiopia, happened to see Moses as he led the army near the walls, and fought with great courage, and admiring the subtlety of his undertakings, and taking him to be the author of the success of the Egyptians, she fell deeply in love with him, and sent to him the most faithful of all her servants to discourse with him about their marriage. He thereupon accepted the offer, on condition that she would procure the delivering up of the city; and gave her the assurance of an oath to make her his wife, and that when he had once taken possession of the city he would not break his oath to her. No sooner was the agreement made than its condition was fulfilled; and when Moses had cut off the Ethiopians he gave thanks to God, and consummated his marriage, and led the Egyptians back to their own land.*

* Josephus.

Now the Egyptians, after they had been preserved by Moses, entertained a hatred to him, and were very eager in compassing their designs against him, suspecting that he would take occasion, from his great success, to raise a sedition and bring innovations into Egypt; so they told the King he ought to be slain. The King had also some intentions of his own to the same purpose; and, being instigated by the elders and wise men, he was ready to undertake to kill Moses. But when Moses learned this he went away privately and joined the army of Kikanus, the King of Ethiopia, at that time suppressing a rebellion in Assyria, and soon became a great favourite with the King and with all his companions. Then Kikanus became sick and died in Ethiopia, and his soldiers buried him and reared a monument over his remains, inscribing upon it the memorable deeds of his life. After the death of King Kikanus the army appointed Moses to be their King and leader. This took place in the hundred and fifty-seventh year after Israel went down into Egypt. The Ethiopians placed Moses upon their throne and set the crown of state upon his head, and they gave him the widow of Kikanus for a wife; but the widow of Kikanus was a wife to Moses in name only. When Moses was made King of Ethiopia the Assyrians again rebelled as they had done before; but Moses subdued them and placed them under yearly tribute to the Ethiopian dynasty. Moses reigned in Ethiopia in justice and righteousness. But the dowager Queen of Ethiopia, Adonith, who was a wife to Moses in name only, said to the people: "Why should this stranger continue to rule over you? Would it not be more just to place the son of Kikanus upon his father's throne, for he is one of you?" The people, however, would not vex Moses, whom they loved, by such a proposition; but Moses voluntarily resigned the power which they had given him, and departed from their land. And the people of Ethiopia made him many rich presents, and dismissed him with great honours.* Moses being still fearful of returning to Egypt, travelled towards Midian, and sat there to rest by a well of water. And the seven daughters of Jethro, the priest of Midian, came there and drew water and filled the troughs to water their father's flock; and Moses helped them, and at the invitation of their father he dwelt with them, and married Zipporah, one of his daughters.

And in process of time the King of Egypt died, and the children of Israel sighed by reason of the bondage; and God sent Moses to them to deliver them. After the enthronement of the next King, Moses and his brother Aaron came before Pharaoh and asked permission for the Israelites to leave Goshen on a three days' journey into the wilderness, to hold a religious festival unto the Lord their God. But Pharaoh refused; and thereupon Moses and Aaron showed miraculous signs and deeds. Still the King persisted in his refusal; till at last the anger of the Lord became great towards Pharaoh. God then commanded Moses and Aaron to prepare the Passover sacrifice, saying: "I will pass over the land of Egypt and slay the first-born, both of man and beast." The Israelites did as they were commanded, and at midnight the angel of the Lord passed over the land and smote the first-born of Egypt, both of man and beast.

* Polano's Talmud.

Then there was a great and grievous cry through all the land, for there was not a house without its dead; and Pharaoh and his people rose up in alarm and consuming grief, and called for Moses and Aaron and bade them be gone, supposing that, if once the Hebrews were gone out of the country, Egypt would be freed from its miseries. They also gave the Israelites gifts, some in order to get them to depart quickly, and others on account of their neighbourhood, and the friendship they had with them.*

So the Hebrews went out of Egypt, while the Egyptians wept, and repented that they had treated them so hardly. And Moses took the bones of Joseph, the builder of the Storehouses of the King, with him; for Joseph had strictly sworn the children of Israel, saying: "God will surely visit you; and ye shall carry up my bones away hence with you." And they took their journey from Goshen, and encamped in Etham, in the edge of the wilderness. This was in the eightieth year of the age of Moses, and the eighty-third of his brother Aaron.

But the King soon regretted that he had let the Hebrews depart, so he resolved to go after them to bring them back. Accordingly he pursued after them with six hundred chariots, fifty thousand horsemen, and two hundred thousand footmen, all armed. On coming up to the Hebrews they seized on the passages by which they imagined the Hebrews might fly, shutting them up between precipices and the sea; for there was on each side a ridge of mountains that terminated at the sea, which were impassable by reason of their roughness, and obstructed their flight.

* Josephus.

Wherefore they were in great distress, as they had no weapons of war for defence, nor was there a way of escape. So there was sorrow and lamentation among the women and children, who had nothing but destruction before their eyes, being encompassed with mountains, the sea, and their enemies, and discerned no way of flying from them.

At this juncture Moses called all the people, and when they were ready he stood on the sea-shore and prayed to God in these words: "Thou art not ignorant, O Lord, that it is beyond human strength and human contrivance to avoid the difficulties which we are now under; but it must be Thy work altogether to procure deliverance to this army, which has left Egypt at Thy appointment. We despair of any other assistance or contrivance, and have recourse only to that hope we have in Thee; and if there be any method that can promise us an escape by Thy providence, we look up to Thee for it. And let it come quickly, and manifest Thy power to us; and do Thou raise up this people to good courage and hope of deliverance, who are deeply sunk into a disconsolate state of mind. We are in a helpless place, but still it is a place that Thou possessest; still the sea is Thine, the mountains also that enclose us are Thine, so that these mountains will open themselves if Thou commandest them; and the sea also, if Thou commandest it, will become dry land. Nay, we might escape by a flight through the air, if thou shouldst determine we should have that way of salvation."* When he ended his prayer, Moses lifted up his hand and smote the sea with his rod, which parted asunder at

* Josephus.

the stroke, and, receding, left the ground dry, as a road and a place of flight for the Hebrews. Seeing the assistance of the Almighty thus vouchsafed in answer to his prayer, he entered in first, and made the Hebrews follow him; they obeyed and went on earnestly, as led by God's presence. The Egyptians supposed at first that they were distracted, and were going rashly upon manifest destruction. But when they saw that they were going a great way without any harm, and that no obstacle or difficulty fell in their journey, they made haste to pursue them, hoping that the sea would be calm for them also. They put their horse foremost, and went down themselves into the sea. By this time the Hebrews had got over to the land on the opposite side without any hurt. Whence the others were encouraged, and more courageously pursued them, as hoping no harm would come to them; but they were mistaken, for as soon as ever the whole Egyptian army was within it, the sea flowed to its own place, and came down with a torrent raised by storms of wind, and encompassed the Egyptians. Showers of rain also came down from the sky, and dreadful thunder and lightning, with flashes of fire. Thunderbolts also were darted upon them; nor was there anything which used to be sent by God upon men as indications of His wrath which did not happen at this time, for a dark and dismal night oppressed them. And thus did the King of Egypt and all his men perish, so that there was not one man left to be a messenger of this calamity to the rest of the Egyptians.* On the next day Moses gathered together the weapons of the

* Josephus.

Egyptians, which were brought on shore by the current of the sea, the force of the winds assisting it; and he armed the Hebrews with them. After returning grateful thanks for this miraculous deliverance, he led the people to Mount Sinai, as he was ordered by God beforehand. Here he instructed them, and prepared them against the time when they should enter the land of Canaan, which country they considered their inheritance, and to which they looked as the destination of their journey. And Moses gave them, among other lessons, the Ten Commandments, which were engraved upon two stone slabs or tables, five on each table, and two and a half upon each side of them. The First Commandment taught that there is but one God, and that they ought to worship Him only; the Second commanded them not to make the image of any living creature, to worship it; the Third, that they must not swear by God in a false matter; the Fourth that they must keep the seventh day, by resting from all sorts of work; the Fifth, that they must honour their parents; the Sixth, that they must abstain from murder; the Seventh, that they must not commit adultery; the Eighth, that they must not be guilty of theft; the Ninth, that they must not bear false witness; the Tenth, that they must not admit the desire of anything that is another's.* These two tables were, for security, placed in a box or ark, made of wood that was naturally strong and could not be corrupted. This ark was called, in the Hebrew language, Eron. Its construction was thus: its length was five spans, but its breadth and height were, each of them, three

* Josephus.

spans. It was covered all over with gold, both within and without, so that the wooden part was not seen. It had also a cover united to it by golden hinges in a wonderful manner; which cover was every way evenly fitted to it, and had no irregularities to hinder its exact conjunction. There were also two golden rings fastened to each of the longer boards, and passing right through the wood; through them gilt bars passed along each board, that it might thereby be moved and carried about as occasion should require; for it was not drawn in a cart by beasts of burden, but borne on the shoulders of the priests. Upon this cover were two images, which the Hebrews call cherubims; they are flying creatures, but their form is not like to that of any of the creatures which men have seen, though Moses said he had seen such beings near the throne of God.*

As the people were dwelling in tents, and were marching towards the land of Canaan by easy marches, Moses made a tent called the Tabernacle, in which he placed the ark containing the two tables. This Tabernacle served as a church in the wilderness, and wherever they travelled they carried it about with them. Moses appointed his brother Aaron to be the High Priest; and after the death of Aaron, Eleazar, his son, became his successor, and the garments of his high office were put upon him. The family of the Levites were the priests.

Moses remained with the Hebrews forty years, and laboured to make them a religious and God-fearing people; but they frequently revolted against him, murmuring whenever they were in distress, and tried

* Josephus.

his patience to the utmost, till he forgot himself, and also complained against God, for which he was forbidden to enter the land of Canaan. Therefore, when he had admonished and repeated to the people all the laws he had given them, he brought them to the border of Canaan, and gave over the charge of the Hebrews to Joshua, his disciple and their commander. Now, as Moses went from them to the place where he wished to vanish out of their sight, they all followed after him weeping; but he beckoned with his hand to those that were remote from him, and bade them stay behind in quiet, while he exhorted those that were near him that they would not mourn so at his departure. Whereupon they thought they ought to grant him that favour, to let him depart according as he himself desired; so they restrained themselves, though weeping still towards one another. All those who accompanied him were the Senate, and Eleazar the High Priest, and Joshua, their commander. Now as soon as they were come to the mountain called Abarim (which is a very high mountain, situate over against Jericho, and one that affords, to such as are upon it, a prospect of the greatest part of the excellent land of Canaan), he dismissed the Senate; and, as he was going to embrace Eleazar and Joshua, and was still discoursing with them, suddenly a cloud stood over him, and he disappeared in a certain valley out of their sight.*

Moses was one hundred and twenty years old when he left the camp of the Israelites. He spent forty years of his life in teaching the Laws of God to the people in the wilderness. He was one that exceeded

* Josephus.

all men that ever were in understanding, and made the best use of what that understanding suggested to him. He had a very graceful way of speaking and addressing himself to the multitude; and as to his other qualifications, he had such a full command of his passions, as if he had hardly any such in his soul, and only knew them by their names, as rather perceiving them in other men than in himself. He was also such a general of an army as is seldom seen, as well as a king and a prophet as was never known, and this to such a degree, that whatsoever he pronounced one would think he heard the voice of God Himself. So the people mourned for him thirty days, nor did any grief so deeply affect the Hebrews as did this upon the departure of Moses; nor were those who had witnessed his conduct the only persons who desired him, but those also who perused the laws he left behind him greatly longed for him, and from those laws learned the extraordinary virtue he was master of.* At this period of his life his eye was not dim, nor his natural force abated. "And Joshua, the son of Nun, was full of the spirit of wisdom, for Moses had laid his hands upon him; and the children of Israel hearkened unto him, and did as the Lord commanded Moses. And there arose not a prophet since in Israel like unto Moses, whom the Lord knew face to face, in all the signs and the wonders, which the Lord sent him to do in the land of Egypt to Pharaoh, and to all his servants, and to all his land, and in all that mighty hand, and in all the great terror which Moses showed in the sight of all Israel."† Although he wrote in the holy books that

* Josephus. † Deuteronomy xxxiv.

he died, it was for fear lest they should say that, because of his extraordinary virtue, he went to God.*

Moses was as we shall see, a great traveller, and acquainted with the vast wilderness that extends from the centre of Africa to the jungles of Bengal, that consists of rugged mountains and of sandy wastes; it was traversed by three river-basins or valley plains. In its centre was the basin of the Tigris and Euphrates. On its east was the basin of the Indus; on its west was the basin of the Nile. Each of these river systems was enclosed by deserts; the whole region resembling a broad yellow field with three green streaks running north and south. The inhabitants of these regions were not in the habit of travelling beyond the confines of their own valleys. They resembled islanders, and they had no ships. But the intermediate seas were navigated by the wandering tribes, who sometimes pastured their flocks by the waters of the Indus, sometimes by the waters of the Nile. It was by their means that the trade between the river-lands was carried on. They possessed the camels and other beasts of burden requisite for the transport of goods. Their numbers and their warlike habits, their intimate acquaintance with the watering-places and seasons of the desert, enabled them to carry the goods in safety through a dangerous land; while the regular profits they derived from the trade, and the oaths by which they were bound, induced them to act fairly to those by whom they were employed. At this time, 1451 B.C., a mighty tide of the Aryans immigrated to the basin or valley plain of the Indus. They called themselves Arya, or

* Josephus.

noble, and spoke a language the common source of Sanskrit, Prakrit, Zand, Persian, and Armenian in Asia. They settled down as agriculturists in the districts surrounding the Indus, their wealth consisting of flocks and herds ; thence, after a time, they overran by successive irruptions the plains of the Ganges, and spread themselves over the regions called Aryavarta, occupying the whole of Central India. They were the promoters of the moral and intellectual progress and civilization in India; and notwithstanding all the diversities of the Hindoo populations throughout India, their religious faith has been preserved in their one language and one literature, furnishing a good evidence of the original unity of the Indo-Aryans. Their leader and legislator was known by the name of Manu, who was no other than Moses. After leaving the camp of the Israelites he travelled to the Indus ; the form of Government he established there was the counterpart or duplicate of the one he established among the Hebrews ; the laws and customs were the very same ; the most careful comparison will confirm the fact. Moses was afraid that the Hebrews would trace his footsteps, so he sank his identity by assuming a foreign name: thus, for Moses he used Manu ; for Abraham, Brahman; for Amram, Ram. All the remarkable Biblical events are familiar to the Brahmans, and the record of the creation as contained in the Bible was given in the Rig-veda of the Hindoos. The narrative of the finding of Moses by the daughter of Pharaoh has a corresponding record, but as he was more than one hundred and twenty years old when he arrived in India, the account is that the Lawgiver was cradled by a large sea-serpent on the bosom of the great waters for ages, whilst he was in a state of somnolence.

The origin of the belief in the Transmigration of the Soul is also taken from an event in the life of Moses, which is recorded in the Hebrew Talmud thus: The Lord said to Moses, " Behold, thy days approach that thou must die." On, this Moses thought that he had committed but a slight offence, which would be pardoned; for ten times had Israel tempted God's wrath and been forgiven through his intercession, as it is written: " And the Lord said, I have pardoned according to thy word." But when he became convinced that he would not be pardoned, he made the following supplication: " Sovereign of the universe, my trouble and my exertion for Israel's sake is revealed and known before Thee. How I have laboured to cause thy people to know Thee, and to believe in Thy Holy Name, and practise Thy holy law, has come before Thee. O Lord, as I had shared their trouble and their distress, I hoped to share their happiness. Behold, now, the time has come when their trials will cease, when they will enter into the land of promised bliss, and Thou sayest to me, Thou shalt not pass over this Jordan. O Eternal, great and just, if thou wilt not allow me to enter into this goodly land, permit me at least to live on here in this world."

Then God answered Moses, saying: " If thou wilt not die in this world, how canst thou live in the world to come ?" But Moses continued: "If thou wilt not permit me to pass over this Jordan, let me live as the beasts of the field; they eat of the herbs and drink of the waters, and live and see the world; let my life be even as theirs."

And God answered: "Let it suffice thee; do not continue to speak unto me any more on this matter." Yet again Moses prayed: "Let me live even as the fowls; they gather their food in the morning, and in the evening they return unto their nests. Let my life be even as theirs."

And again God said: "Let it suffice thee; do not continue to speak to me any more on this matter." Then Moses proclaimed: "He is the Rock; His work is perfect, and His ways are just; the God of Truth, just and upright is He."*

The Persians, known in India as Parsees, are worshippers of the element of fire. This fire-worship originated from an event that took place in Persia when the Hebrews were captives in that country. The King of Persia gave the Hebrews leave to sacrifice to the Lord as Moses had commanded them; and when the prophet Nehemiah had prepared the sacrifice, the priests and the Israelites offered up this prayer: "O Lord, Lord God, Creator of all things, Who art fearful and strong, and righteous and merciful, and the only and gracious King, the only giver of all things, the only just, almighty, and everlasting, Thou that deliverest Israel from all trouble, and didst choose the fathers, and sanctify them: Receive the sacrifice for Thy whole people Israel, and preserve Thine own portion, and sanctify it. Gather those together that are scattered from us, deliver them that serve among the heathen, look upon them that are despised and abhorred, and let the heathen know that

* Polano's Talmud.

Thou art our God. Punish them that oppress us, and with pride do us wrong. Plant Thy people again in Thy holy place, as Moses hath spoken." And the priests sang psalms of thanksgiving.

Now when the sacrifice was consumed, Nehemiah commanded the water that was left to be poured on the great stones. When this was done, there was kindled a flame; but it was consumed by the light that shined from the altar. So when this matter was known, it was told the King of Persia that, in the place where the priests that were led away had hid the fire, there appeared water, and that Nehemiah had purified the sacrifices therewith. Then the King, inclosing the place, made it holy, after he had tried the matter and convinced himself of the fact.*

The Mohammedans are the followers of Mohammed, and the Koran that he gave them, he told his followers, "is not a new invented fiction, but a confirmation of those Scriptures which have been revealed to Moses before it, and a distinct explication of everything necessary in respect either to faith or practice, and a direction and mercy unto people who believe."†

As for the Israelites, though they are now scattered over the face of the whole earth, yet the Tabernacle, and the Altar of Incense, and the Ark containing the two Stone Tables on which were engraven the Ten Commandments given by God, by the hand of Moses, are still in Mount Abarim, hidden there by Jeremiah the prophet, before the sack and burning of the Temple of Solomon by the Babylonians. They are in a cave, wherein Jeremiah laid them and stopped the door, saying, "As for that place, it shall be

---

* 2 Maccabees i. † Al Koran, chap. xii.

unknown until the time that God gather his people again together, and receive them unto mercy. Then shall the Lord show them these things, and the glory of the Lord shall appear, and the cloud also, as it was showed under Moses, and as when Solomon desired that the place might be honourably sanctified."*

After the departure of the Israelites from the land of Egypt, that country was reduced to the lowest depth of misery. The King, with all his chariots, horsemen, and footmen were all overwhelmed and destroyed; there was no firstborn of man (or beast) to mourn the loss of their kindred. The land was desolate, and the Storehouses of the King stood out in their grandeur to remind the survivors of their ingratitude to the relatives of the man who built them, to preserve the Egyptians during the seven years of the grievous famine that afflicted the land of Egypt. They must have avoided the sight of these monuments, thereby to forget the misery and desolation they had brought on themselves by their cruel treatment of the Hebrews. The Egyptian priests knew what these buildings were, for they were the historians of their country; but when Herodotus visited Egypt and made minute inquiries regarding the Pyramids, they gave him a confused account, telling him, however, that for one hundred and six years the Egyptians suffered all kinds of calamities, and that for this length of time the temples were closed and never opened. From the hatred they bore them, the Egyptians were not willing to mention the names of their kings, but called the large Pyramids after Philition (Zaphnath-paaneah, Psothom Phanech), a

* 2 Maccabees ii.

shepherd who at that time kept his cattle in those parts.* Philition is a corruption of the other two names given to Joseph by Pharaoh; while the shepherds were the brothers of Joseph, and Goshen —Gizeh of our time—the region where they dwelt, as commanded by the King. The Greeks could make nothing out of the information gathered by Herodotus.

In course of time the first Republic of France sent a traveller into Upper and Lower Egypt, and the inhabitants of the land of Egypt had so far forgotten the events of the past that they showed him an enclosed space as the granaries of Joseph. The traveller says: "You see at ancient Cairo the granaries of Joseph, if the name of granaries can with propriety be given to a vast space of ground surrounded with walls twenty feet in height, and divided into a sort of courts which have no roof, or any other covering whatever, in which are deposited the grains brought out of Upper Egypt for the revenue, where they are the food of a multitude of birds, and the receptacle of their ordure. The walls of this enclosure are of a bad construction; they have nothing in their appearance which announces an ancient building, and the love of the marvellous alone could have attributed its elevation to the patriarch Joseph."* The French Government gained nothing, and its attention was diverted from the Storehouses of the King. Since that time many explorers have gone to the Pyramids, and spent princely fortunes in trying to solve the mystery as to what they were and who built them.

* Herodotus, *Euterpe*, ii.
† Sonnini, *Travels in Upper and Lower Egypt.*

But the Arabs are too cunning and too indolent to tell the truth; for they know from experience that, if the truth were known, they would be made to assist in repairing the Storehouses of the King, just as many of the people were set to cut the Suez Canal, when the French discovered an old undertaking of the reign of Necho, which had been left unfinished because the oracle declared that the king was making the canal for a barbarian. Wherefore the Arabs reckon that, ignoring all knowledge, they gain a good livelihood as guides, by taking travellers to the Pyramids, which is little trouble to them, but brings them "plenty backsheesh."

CHAPTER III.

TOWER OF BABEL—THE MODEL.

THE Pyramids were, without doubt, copied from and built after the model of the Tower of Babel. At the time that Joseph was entrusted by Pharaoh with the task of making provision against the approaching famine that he predicted would take place, the building of the City and Tower of Babel by Nimrod the son of Cush, the son of Ham, the son of Noah, and the confusion of tongues that followed, were of comparatively recent date. Abraham's father Terah was in the service of King Nimrod during their erection.

We are told in the Scriptures that "the whole earth was of one language and of one speech. And it came to pass, as they journeyed from the east, that they found a plain in the land of Shinar; and they dwelt there. And they said one to another, Go to, let us make brick, and burn them throughly. And they had brick for stone, and slime had they for mortar. And they said, Go to, let us build us a city and a tower, whose top may reach unto heaven; and let us make us a name, lest we be scattered abroad upon the face of the whole earth."*

In this description the motive assigned for the

* Gen. xi.

building of the above-mentioned city and tower is that the people over whom Nimrod reigned might be preserved together with renown. They found a plain by the river Euphrates that suited their purpose, resembling the plain of Egypt by the river Nile. In Shinar there was no stone, so brick was used in its stead. This plain was fertile and produced much corn. The settlers anticipated another Deluge, and on that account they provided themselves with the means of subsistence when that calamity might recur on the earth. The precaution they took for this event was to build a place of safety, with a granary that would hold a sufficient amount of corn to last during the whole period of the visitation. They built a gigantic granary resembling the great Pyramid of Jeezeh, which they filled with corn. Joseph imitated this example in Egypt.

The same event is thus recorded in the Talmud:— "Cush, the son of Ham and grandson of Noah, married in his old age a young wife, and begat a son, whom he called Nimrod, because in those days the people were beginning to rebel again against the Lord's command, and Nimrod signifies 'Rebellion.' Now Nimrod grew up, and his father loved him exceedingly, because he was the child of his old age. When Nimrod was forty years old his brethren, the sons of Ham, quarrelled with the sons of Japhet. And Nimrod assembled the tribe of Cush, and went forth to battle with the sons of Japhet. And he addressed his army, saying, 'Be not dismayed, and banish fear from your hearts. Our enemies shall surely be your booty, and ye shall do with them as ye please.' Nimrod was victorious, and the opposing armies became his subjects. And when he and his soldiers returned home rejoicing, the people gathered around and made him king, and placed a crown upon his head. And he appointed counsellors, judges, chiefs, generals, and captains. He established a national government, and he made Therach, the son of Nahor, his chief officer. When Nimrod had thus established his power he decided to build a city, a walled town, which should be the capital of his country. And he selected a certain plain and built a large city thereon, and called it Shinar. And Nimrod dwelt in Shinar in safety, and gradually became ruler over all the world; and at that time all the people of the earth were of one language and of one speech. Nimrod in his prosperity did not regard the Lord. He made gods of wood and stone, and the people copied his doings. His son Mordan served idols also, from which we have, even to this day, the proverb, 'From the wicked wickedness comes forth.'

"And it came to pass about this time that the officers of Nimrod and the descendants of Phut, Mitzrayim, Cush, and Canaan took counsel together, and they said to one another, 'Let us build a city, and also in its midst a tall tower for a stronghold, a tower the top of which shall reach even to the heavens. Then shall we truly make for ourselves a great and mighty name, before which all our enemies shall tremble. None will then be able to harm us, and no wars may disperse our ranks.' And they spoke these words to the King, and he approved of their design. Therefore these families gathered together and selected a suitable spot for their city and its tower on a plain towards the east in the land of Shinar.

"And while they were building rebellion budded in their hearts, rebellion against God, and they imagined that they could scale the heavens and war with Him. They divided into three parties. The first party said, 'We will ascend to heaven and place there our gods and worship them.' The second party said, 'We will pour into the heavens of the Lord and match our strength with His.' And the third party said, 'Yea, we will smite Him with arrow and with spear.'

"And God watched their evil enterprise and knew their thoughts, yet they builded on. If one of the stones which they had raised to its height fell, they were sad at heart, and even wept; yet when any of their brethren fell from the building and were killed, none took account of the life thus lost. Thus they continued for a space of years, till God said, 'We will confuse their language.' Then the people forgot their language, and they spoke to one another in a strange tongue. And they quarrelled and fought on account of the many misunderstandings occasioned by this confusion of language, and many were destroyed in these quarrels, till at last they were compelled to cease building.

"The tower was exceedingly tall. The third part of it sank down into the ground, a second third was burned down, but the remaining third was standing until the time of the destruction of Babylon. Thus were the people dispersed over the globe, and divided into nations."*

* Polano's Talmud.

In this narrative the object of these wicked idolaters was to ascend and carry war into heaven against God. To accomplish this object or design they built the city and tower; the latter served for the granary as well as the stronghold of the new city.

Abraham was born about this time. His father Terah was then in the service of King Nimrod, in Babylon. Owing to the idolatry and the wickedness of the people, Abraham left the country with his wife and nephew, and settled in the land of Canaan. When Joseph was a child he must have heard from his father the story of those eventful times, when Abraham dwelt in the country wherein he was born. In due time he availed himself of the knowledge thus imparted to him in his early days.

Modern travellers have found many remains of Pyramids in the ancient kingdom of Babylonia. There was, therefore, nothing new or wonderful in the fact of Joseph erecting granaries throughout Egypt when a severe famine was expected. These granaries or Pyramids began in the Delta, which was most fertile and yielded the largest amount of corn. The Pyramids here are the finest as well as the largest; the rest are erected along the western shore of the Nile as far as Ethiopia, which was a province of Egypt. This province revolted in the lifetime of Moses. He went there as commander of the Egyptian forces and suppressed the rebellion. The ruins in Meroë and Axum, and other places in Ethiopia, attest the truth of this statement.

Egyptologists have spent much time and labour in pursuit of their science, but, very unfortunately, their researches have been directed by misleading guides.

The authorities they took for their guidance were the Greek and Roman writers, who knew nothing about the events that took place before Egypt became a province of Alexander the Great and of the emperors of Rome.

The oldest and best records of Egypt and the ancient world were written by the inspired historian Moses, and these records, or a small portion of them, were translated from the Hebrew into the Greek language by seventy Jewish elders for the King Ptolemy Philadelphus in the year 284 B.C.; so that before this time the outer or the Gentile world was in utter ignorance regarding the history of Egypt, as well as that of the Jews. The authors held in veneration by Egyptologists are Manetho and Herodotus. Manetho's ignorance as to the history of his own country is shown by Flavius Josephus; and Herodotus wrote his account of the Pyramids from hearsay. The priests who related the anecdotes concerning the kings Cheops and his brother Chephren, and the shepherd Philition, knew nothing themselves as to the real truth, for the whole account is in confusion, worse confounded by their stupendous ignorance.

The writings of these two authors have misled every Egyptologist. Had the Bible, the Jewish records called the Talmud, and Flavius Josephus been studied instead, Egyptologists would have learnt the truth, and nothing but the truth, and their time and labour would have been rewarded most satisfactorily. The reader of this work will find extracts in the later portion of it, which will repay the trouble of perusal.

The testimony of recent travellers proves the reality of the existence of granaries in Babylon, and the indisputable fact that the Pyramids were built in imitation of them. The following is an instance:—*

"On the 9th December 1811 Mr. Rich made an expedition to the Birs-i-Nimrúd. He found vestiges of mounds all round it to a considerable extent, and the country traversed by canals in every direction. The soil round it is sandy. Close to the Birs, or at about a hundred yards from it, and parallel with its southern front, is a high mound, almost equal in size to that of the Kasr.

"'The Birs,' says he, 'is an enormous mound. At the north end it rises, and there is an immense brick wall, thirty-seven feet high and twenty-eight in breadth, upon it. This wall is not in the centre of the north summit of the mound, but appears to have formed the southern face of it. The other parts of the summit are covered by huge fragments of brickwork, tumbled confusedly together; and what is most extraordinary is that they are partly converted into a solid vitrified mass. The layers are in many parts perfectly distinguishable; but the whole of these lumps seem to have undergone the action of fire. Several lumps of the same matter have rolled down, and remain partly on the side of the mound and partly in the plain. The large wall on the southern face of the summit is built of burnt bricks, with writing on them, and so close together that no cement is discoverable between the layers. Small

* W. T. W. Vaux, *Nineveh and Persepolis.*

square apertures are left, which go quite through the building, and are arranged in a kind of quincunx form. Down the face of the wall the bricks have been separated, leaving a large crack. On the side towards the mound of Ibrahím Khalil, the mound slopes gradually down, and up nearly half its height is a flat road running round this part of it, twenty of my paces broad.

"'From this the mound slopes more gradually to the plain or valley between it and the mound of Ibrahím Khalil, and is worn into deep ravines or furrows, like the Mujelibé. On the other or north face of this pile it slopes down more abruptly at once into the plain, with only hollows or paths round it, the road before mentioned, which from that part appears to surround the building, losing itself before it reaches this. On the north-west face, where it also slopes down into the plain, are vestiges of building in the side, exactly similar in appearance and construction to the wall on the top, with the holes or apertures which are mentioned in the description of that. At foot of all is, seemingly, a flat base of greater extent, but very little raised above the level of the plain. The whole sides of the mound are covered with pieces of brick, both burnt and unburnt, bitumen, pebbles, spar, black stone, the same sand or limestone which covers the canal at the Kasr, and even fragments of white marble. No reeds were to be seen in any part of the building, though I saw one or two specimens of burnt bricks which evidently had reeds in their composition, and some had the impression of reeds on their cement. I saw also several bricks which were thickly coated with bitumen on their lower face. In the lowest part of the mound opposite Ibrahím Khalil, the mounds are most evidently composed of unburnt bricks, the layers being in great measure visible. This would lead one to suppose that it was not originally part of the great pile, were not specimens of this kind of bricks found in it also.

"'The circumference of the base—not the low one—is 762 yards. The whole height of it, from this measured base to the summit of the tower or wall, is 235 feet; but there can be no doubt that it was much higher. The form is more oblong than square. I found the longest side to be 248 of my paces. Fortunately for the preservation of the ruin, it is too far from the Euphrates for the Arabs to think it worth their while to excavate for bricks; while they are so closely joined together, that it is impossible to procure them quite unbroken.'

"Mr. Rich will not admit this tower to be that of Belus, because, according to his view, it is on the wrong side of the river.

"The whole height of the Birs-i-Nimrúd above the plain to the summit of the brick wall is 235 feet. The brick wall itself, which stands on the edge of the summit, and was undoubtedly the face of another stage, is 37 feet high. In the side of the pile, a little below its summit, is very clearly to be seen part of another brick wall, precisely resembling the fragment which crowns the summit, and still encasing and supporting its part of the mound. This is clearly indicative of another stage of greater extent.

"Without forming any conjecture as to what

might have been its original construction, the impression made by the sight of it is, that it was a solid pile, composed in the interior of unburnt brick, and perhaps earth or rubbish; that it was constructed in receding stages, and faced with kiln-burnt bricks having inscriptions on them, laid in a very thin layer of lime cement; and that it was reduced by violence to its present ruinous condition. The upper stones have been forcibly broken down, and fire has been employed as an implement of destruction, though it is not easy to say how or why. The facing of fine bricks has been partly removed and partly covered by the falling down of the mass which it supported and kept together.

"A still later traveller, Mr. Buckingham, is of opinion that the traces of four stages are clearly discernible.

"As to Major Rennell's doubt whether the ruin was artificial, Mr. Rich observes that, 'so indisputably evident is the fact of the whole mass being from top to bottom artificial, that he should as soon have thought of writing a dissertation to prove that the Pyramids are the work of human hands as of dwelling upon this point. The Birs-i-Nimrúd,' he adds, 'is, in all likelihood, at present nearly in the state in which Alexander saw it, if we give any credit to the report that ten thousand men could only remove the rubbish, preparatory to repairing it, in two months. If, indeed, it required one half of that number to disencumber it, the state of dilapidation must have been complete.

"'The immense masses of vitrified brick which are seen on the top of the mound appear to have marked its summit since the time of its destruction. The rubbish about its base was probably in much greater quantities, the weather having dissipated much of it in the course of so many revolving ages; and possibly portions of the interior facing of fine brick may have disappeared at different periods.'"

CHAPTER IV.

THE PYRAMIDS AS GRANARIES.

THE land of Shinar, with its desolate tower, the marvellous prototype of the Great Pyramid of Jeezeh, passed from one conqueror to another; and when the descendants of the Prophet Mohammed became rulers of the east and west, the Caliph Al Mamoun, in the year A.D. 820, came from Bagdad to El Fostat, an earlier Cairo, and determined to enter the largest Pyramid and examine its contents, for he believed from the reports brought to him that it contained untold treasures. He ordered his Mohammedan workmen to begin at the middle of the northern side of the Great Pyramid. These men worked on unceasingly by night and by day. Weeks and months were consumed in these toilsome exertions; so persevering, however, were they, that, though progressing slowly, they at length penetrated no less than one hundred feet in depth from the entrance. By that time, they were becoming thoroughly exhausted, and began to despair of the hard and hitherto fruitless labour, when one day they heard a great stone fall evidently in some hollow space within not more than a few feet on one side of them. In the fall of that particular stone there seems to have been somewhat more than an accident.

They instantly pushed on in the direction of the strange noise. Breaking through a wall surface, they burst into the hollow way, very dark and dreadful to look at, and difficult to pass. It was the inclined and descending entrance-passage of the Pyramid, where the Romans and others passed up and down in their occasional visits to the subterranean chamber and its unfinished, unquarried-out floor.

A large angular-fitting stone, that had been for ages, with its lower flat side, a smooth and polished portion of the ceiling of the inclined and narrow entrance-passage, quite undistinguishable from any other part of the whole of its line, had now dropped on to the floor before their eyes, and revealed that there was just behind it the end of another passage, clearly ascending therefrom towards the south. That ascending passage itself was still closed a little further up by a portcullis or stopper, formed by a series of huge granite plugs, of square wedge-like shape, dropped or slid down, and then jammed in immovably from above. To break this in pieces within the confined space, and pull out the fragments there, was entirely out of the question; so the workmen broke through the smaller ordinary masonry, and thus up again by a huge chasm—still visible, and used by visitors into the interior—to the ascending passage, at a point past the terrific hardness of its lower granite obstruction. They found up there beyond the portcullis the passage-way still blocked, but the filling material at that part was only limestone; so, making themselves a very great hole in the masonry along the western side, they there wielded their tools on the long blocks which presented themselves to their view. But as fast as they broke up and pulled out the pieces of one of the blocks in this ascending passage, other blocks, also of such a size as to completely fill it, slid down from above, and where there should have been free passage there was still an obstruction of solid stone. The men despair; but the Caliph, being present, insists that, whatever the number of stone plugs still to come down from the mysterious reservoir, his men shall hammer and hammer them, one after the other, and bit by bit, to little pieces, at the only opening where they can get at them, until they at last come to the end. So the work goes on, till at length the ascending passage, beginning just above the granite portcullis, leading thence upward and to the south, becomes free from obstruction.

On they rush, up one hundred and ten feet of the steep incline, crouching hands and knees and chin together, through a passage of polished white limestone, forty-seven inches in height and forty-one in breadth. They suddenly emerge into a long high gallery, all black as night and in death-like silence; still ascending, they see another low passage. On their right hand is the dark, ominous-looking mouth of a deep well, in which not even at a depth of more than 140 feet is the water reached; while onwards and above them is a continuation of the gallery leading them on.

The way was narrow, not more than six feet broad anywhere, and contracted to three feet at the floor, but twenty feet high, and of polished marble-like stone throughout. Ascending at an angle of 26°, these men had to push their dangerous and slippery way for about a hundred feet still further ; then an obstructing three-foot step to climb over ; next a low doorway ; then a hanging portcullis to pass, almost to creep under; and then another low doorway, with awful blocks of red granite on either side, above, and below.

After this they leaped without further obstruction at once into the grand chamber, a right noble apartment now called the King's Chamber, about thirty-four feet long, seventeen broad, and nineteen high, of polished red granite throughout, in blocks squared and put together with exquisite skill. In this apartment they found—nothing, except an empty stone chest or box or coffer without a lid !*

The Caliph Al-Mamoun was amazed, for he had arrived at the very furthest part of the interior of the Great Pyramid he had so long desired to take possession of, and had now found absolutely nothing that he could make any use of, or saw the smallest value in. He returned to El Fostat greatly disappointed, and the Grand Gallery, the King's Chamber, and the stone coffer without a lid were troubled by him no more; for after this he left Egypt and returned to his imperial residence in Bagdad, where he died in A.D. 842.

The entrance into the Great Pyramid in use in our time is the one thus made by this prince. The granite chest or coffer without a lid, found in the King's Chamber above-mentioned, was not a sarco-

* Piazzi Smyth, *Our Inheritance in the Great Pyramid.*

phagus, or a coffin, but simply a corn measure, and nothing else, which holds about four English quarters. It was placed in that chamber by the inspired builder Joseph, the great-grandson of Abraham the Hebrew, the friend of God; the Pyramid being a gigantic granary holding corn, and this the measure by which he ascertained the quantity stored in it. The passages in the walls, called air-channels by Egyptologists, were apertures through which the corn was thrown from without into the chamber, and thence into the vast receptacles below. The grain was brought from the fields to the apertures up the steps, before the casing-stones were fitted to the whole edifice, which, being afterwards polished, kept the contents secure from moth and mildew.

When Joseph died "his body was embalmed and afterwards laid in the ground near the banks of the Nile."* The locality that exactly answers this place of sepulture has been discovered in modern times. "The structure found there is situated about a thousand feet south-east of the Pyramid building, and still to be seen, descended into, and measured, is a colossally large and deep burial pit, on the square and level bottom of which rests an antique rude sarcophagus of very gigantic proportions. But deep as is the pit containing it, it is surrounded by a grand rectangular trench which goes down deeper still, cut clearly in solid limestone rock the whole of the way down; and to such a depth does it reach at last as to descend below the level of the adjacent waters of the Nile at inundation time. Then, as the waters of that river necessarily percolate the hygroscopic rock of the

* Polano's Talmud.

hill up to their own level, the lower depths of the trench are filled with Nile water, and the grand old sarcophagus of the interior pit does then rest in a manner on an island surrounded by the waters of the Nile; and it is the only known tomb on the Jeezeh hill which is gifted with that peculiarity or privilege."*

This is the tomb of which Herodotus speaks as the resting-place of the builder of the Great Pyramid, to whom he gives the names of Chemmis, Cheops, Xufu, Suphis, Philition the Shepherd, &c. All these appellations belong to no other person than Zaphnath-paaneah, the Viceroy of Pharaoh, King of Egypt, the great-grandson of Abraham the Hebrew, the friend of God!

The sarcophagus is empty, for the bones of Joseph were carried away by the children of Israel when they took their departure from Egypt under the leadership of Moses and Aaron.

Visitors who enter the Pyramid get covered with a fine grey dust or powder similar to that found in large rooms or buildings wherein grain has been stored; for any person entering such places, though emptied of their contents, but left unswept, would get covered with a grey powder fallen from corn, or rice, or wheat, &c., which in every respect resembles this fine grey dust. In confirmation of this the following is an instance:—

"Last month (1877) an American newspaper, recounting a recent visit to the King's Chamber of the Great Pyramid, mentions how the clergyman of the party, the Rev. Dr. ——, insisted on laying himself down full length inside the coffer. He had heard the

* Piazzi Smyth, *Our Inheritance in the Great Pyramid.*

inspiration, and scientific metrological theory of the Great Pyramid duly related by Dr. Grant, and had not denied it; but so strongly was he imbued with the mere tombic idea of the Egyptians, that he held, as he lay there, with the notion that he was lying down in a royal coffin; and when he, Dr. ——, rose up from that open granite chest and found himself filthy, horrible, odious, with fine grey dust begriming his hair and transfusing his clothes, he had a great deal of trouble about it; for not until he had got right away from Egypt, and obtained the help of the steward's assistant on board ship to give the clothes an extra beating over the waves of the rolling sea, was the last of the penetrating powdery stuff got rid of."*

Colonel Howard Vyse also found a substance of this description when he entered the Pyramids, of which he gave a minute account in his work on the Pyramids of Egypt. It is as follows:—"For a day or two after the chamber had been opened those who remained in it became blackened as if by a London fog. As this effect gradually disappeared, I conceive it to have been occasioned by the blasting and by the sudden admission of the air.

"Upon first entering the apartment, a black sediment was found, of the consistence of a hoar-frost, equally distributed over the floor, so that footsteps could be distinctly seen impressed on it, and it had accumulated to some depth in the interstices of the blocks. Some of this sediment which was sent to the French establishment near Cairo was said to contain ligneous particles. When analysed in England

* Piazzi Smyth, *Our Inheritance in the Great Pyramid.*

it was supposed to consist of the exuviæ of insects; but as the deposition was equally diffused over the floor, and extremely like the substance found on the 25th instant (1837) at the Second Pyramid, it was most probably composed of particles of decayed stone. If it had been the remains of rotten wood, or of a quantity of insects that had penetrated through the masonry, it would scarcely have been so equally distributed; and if caused by the latter, it is difficult to imagine why some of them should not have been found alive when the place was opened evidently for the first time since the Pyramid was built."

Previous to the visitation of the seven years' famine, these granaries were built and stored, and the casing-stones fitted with cement and polished, making these edifices appear like natural rocks. Bruce, the great traveller, and other old travellers of those days, mistook them for such (natural rocks) and paid no attention to them whatever.

When the time arrived that the Storehouses of the King were required to be tapped, and food distributed to the famine-stricken people, the exterior of these buildings was left entire, and the operation of taking out the grain carried on by means of long shafts bored in the adjacent ground to a depth reaching the foundation of the Pyramid, where there were openings from which the contents could be tapped. These could be opened and shut at pleasure, as Joseph ordered that all the granaries should be closed with the exception of one, where he hoped to see his brothers when they came to buy corn in Egypt.

Colonel Howard Vyse gives a description of one of these entrances, thus:—"The Pyramid of Saccara.

This Pyramid was built in steps, or degrees, and was entered from a sort of well, or shaft, made in the sand on the northern side. The passage, which was long and winding, and apparently in many places forced, led to a lofty chamber, in the roof of which wood had been employed. Various forced passages wound around this chamber, and conducted to openings, or windows, which looked down into it from a considerable height.* These passages were much encumbered with rubbish, pieces of alabaster, and decayed wood; and in one place there was an accumulation of large blocks of polished granite, raised up by small fragments of stone sufficiently high to admit of a man's crawling beneath them. For what purpose they were so placed we did not find out."

* These are passages by which the grain was thrown down into the building from the outside before the casing-stones were fixed.—J. V. G.

CHAPTER V.

THE HEBREWS IN EGYPT.

In the Talmud it is recorded that after Joseph's marriage with Asenath, daughter of Potipherah the priest of On, "he built for himself a palace, elegant and complete in its details and surroundings, so elaborate that three years' time was required for its completion." A man so wise and so powerful as to be looked upon by the Egyptians as their king was certainly able to make a suitable provision for the anticipated advent of his beloved father, as well as for all his brothers, who came with their entire households, and possessions in flocks and herds, &c., for the famine was over the whole earth.

The large palace called the Labyrinth by Herodotus, would correspond with such a provision for their accommodation and comfort. Herodotus saw this palace himself in the year 448 B.C., and he describes it thus:—"The Egyptians having become free, after the reign of the priest of Vulcan, for they were at no time able to live without a king, established twelve kings, having divided all Egypt into twelve parts. These having contracted intermarriages, reigned, adopting the following regulations: that they would not attempt the subversion of one another, nor one seek to acquire more than another, and that they should maintain the strictest friendship. They made these regulations and strictly upheld them, for the following reason: it had been foretold them by an oracle, when they first assumed the government, 'that whoever among them should offer a libation in the temple of Vulcan from a brazen bowl should be king of all Egypt,' for they used to assemble in all the temples. Now, they determined to leave in common a memorial of themselves; and having so determined, they built a Labyrinth, a little above the lake of Mœris, situated near that called the city of crocodiles. This I have myself seen, and found it greater than can be described. For if anyone should reckon up the buildings and public works of the Grecians, they would be found to have cost less labour and expense than this Labyrinth; though the temple in Ephesus is deserving of mention, and also that in Samos. The Pyramids likewise were beyond description, and each of them comparable to many of the great Grecian structures. Yet the Labyrinth surpasses even the Pyramids. For it has *twelve* courts enclosed with walls, with doors opposite each other, six facing the north, and six the south, contiguous to one another; and the same exterior wall encloses them. It contains two kinds of rooms, some under ground and some above ground over them, to the number of three thousand, fifteen hundred of each. The rooms above ground I myself went through and saw, and relate from personal inspection. But the underground rooms I only know from report, for the Egyptians who have charge of the building would on no account show me them, saying that there were the sepulchres of the kings who originally built this Labyrinth, and of the sacred crocodiles. I can therefore only relate what I have learned by hearsay concerning the lower rooms; but the upper ones, which surpass all human works, I myself saw; for the passages through the corridors, and the windings through the courts, from their great variety, presented a thousand occasions of wonder as I passed from a court to the rooms, and from the rooms to halls, and to other corridors from the halls, and to other courts from the rooms. The roofs of all these are of stone, as also are the walls; but the walls are full of sculptured figures. Each court is surrounded with a colonnade of white stone, closely fitted. And adjoining the extremity of the Labyrinth is a Pyramid forty orgyæ in height,* on which large figures are carved, and a way to it has been made under ground."†

This curious record of these twelve kings can be easily explained by referring to the book of Genesis, chapter xlvii. This chapter corroborates it, for the Israelites, the twelve sons of Jacob, had absolute power given them by Pharaoh, and had the whole land of Egypt under their control; for "Pharaoh spake unto Joseph, saying, 'Thy father and thy brethren are come unto thee. The land of Egypt is before thee; in the best of the land make thy father and brethren dwell: in the land of Goshen let them dwell; and if thou knowest any men of activity among them, then make them rulers over my cattle.'"

* One hundred and sixty cubits high.—J. V. G.
† Herodotus, *Euterpe*, ii.

Owing to the severity of the famine every Egyptian had to part with his cattle, and "Joseph gave them bread in exchange for horses, and for the flocks, and for the cattle of the herds, and for the asses: and he fed them with bread for all their cattle for that year."

But as the famine still continued, the poor Egyptians, when they had exchanged all they possessed for bread, sold even their own persons. When the whole country was in this desperate condition, the Hebrews governed the nation for Pharaoh, who placed implicit faith in their wisdom and probity. These were the men styled by Egyptologists "Shepherd Kings," and this period or epoch is mentioned by Manetho, the Egyptian historian, in the record written in the Greek language, of which he was a master; it is as follows:—

"There was a king of ours, whose name was Timaus.* Under him it came to pass, I know not how, that God was averse to us, and there came, after a surprising manner, men of ignoble birth out of the eastern parts, and had boldness enough to make an expedition into our country, and with ease subdued it by force, yet without our hazarding a battle with them.† So when they had gotten those that governed us under their power, they afterwards burnt down our cities and demolished the temples of the gods, and used all the inhabitants after a most barbarous manner; nay, some they slew, and led

---

* The Pharaoh of Joseph.—J. V. G.

† A malicious, culpable suppression of the truth. These people were the Hebrews who came from Canaan to Joseph during the famine.—J. V. G.

their children and their wives into slavery.* At length they made one of themselves king, whose name was Salatis.† He also lived at Memphis, and made both the upper and lower regions pay tribute, and left garrisons in places that were most proper for them.‡

"He chiefly aimed to secure the eastern part, as foreseeing that the Assyrians, who had then the greatest power, would be desirous of that kingdom and invade them; and as he found in the Saite Nomos (Seth-roite) a city very proper for his purpose, and which lay upon the Bubastic Channel, but, with regard to a certain theologic notion, was called Avaris, this he rebuilt, and made very strong by the walls he built about it, and by a most numerous garrison of 240,000 armed men whom he put into it to keep it. Thither Salatis came in summer-time, partly *to gather his corn* and pay his soldiers their wages, and partly to exercise his armed men, and thereby to terrify foreigners.

"When this man had reigned thirteen years, after him reigned another, whose name was Beon, for forty-four years; after him reigned another, called Apachnas, thirty-six years and seven months; after him Apophis reigned sixteen years; and then Jonias, fifty years and one month; after all these, Assis,§ forty-nine years and two months. And these

---

* They sold themselves for food and became slaves to Pharaoh.—J. V. G.

† Joseph, made governor by Pharoah.—J. V. G.

‡ To guard the Pyramids from being broken into, as the people at that time knew that they were granaries.—J. V. G.

§ These men were the brethren that Joseph presented to Pharaoh immediately on their arrival, and who were appointed by him to be rulers over his cattle. Gen. xlvii. 6.—J. V. G.

six were the first rulers among them, who were all along making war with the Egyptians, and were very desirous gradually to destroy them to the very roots. This whole nation was styled Hycsos, that is, Shepherd Kings; for the first syllable *Hyc*, according to the sacred dialect, denotes a king, as is *sos* a shepherd, but this according to the ordinary dialect, and of these is compounded Hycsos; but some say that these people were Arabians. It is also said that this word does not denote kings, but, on the contrary, denotes captive shepherds, and this on account of the particle *Hyc*; for that *Hyc*, with the aspiration, in the Egyptian tongue again denotes shepherds, and expressly also; and this seems the more probable opinion and more agreeable to ancient history.

"These people, whom we have before named kings, and called shepherds also, and their descendants, kept possession of Egypt 511 years. After these, the kings of Thebais and of the other parts of Egypt made an insurrection against the shepherds, and that then a terrible and long war was made between them. That under a king whose name was Alisphragmuthosis,* the shepherds were subdued by him, and were, indeed, driven out of other parts of Egypt, but were shut up in a place that contained 10,000 acres; this place was named Avaris. The shepherds built a wall round all this place, which was a large and strong wall, and this in order to keep all their possessions and their prey within a place of strength, but that Thummosis,† the

---

* This Alisphragmuthosis is meant for Moses, the son of the daughter of Pharaoh, by adoption.—J. V. G.

† Thummosis was not the son, but brother, of Moses—Aaron. —J. V. G.

son of Alisphragmuthosis made an attempt to take them by force and by siege with 480,000 men to lie round about them ; but that, upon his despair of taking the place by that siege, they came to a composition with them, that they should leave Egypt, and go without any harm to be done to them, whithersoever they would ; and that, after this composition was made, they went away with their whole families and effects, not fewer in number than 240,000, and took their journey from Egypt, through the wilderness, for Syria ;* but that, as they were in fear of the Assyrians, who had then dominion over Asia, they built a city in that country which is now called Judea, and that large enough to contain this great number of men, and called it Jerusalem."†

Manetho is altogether in a mist, for he seems unwilling to state the truth, and still he is compelled, as a historian, to write something, though against his will. His malice against the Hebrews is manifest throughout. To give an account of the overthrow of the Egyptians at the Red Sea, he invents this story :—

"After those that were sent to work in the quarries had continued in that miserable state for a long while, the King was desired that he would set apart the city Avaris,‡ which was then left desolate of the shepherds, for their habitation and protection, which desire he granted them.

"Now this city, according to the ancient theology, was Trypho's city. But when the men were gotten

---

* The exodus of the Children of Israel for the Land of Promise.—J. V. G.

† Josephus, *Against Apion*.   ‡ Goshen.—J. V. G.

into it, and found the place fit for a revolt, they appointed themselves a ruler out of the priests of Heliopolis, whose name was Osarsiph, and they took their oaths that they would be obedient to him in all things. He then, in the first place, made this law for them: that they should neither worship the Egyptian gods, nor should abstain from any one of those sacred animals which they have in the highest esteem, but kill and destroy them all; that they should join themselves to nobody but to those that were of this confederacy.

"When he had made such laws as these, and many more such as were mainly opposite to the customs of the Egyptians, he gave order that they should use the multitude of the hands they had in building walls about their city,* and make themselves ready for a war with King Amenophis†, while he did himself take into his friendship the other priests, and those that were polluted with them, and sent ambassadors to those shepherds who had been driven out of the land by Tethmosis to the city called Jerusalem, whereby he informed them of his own affairs, and of the state of those others that had been treated after such an ignominious manner, and desired that they would come with one consent to his assistance in this war against Egypt. He also promised that he would, in the first place, bring them back to their ancient city and country Avaris, and provide a plentiful maintenance for their multitude; that he would protect them and fight for them as

---

* Building treasure-cities for Pharaoh — Pithom, and Raamses.
† The new king, who knew not Joseph.

occasion should require, and would easily reduce the country under their dominion.

"These shepherds were all very glad of this message, and came away with alacrity altogether, being in number 200,000 men, and in a little time they came to Avaris. And now Amenophis, the King of Egypt, upon his being informed of their invasion, was in great confusion, as calling to mind what Amenophis, the son of Papis, had foretold him; and, in the first place, he assembled the multitude of the Egyptians, and took counsel with their leaders, and sent for their sacred animals to him, especially for those that were principally worshipped in their temples, and gave a particular charge to the priests distinctly, that they should hide the images of their gods with the utmost care.

"He also sent his son Sethos, who was also named Ramesses from his father Rhampses, being but five years old, to a friend of his. He then passed on with the rest of the Egyptians, being 300,000 of the most warlike of them, against the enemy, who met them. Yet did he not join battle with them; but, thinking that would be to fight against the gods, he returned back and came to Memphis, where he took Apis and the other sacred animals which he had sent for to him, and presently marched into Ethiopia, together with his whole army and multitude of Egyptians;* for the King of Ethiopia was under an obligation to him, on which account he received him, and took care of

---

* The true and authentic version is in the Bible, written by Moses. They were overwhelmed in the Red Sea, instead of retiring into Ethiopia!—J. V. G.

all the multitude that was with him, while the country supplied all that was necessary for the food of the men.

"He also allotted cities and villages for this exile, that was to be from its beginning during those fatally-determined thirteen years. Moreover, he pitched a camp for his Ethiopian army, as a guard to King Amenophis, upon the borders of Egypt. And this was the state of things in Ethiopia. But for the people of Jerusalem, when they came down together with the polluted Egyptians, they treated the men in such a barbarous manner, that those who saw how they subdued the fore-mentioned country, and the horrid wickedness they were guilty of, thought it a most dreadful thing, for they did not only set the cities and villages on fire, but were not satisfied till they had been guilty of sacrilege, and destroyed the images of the gods, and used them in roasting those sacred animals that used to be worshipped, and forced the priests and prophets to be the executioners and murderers of those animals, and then ejected them naked out of the country.

"It was also reported that the priest who ordained their polity and their laws was by birth of Heliopolis, and his name Osarsiph, from Osiris, who was the god of Heliopolis; but that when he was gone over to these people his name was changed, and he was called Moses."*

At this period the land of Egypt was in a most desolate condition. The hand of God was upon it, for evil plagues were sent, and nothing that did harm to the land and its people was withheld during the

* Josephus, *Against Apion.*

time that Moses and Aaron were negotiating with the King to let the Hebrews go a short journey into the wilderness to hold a festival to the Lord. Pharaoh refusing them leave to do so, the last and direst plague was sent, the death of the first-born in the land of Egypt, "from the first-born of Pharaoh that sat on his throne unto the first-born of the captive that was in the dungeon, and all the first-born of cattle."

Then "Pharaoh rose up in the night, he and all his servants, and all the Egyptians; and there was a great cry in Egypt, for there was not a house wherein there was not one dead." In his hour of affliction the King desired these Hebrews to depart, with everything they possessed. When the permission was obtained, the Israelites borrowed from the Egyptians jewels of gold and jewels of silver, and raiment, and the Egyptians lent unto them such things as they required. And they spoiled the Egyptians. After this they took their departure towards the Red Sea.

Pharaoh, when he recovered from his paroxysm of grief, wished to revoke the permission and get the Hebrews back to work for him again. So he called his people together, and, making ready his chariot, he took them with him. "And he took six hundred chosen chariots, and all the chariots of Egypt, and captains over every one of them, and he pursued after the children of Israel; and the children of Israel went out with an high hand." And Pharaoh with all his forces "overtook them encamping by the sea, beside Pi-hahiroth, before Baal-zephon."

Now at this place there was no retreat for the

Israelites by land. They were compelled to effect their escape from their pursuers by crossing the sea to the opposite shore. Seeing the dangerous position they were in, Moses, the man gifted with supernatural resources, contrived to make a passage through the sea, and, a strong east wind assisting him throughout the night, he accomplished the construction of a road for himself and his followers, which should also serve as a trap to engulph their enemies after they had effected their own escape.

He, the builder of the monuments now extant in Ethiopia and Upper Egypt, and in other parts of the habitable earth (of which mention will be made in the course of this narrative)—he it was who contrived and made this passage during the night, while the Egyptians rested after their weary march. It was the sublimest effort of mechanical skill!

When day dawned the passage was ready, and Moses stood by and saw all his people walk down from the Egyptian shore into the dry road in the sea prepared for them. The waters were divided; "and the waters were a wall unto them on their right hand and on their left. And the Egyptians pursued and went in after them to the midst of the sea, even all Pharaoh's horses, his chariots, and his horsemen."

When the Israelites gained the Arabian shore, and the Egyptians were in the middle between the two shores, Moses threw back the waters that were driven aside, and the waters returned and covered all the host of Pharaoh that came into the sea; there escaped not so much as one of them! And the Israelites saw the Egyptians dead upon the sea-shore; "and the people feared the Lord, and believed the Lord, and His servant Moses."

At this crisis there were only women and children left in Egypt, and these in the deepest grief for the death of their first-born sons. No one came back from the camp to relate the terrible catastrophe to these unfortunate widows and orphans; and there was neither priest nor grown-up man to record the events of this period in the sacred books of the nation. Consequently, when Manetho compiled his history from the sacred records, he was unable to relate the events of this period clearly and without contradiction.

He accounts for the non-appearance of the King Amenophis and his forces in Egypt, after his pursuit of the Hebrews, by saying that he retired into Ethiopia, and remained there thirteen years as the guest of the king and people of Ethiopia. The son of this Pharaoh, whom Manetho calls Sethos, was at this time, when his father was drowned, five years old; so that at the end of these thirteen years he attained his majority, and the children that were his contemporaries were old enough to help themselves. These thirteen years form a gap in the history of Egypt.

After the departure of the Israelites, Egypt became a complete wilderness, and the Egyptians were so crushed and desolate that they seemed to have become almost extinct. They mourned and grieved so long that they appear to have quite forgotten even the names of their kings and the history of their nation. No wonder the Nile was termed the Lethe by classic writers.

The present Egyptians, the real descendants of

Mizraim, are the Copts and the Fellaheen,—poor wretched specimens of humanity—and if these represent their ancestors, it conclusively proves to every traveller, when he stands in mute admiration on the stupendous monuments of past grandeur, that they never were the founders of such works of art and magnificence ; they never were the players on the harp and other musical instruments depicted on the walls of palaces, nor the refined occupants of those noble apartments, representing the highest culture and intelligence—apartments furnished with chairs, sofas, and tables, and embellished with pictures of battles and banquets, marriage-processions, funerals, and other subjects of the greatest interest. The real Egyptians were not the founders or builders of any of those monumental remains which make Egypt the land of wonders and the favourite resort of the learned.

The descendants of Abraham the Hebrew were the guiding intellects that ruled Egypt for her Pharaohs, who possessed discernment enough to appoint them to rule their kingdom on account of their wisdom and activity.

About the year 1900 B.C. Abraham went down to Egypt from Canaan because of the famine. And when he had seen and spoken to Pharaoh, that monarch "gave him leave to enter into conversation with the most learned among the Egyptians, from which conversation his virtue and his reputation became more conspicuous than they had been before. For whereas the Egyptians were formerly addicted to different customs, and despised one another's sacred and accustomed rites, and were very angry one with another on that account, Abram conferred with each of them, and, confuting the reasonings they made use of every one for their own practices, demonstrated that such reasonings were vain and void of truth; whereupon he was admired by them in those conferences as a very wise man, and one of great sagacity, when he discoursed on any subject he undertook; and this not only in understanding it, but in persuading other men also to assent to him. He communicated to them arithmetic, and delivered to them the science of astronomy; for, before Abram came into Egypt, they were unacquainted with those parts of learning, for that science came from the Chaldeans into Egypt, and from thence into Greece and elsewhere."*

This visit has been mentioned by the Greek and Roman writers, who state these visitors to be Shepherd Kings, the Hycsos. Abraham was immensely wealthy, for the Bible says that "Abram went up out of Egypt, he and his wife Sarai, and all that he had, and Lot, his nephew, with him, into the south. And Abram was very rich in cattle, in silver, and in gold."

The ruins that are now existing in the Vostani, or Middle Egypt—comprising the provinces of Fayoum, Beni-Souef, and Minieh—and in the Bahari, or Lower Egypt—comprising the provinces of Bahireh, Rosetta, Damietta, Gharbiyeh, Menouf, Mansoura, and Sharkeyeh—were the constructions and erections of Joseph, otherwise called Zaphnath-paaneah, and his eleven brothers; while those found in the Saïd, or Upper Egypt—comprising the provinces of Thebes,

* Josephus.

Djergeh, and Siout—as well as those in Nubia and Ethiopia, sometimes called Abyssinia, owe their erection to Moses, the descendant of Levi, one of the brothers of Joseph.

Being the adopted son of Princess Thurmuthis, daughter of Pharaoh, Moses ruled Egypt as his ancestors had done before his time. His return after the siege and re-conquest of Meroë, and the entrance in state of his bride, the Princes Tharbis, daughter of the King of Ethiopia, are commemorated on the walls of the palace in Upper Egypt. He became very hateful to the Egyptians on account of his great acts and the power he displayed, so that they conspired against him.

To save his life Moses left Egypt, and meeting Kikanus, the King of Ethiopia, returning home from an incursion into Assyria, Moses went with him and his army. After a residence of nine years with the King, the Ethiopians elected Moses to the throne of Ethiopia on the death of Kikanus. This event took place in the hundred and fifty-seventh year after Israel went down into Egypt.*

On the son of the King coming of age, Moses abdicated and left Ethiopia. The Ethiopians made him many rich presents, and sent him away with great honours.

In Abyssinia there is a colony of people quite distinct from the Ethiopians. They differ totally from them in personal appearance, being fair and handsome, and decidedly of the Jewish type. In religion and customs and language they resemble the Jews; the characters of their writing are similar

* The Talmud.

to the Hebrew. This people must have entered Ethiopia with Moses, and stayed behind when he went away and entered Midian. The place they occupy is called Amhara, situate on a hill, and their language Amharic.

CHAPTER VI.

THE SPHINX—THE ENTRANCE.

THE Great Sphinx that is on the Mokattam Hill, facing the large Pyramids of Jeezeh, is the link of union between the north and south of Egypt, as well as the union of the works of those great men living at different periods of time as rulers of Egypt—Joseph and Moses. The following account of this Sphinx is taken from a work called *View of Ancient and Modern Egypt*, by the Rev. Michael Russell, LL.D.

"Our account of the mechanical productions of ancient Egypt would be incomplete did we not mention the Great Sphinx, which has always been regarded as an accompaniment, and sometimes even as a rival, to the Pyramids. The latest information in regard to this stupendous figure was obtained through the persevering labours of Mr. Caviglia, whose name has been already mentioned with so much honour.

"After the most fatiguing and anxious endeavours during several months, he succeeded in laying open the whole statue to its base, and exposing a clear area extending to a hundred feet from its front. 'It is not easy,' says Mr. Salt, who witnessed the process of excavation, 'for any person unused to operations of this kind to form the smallest idea of the difficulties which he had to surmount, more especially when working at the bottom of the trench; for, in spite of every precaution, the slightest breath of wind, or concussion, set all the surrounding particles of sand in motion, so that the sloping sides began to crumble away, and mass after mass to come tumbling down, till the whole surface bore no unapt resemblance to a cascade of water. Even when the sides appeared most firm, if the labourers suspended their work but for an hour, they found on their return that they had the greatest part of it to do over again. This was particularly the case on the southern side of the paw, where the whole of the people—from sixty to a hundred—were employed for seven days without making any sensible advance, the sand rolling down in one continued torrent. But the discovery amply rewarded the toil and expense which were incurred in revealing the structure of this wonderful work of art.

"'The huge legs stretched out fifty feet in advance from the body, which is in a cumbent posture; fragments of an enormous beard were found resting beneath the chin; and there were seen all the appendages of a temple, granite tablet, and altar, arranged on a regular platform immediately in front. On this pavement, and at an equal distance between the paws of the figure, was the large slab of granite just mentioned, being not less than fourteen feet high, seven broad, and two thick. The face of this stone, which fronted the east, was highly embellished with sculptures in bas-relief, the subject representing two sphinxes seated on pedestals, and priests holding out offerings, while there was an inscription in hieroglyphics most beautifully executed; the whole design being covered at top, and protected, as it were, with the sacred globe, the serpent, and the wings.

"'Two other tablets of calcareous stone, similarly ornamented, were supposed, together with that of granite, to have constituted part of a miniature temple, by being placed one on each side of the latter, and at right angles to it. One of them, in fact, was still remaining in its place; of the other, which was thrown down and broken, the fragments are now in the British Museum.

"'A small lion, couching in front of this edifice, had its eyes directed towards the main figure. There were besides several fragments of other lions rudely carved, and the fore-part of a sphinx of tolerable workmanship; all of which, as well as the tablets, walls, and platforms on which the little temple stood, were ornamented with red paint, a colour which seems to have been, in Egypt as well as in *India*, appropriated to sacred purposes. In front of the temple was a granite altar, with one of the four projections or horns still retaining its place at the angle. From the effects of fire evident on the stone, it is manifest that it had been used for burnt-offerings.

"'On the side of the left paw of the Great Sphinx were cut several indistinct legends in Greek characters, addressed to different deities.* On the second digit of the same was sculptured, in pretty deep letters, an inscription in verse, of which the

* Done by Greeks in modern times.—J. V. G.

subjoined translation was given by the late Dr. Young, whose extensive knowledge of antiquities enabled him at once to restore the defects of the original, and to convey its meaning in Latin as well as in English.

"'Thy form stupendous here the gods have placed,
    Sparing each spot of harvest-bearing land;
And with this mighty work of art have graced
    A rocky isle, encumber'd once with sand:
Not that fierce Sphinx that Thebes erewhile laid waste,
But great Latona's servant, mild and bland:
Watching that prince beloved who fills the throne
Of Egypt's plains, and calls the Nile his own.
That heavenly monarch who his foes defies,
Like Vulcan powerful, and like Pallas wise.'

"This remarkable statue is again as much under the dominion of the desert as it was half a century ago; and, consequently, it now meets the eye of the Egyptian traveller shrouded in sand to the same depth as before.

"Dr. Richardson relates that the wind and the Arabs had replaced the covering on this venerable piece of antiquity, and hence the lower parts were quite invisible. The breast, shoulders, and neck, which are those of a human being, remain uncovered, as also the back, which is that of a lion; the neck is very much eroded, and, to a person near, the head seems as if it were too heavy for its support. The head-dress has the appearance of an old-fashioned wig, projecting out about the ears like the hair of the Berberi Arabs;* the ears project considerably, the nose is broken, the whole face has been painted

---

* The consort of Moses was from Meroë, and she must have had her hair dressed in that fashion.—J. V. G.

red, which is the colour assigned to the ancient inhabitants of Egypt, and to all the deities of the country except Osiris. The features are Nubian, or what, from ancient representations, may be called ancient Egyptian, which is quite different from the negro feature. The expression is particularly placid and benign; so much so, that the worshipper of the Sphinx might hold up his god as superior to all the other gods of wood and stone which the blinded nations worshipped.

"Pococke found the head and neck—all that were above ground—to be twenty-seven feet high; the breast was thirty-three feet wide; and the entire length about a hundred and thirty. Pliny estimated it at a hundred and thirteen feet long and sixty-three in height. According to Dr. Richardson, the stretch of the back is about a hundred and twenty feet, and the elevation of the head above the sand from thirty to thirty-five, a result which accords pretty nearly with the measurement of Coutelle. It is obvious, at the same time, that the discrepancy in these reports as to the elevation of the figure must be attributed to the varying depth of the sand, which appears to have accumulated greatly since the days of the Roman naturalist.

"There is no opening found in the body of the statue, whereby to ascertain whether it is hollow or not; but we learn from Dr. Pococke that there is an entrance both in the back and in the top of the head, the latter of which, he thinks, might serve for the arts of the priests in uttering oracles, while the former might be meant for descending to the apartments beneath."

Colonel Howard-Vyse made ineffectual attempts to pierce the Sphinx; the result, in the back of the statue, he gives in these words :—

"The boring-rods were broken, owing to the carelessness of the Arabs, at the depth of twenty-seven feet in the back of the Sphinx. Various attempts were made to get them out, and on the 21st of July* gunpowder was used for that purpose; but, being unwilling to disfigure this venerable monument, the excavation was given up, and several feet of boring-rods were left in it. During the operation a very beautiful fossil of a reed was discovered, which is now in the British Museum."

Respecting the attempt near the shoulder, he says :—"The operations carried on at the Sphinx were suspended, and the hole made near the shoulder, about twenty-five and a half feet in depth, was plugged up."

It was Moses who had the Sphinx cut out of the solid rock on which it stands. The features and the head-dress of the statue represent in colossal proportions the features and the head-dress of his beloved Ethiopian bride, who was "black but comely."

The statue served as the royal entrance into the Great Pyramid, near which it is constructed. That this Pyramid has been entered from this direction is evident from the fact that a ramp-stone has been taken away from its place by some person who approached it by a subterranean passage.

"The original builders,† then, were not those

---

* A.D. 1837.

† Piazzi Smyth, *Our Inheritance in the Great Pyramid.*

who knocked out from within on the well side that now lost ramp-stone, and exposed the inlet to the well-mouth as it is presently seen, near the north-west corner of the Grand Gallery. Neither was Al Mamoun the party, for no one could have done it except by entering the well from the very bottom-most depths of the subterranean region; and he, the son of Caliph Haroun Al Raschid, and all his crew, did not descend further down the entrance-passage than merely to the level of his own forced hole, which is not subterranean at all. Nor is the credit claimed for any of his Arab successors, who rather alluded to the well as an already existing feature in their earliest time, and one they did not understand; in large part, too, because they had only seen, and only knew of, the upper end of it in the north-west corner of the Grand Gallery floor; and there it was simply a deep hole, the beginning of darkness and the shadow of death.

"Who, then, did burst out that now missing ramp-stone? Who, indeed! For the whole band of Egyptological writers we have mentioned appear to be convinced that ages before Caliph Al Mamoun made his way by blundering and smashing,—long ages, too, before Mohammed was born, and rather at and about the period of Judah being carried captive to Babylon,—the Egyptians themselves had entered the Great Pyramid by cunning art and tolerable understanding of its mere methods of construction, and had closed it again when they left."

Yes; this Sphinx was the grand royal entrance by which Moses and his consort entered into the interior of the Great Pyramid. He, being inspired by Heaven, had foreseen that in future ages the knowledge of this entrance would be forgotten; he therefore removed the ramp-stone and left the space it occupied open, so as to excite the curiosity of those who might visit the spot.

He also left the world a specimen of this entrance in a wooden statue, built far away, that this wooden construction might serve to unriddle the passage in the Sphinx, which leads into the Great Pyramid. The openings in the head and back of the Sphinx were to give light and air to the passage. The following is a description of the wooden statue, taken from Captain Meares' voyages :—*

"After the English had been for some time in King George's Sound, the Americans began to make use of sails of mats, in imitation of my ship. Not long after this the English were waited upon by Wicananish, a prince of greater wealth and power than any they had yet seen, who invited them to visit his kingdom, which lay at some distance to the southward, that a commercial intercourse might be established for the advantage of both parties.

"The invitation was accepted, and Wicananish himself met the 'Felice' at some distance from the shore with a small fleet of canoes, and, coming on board, piloted them into the harbour. They found the capital to be at least three times the size of Nootka. The country round was covered with impenetrable woods of great extent, in which were trees of enormous size.

"After the King and his chiefs had been enter-

---

* Tytler, *Historical View of the Progress of Discovery on the more Northern Coasts of America.*

tained on board, the English were in return invited to a feast by Wicananish; and it is not easy to conceive a more interesting picture of savage life than witnessed on this occasion. On entering the house, we were absolutely astonished at the vast area it enclosed.

"It contained a large square, boarded up close on all sides to the height of twenty feet with planks of an uncommon breadth and length. Three enormous trees, rudely carved and painted, formed the rafters, which were supported at the ends and in the middle by gigantic images, carved out of huge blocks of timber. The same kind of broad planks covered the whole to keep out the rain; but they were so placed as to be removable at pleasure, either to receive the air and light or to let out the smoke. In the middle of this spacious room were several fires, and beside them large wooden vessels filled with fish soup. Large slices of whale's flesh lay in a state of preparation, to be put into similar machines filled with water, into which the women, with a kind of tongs, conveyed hot stones from very fierce fires, in order to make it boil.

"Heaps of fish were strewed about; and in this central part of the square, which might properly be called the kitchen, stood large seal-skins filled with oil, from whence the guests were served with that delicious beverage. The trees that supported the roof were of a size which would render the mast of a first-rate man-of-war diminutive on a comparison with them; indeed, our curiosity as well as our astonishment was at its utmost stretch when we considered the strength which must have been required to raise these enormous beams to their present elevation, and how such strength could be commanded by a people wholly unacquainted, as we supposed, with the mechanic powers.

"The door by which we entered this extraordinary fabric was the mouth of one of these images, which, large as it may, from this circumstance, be supposed to have been, was not disproportioned to the other features of its colossal visage. We ascended by a few steps on the outside; and, after passing the portal, descended down the chin into the house, where we found new matter for wonder in the number of men, women, and children who composed the family of the chief, which consisted of at least 800 persons. These were divided into groups according to their respective offices, which had distinct places assigned them.

"The whole of the interior of the building was surrounded by a bench, about two feet from the ground, on which the various inhabitants sat, ate, and slept. The chief appeared at the upper end of the room, surrounded by natives of rank, on a small raised platform, round which were placed several large chests, over which hung bladders of oil, large slices of whale's flesh, and proportionable gobbets of blubber.

"Festoons of human skulls, arranged with some attention to uniformity, were disposed in almost every part where they could be placed, and, however ghastly such ornaments appeared to European eyes, they were evidently considered by the courtiers and people of Wicananish as a very splendid and appropriate decoration of the royal apartment.

"When the English appeared, the guests had made a considerable advance in their banquet. Before each person was placed a large slice of boiled whale, which, with small wooden dishes filled with oil and fish-soup, and a mussel-shell instead of a spoon, composed the economy of the table. The servants busily replenished the dishes as they were emptied, and the women picked and opened some bark, which served the purpose of towels. The guests despatched their messes with astonishing rapidity and voracity, and even the children, some of them not above three years old, devoured the blubber and oil with a rapacity worthy of their fathers. Wicananish, in the meantime, did the honours with an air of hospitable yet dignified courtesy, which might have graced a more cultivated society."

The Sphinx was cut or carved on Moses' return from Meroë, and prior to his departure for Ethiopia, where he was elected King. He carefully closed the mouth, which was the door of the passage, that it should never be opened till the fulness of time arrived. But to prevent the monument from being broken into by strangers, he instructed the above-mentioned savages to make the large image, with a door in its mouth, that it might in the future serve as a key to solve the mystery of the Sphinx in connection with the Great Pyramid.

CHAPTER VII.

MISSION OF MOSES IN THE EAST.

DURING his reign in Ethiopia, Moses erected the Sphinxes and other monuments, and left inscriptions and bas-reliefs as tokens of his presence in that country. From thence he went to Midian, where he did not remain idle, for there are mines there which he must have had worked. He was commissioned by the Almighty to deliver the Israelites and bring them out of Egypt, and, after teaching them how to govern themselves, to lead them to the Land of Promise. During the forty years that the Hebrews sojourned in the desert, Moses wrote inscriptions on the rocks—all resembling those he left in Thebes—in order to show to future generations the route by which he led his people.

At the foot of Mount Hor there is a remarkable place, called by the Arabs Wady Mousa, or the Valley of Moses; and the whole of this wild region is celebrated for its beautiful architectural remains. Travellers of our time are told by the Arabs that a great prince dwelt there, and they show them a noble edifice as Pharaoh's Castle, and another equally beautiful as the Palace of Pharaoh's daughter. The following extract, taken from the account given by an American traveller, Mr. Stephens, describes these edifices :—*

"At the entrance of the city there was not a creature to dispute our passage; its portals were wide open, and we passed along the stream down into the area, and still no man to oppose us. In front of the great temple, the pride and beauty of Petra, I saw a narrow opening in the rocks, exactly corresponding with my conception of the object for which I was seeking. A full stream of water was gushing through it, and filling up the whole mouth of the passage.

"Mounted on the shoulders of one of my Bedouins, I got him to carry me through the swollen stream at the mouth of the opening, and set me down on a dry place a little above, whence I began to pick my way, occasionally taking to the shoulders of my follower, and continued to advance more than a mile. I was beyond all peradventure in the great entrance I was seeking. There could not be two such, and I should have gone on to the extreme end of the ravine.

"For about two miles it lies between high and precipitous ranges of rocks, from five hundred to a thousand feet in height, standing as if torn by some great convulsion, and barely wide enough for two horsemen to pass abreast. At the end was a large open space, with a powerful body of light thrown down upon it, and exhibiting in one full view the façade of a beautiful temple, hewn out of the rock, with rows of Corinthian columns and ornaments,

* Laborde, *Journey through Arabia Petræa, to Mount Sinai, and the excavated City of Petra, the Edom of the Prophecies.*

standing out fresh and clear as if but yesterday from the hands of the sculptor.

"Though coming directly from the banks of the Nile, where the preservation of the temples excites the admiration and astonishment of every traveller, we were roused and excited by the extraordinary beauty and excellent condition of the great temple at Petra (Wady Mousa). The whole temple, its columns, ornaments, porticoes, and porches, are cut out from and form part of the solid rock; and this rock, at the foot of which the temple stands like a mere print, towers several hundred feet above, its face cut smooth to the very summit, and the top remaining wild and misshapen as Nature made it.

"The whole area before the temple is perhaps an acre in extent, enclosed on all sides, except at the narrow entrance, and an opening to the left of the temple, which leads into the area of the city by a pass through perpendicular rocks five or six hundred feet in height.

"Ascending several broad steps, we entered under a colonnade of four Corinthian columns, about thirty-five feet high, into a large chamber of some fifty feet square and twenty-five feet high. The outside of the temple is richly ornamented, but the interior is perfectly plain, there being no ornament of any kind upon the walls or ceiling; on each of the three sides is a small chamber; and on the back wall of the innermost chamber I saw the names of Messrs. Leigh, Banks, Irby, and Mangles, the four English travellers who with so much difficulty had effected their entrance to the city; of Messieurs Laborde and Linant, and several others.

"Leaving the temple and the open area on which it fronts, and following the stream, we entered another defile much broader than the first, on each side of which were ranges of tombs, with sculptured doors and columns ; and on the left, in the bosom of the mountain, hewn out of the solid rock, is a large theatre, circular in form, the pillars in front fallen, and containing thirty-three rows of seats, capable of containing more than three thousand persons. Above the corridor was a range of doors opening to chambers in the rocks, the seats of the princes and wealthiest inhabitants of Wady Mousa (Petra), and not unlike a row of private boxes in a modern theatre. The whole theatre is at this day in such a state of preservation that if the tenants of the tombs around could once more rise into life, they might take their old places on its seats and listen to the declamation of their favourite player.

" Though I had no small experience in exploring catacombs and tombs, these were so different from any I had seen that I found it difficult to distinguish the habitations of the living from the chambers of the dead. The façades or architectural decorations of the front were everywhere handsome ; and in this they differed materially from the tombs in Egypt. In the latter the doors were simply an opening in the rock, and all the grandeur and beauty of the work within ; while here the door was always imposing in its appearance, and the interior was generally a simple chamber, unpainted and unsculptured.* I say that I could not distinguish the dwellings from

* This being the camp of the Children of Israel, these chambers were the dwellings of the living.—J. V. G.

the tombs; but this was not invariably the case. Some were clearly tombs, for there were pits in which the dead had been laid, and others were as clearly dwellings, being without a place for the deposit of the dead. One of these last particularly attracted my attention. It consisted of one large chamber, having on one side, at the foot of the wall, a stone bench about one foot high and two or three broad, in form like the divans in the East at the present day; at the other end were several small apartments, hewn out of the rock, with partition-wall left between them, like stalls in a stable, and these had probably been the sleeping apartments of the family.

"There were no paintings or decorations of any kind within the chamber; but the rock out of which it was hewn, like the old stony rampart that encircled the city, was of a peculiarity and beauty that I never saw elsewhere, being a dark ground, with veins of white, blue, red, purple, and sometimes scarlet and light orange, running through it in rainbow streaks; and within the chambers, where there had been no exposure to the action of the elements, the freshness and beauty of the colours in which these waving lines were drawn gave an effect hardly inferior to that of the paintings in the tombs of the Kings at Thebes.

"Farther on, in the same range—though, in consequence of the steps of the streets being broken, we were obliged to go down and ascend again before we could reach it—was another temple, like the first, cut out of the solid rock, and, like the first, too, having for its principal ornament a large urn, shattered and bruised by musket-balls; for the ignorant Arab, believing that gold is concealed in it, day after day, as he passes by, levels at it his murderous gun, in the vain hope to break the vessel and scatter a golden shower on the ground."

From this encampment Moses led the Hebrews to the plains of Moab, and after taking a survey of Canaan from the top of Mount Pisgah, that is over against Jericho, he bade them a last farewell. He was then a hundred and twenty years old; "his eye was not dim, nor his natural force abated. And the children of Israel wept for Moses in the plains of Moab thirty days," and Joshua became their leader in the place of Moses. It is also recorded, that "there arose not a prophet since in Israel like unto Moses, whom the Lord knew face to face, in all the signs and wonders, which the Lord sent him to do in the land of Egypt to Pharaoh, and to all his servants, and to all his land . . . and in all the great terror which Moses showed in the sight of all Israel."

Josephus the Jewish historian gives an account of the departure of Moses from the children of Israel thus:—*" Now as soon as they were come to the mountain called Abarim (which is a very high mountain, situate over against Jericho, and one that affords, to such as are upon it, a prospect of the greatest part of the excellent land of Canaan), he dismissed the senate; and as he was going to embrace Eleazar and Joshua, and was still discoursing with them, a cloud stood over him on the sudden, and he disappeared in a certain valley, although he wrote in the Holy Books that he died,

* Josephus, *Antiquities of the Jews.*

which was done out of fear, lest they should venture to say that, because of his extraordinary virtue, he went to God."

Modern travellers have found remains of architecture and sculpture, which serve as landmarks in the royal progress towards the East. No doubt Moses had these works executed that they might give ample proof of his presence in all those countries wherein the remains exist—countries far divided from each other—and so that by them his route could easily be followed from Ethiopia to the place where he ended his pilgrimage on earth.

From Mount Abarim he took his journey eastward, evidently with a large caravan, consisting of his faithful followers, and forming a formidable escort. The first place at which they halted for any length of time is in Persia, where there are unmistakable signs of his sojourn. The following is an account given by Mr. Morier, who accompanied Sir Harford Jones Brydges on the mission to Persia in 1809:—*

"The sculptures are situated at the distance of about fifteen miles from Kázerún. About seven miles from it I passed the ruined village of Derses; and, leaving two tombs, one on the right hand and the other on the left of the road, came to the bed of a torrent, over which there seems to have been built an aqueduct, for, on each side of its banks, there are remains of masonry, and traces of its conduit may be perceived on the southern bank.

"The extent of the ruins of Shahpúr to the southward is bounded by a beautiful stream of water. Over the spring from which it issues the road is sustained

* Vaux, *Nineveh and Persepolis.*

by fragments of architecture, which are part of the entablature of some public building, and, by their dimensions, must have once been magnificent.

"Immediately after passing the spring, we came upon the ruins of Shahpúr. When standing on an eminence, we computed the whole to be comprised, on a rough calculation, within a circumference of six miles. This circumference enclosed a tract of plain, and a hill, on which the remains of the ancient citadel formed a conspicuous and commanding object. Whether by the caprice of Nature or by the labour of man, this hill or acropolis is distinctly separated from the great range of mountains forming the most eastern boundary of the plain of Kázerún.

"Between this and another imposing mass of rock runs the beautiful river of Shahpúr. We reckoned the space between the two rocks at thirty yards, which formed a little plain of verdure and shrubbery, intersected, indeed, by the stream of the river. The opening between the two grand masses presented a landscape the most varied, the most tranquil, the most picturesque, and, at the same time, the most sublime, that imagination can form.

"A black and stupendous rock flanked the right of the picture; while another still more extraordinary rock, as richly illumined as the other was darkened, supported the left. Between both a distant range of mountains, whose rocks were terminated by a plain, filled up the interstices, forming a fine aërial perspective; whilst the river and rich shrubbery completed a most enlivening foreground.

"The hill on which the remains of the citadel stand is covered by ruins of walls and turrets. On its eastern aspect the nature of the fortification can be traced easily ; for walls fill the chasms from rock to rock, forming altogether a place of defence admirably strong. The first object which arrested our attention was a mutilated sculpture of two colossal figures on horseback, carved on the superfices of the rock. The figure on the right was most injured ; the only part, indeed, which we could ascertain with precision was one of the front and two of the hinder feet of a horse, standing over the statue of a man, who was extended at his full length, his face turning outwardly, and reposed upon his right hand, and his attire bearing marks of a Roman costume. A figure in the same dress was placed in an attitude of supplication at the horse's knees, and a head in alto-relievo just appeared between the hinder feet. The equestrian figure on the left is not quite so much mutilated, the horse and parts of the drapery on the thighs being still well preserved.

"The next piece of sculpture (which, like the former, was carved upon the mountain of the citadel) is perfect in all its parts. It consists of three grand compartments; the central and most interesting represents a figure on horseback, whose dress announces a royal personage. His head-dress is a crown, on which is placed a globe; his hair flows in very large and massy curls over both shoulders, whilst a slight mustachio just covers his upper lip, and gives much expression to a countenance strongly indicative of pride and majesty.

"His body is clothed with a robe, which falls in many folds to his girdle, and then extends itself over his thigh and legs as low as his ancle. A quiver hangs by his side; in his right hand he holds the hand of a figure behind him, which stands so as to cover the whole hind quarter of his horse, and which is dressed in the Roman tunic and helmet. A figure, habited also in the Roman costume, is on its knees before the head of the horse, with its hands extended and with a face betraying entreaty. Under the feet of the horse is another figure extended, in the same attire and character as that of the other two Roman figures.

"To the right of the tablet stands a figure with his hands also extended, but dressed in a different manner, and, as far as we could judge, with features more Egyptian than European. In the angle between the King's head and the horse's is a Victory displaying the scroll of fame. A figure (part of which is concealed by the one on its knees) completes the whole of this division.

"The second grand compartment, which is on the right, is divided again into six sub-compartments, in each of which are carved three figures, the costumes and general physiognomies of which are all different. They appear mostly in postures of supplication, and, I should suspect, are representations of vanquished people.

"On the left, in the third grand compartment, are rows of horsemen, divided by one line into two smaller compartments. They have all the same characteristic dress and features as the royal figure in the centre, and certainly represent his forces. The whole of this most interesting monument is sculptured in a very hard rock, which bears the finest polish, and which we pronounced to be a coarse species of jasper. The figures on foot are in height five feet nine inches: figures on horseback, from the rider's cap to the horse's hoofs, six feet ten inches in length; the grand tablet eleven feet eleven inches.

"Having examined these, we next crossed the river to the sculptures on the opposite rock. The first is a long tablet containing a multitude of figures. The principal person (who is certainly the King represented in the former tablet) is placed in the very centre of the piece, alone in a small compartment, and is seated with a sword placed betwixt his legs, on the pommel of which rests his left hand. On his right, on the uppermost of two long slips, are many men, who seem to be a mixture of Persians and Romans, the former conducting the latter as prisoners. Under these, in the lower step, are others, who by their wigs appear to be Persians. Their leader bears a human head in both hands, and extends it towards the central figure. On the left are four small compartments. The first (nearest that figure, and the highest from the ground) incloses a crowd of men, whose arms are placed over one another's shoulders. Below these are five figures, one of whom leads a horse without any more furniture than a bridle.

"The other two compartments are filled up with eight figures each. We considered this to represent in general a King seated in his room of audience, surrounded by his own people, and by nations tributary to him. The length is eleven yards four inches. On the left of this were two colossal figures on horseback carved in alto-relievo. The one to the right had all the dress, character, and features of the

King above described; the other on the left appeared also a royal personage, but differing in dress and in the furniture of his horse. Both had their hands extended, and held a ring, which we conceived to be emblematical of peace.

"After having re-passed the river, we walked over the numerous mounds of stones and earth which cover the ruined buildings of Shahpúr, and which, if ever explored, would discover innumerable secrets of antiquity. We were conducted by the peasants who were with us to the remains of a very fine wall, which in the symmetry of its masonry equalled any Grecian work that I have ever seen. Each stone was four feet long, twenty-seven inches thick, and cut to the finest angles.

"The wall formed the front of a square building, the area of which is fifty-five feet. At the top were placed sphinxes couchant, a circumstance which we ascertained from discovering accidentally two eyes and a mutilated foot, at the extremity of one of the upper stones. In this wall there is a window, which is arched by the formation of its upper stone. Behind this square building we traced most correctly the configuration of a theatre, thirty paces in length and fourteen in breadth. The place resembled, at least, those called theatres which I have seen in Greece. From a comparison of their positions, we were led to suppose that the building still extant must have been connected with the other behind it, and may have formed, perhaps, the entrance to it."*

These commemorative sculptures denote that

* Vaux, *Nineveh and Persepolis*.

the stranger King (Moses) and his forces took possession of Derses near Shahpúr by conquest; and the length of time he remained in the country may be inferred from the interregnum, or unrecorded interval, between the Assyrian epochs of Nimrúd and Khorsabad. The supposed duration of that period is about sixty or seventy years, and it began just about the time that Moses left the children of Israel, so that it synchronises with the arrival of Moses in the country, and his residence there fills up the gap.

The number of his followers must have increased during the years that Moses travelled from one country to another, and he was likely in consequence to leave some of them to colonise, and to teach his doctrine, and to carry on the ordinances of his religion, in every region that was suitable for that purpose.

The Afghans, whose country lies nearest to Persia, claim descent from the Jews, and the people of Kafiristan are unmistakably Jews. These inhabit a mountainous country adjoining Afghanistan, on the north-west of Cashmere.

"The Caufirs* have no general name for their nation. Each tribe has its peculiar name, for they are all divided into tribes, though not according to genealogy, but to geographical position, each valley being held by a separate tribe. The Mussulmans confound them all under the name of Caufir, or infidel, and call their country Caufiristaun. They also call one division of them Seeaposh (black-vested),

* Mountstuart Elphinstone, *Account of the Kingdom of Cabul.*

or Tor Caufirs (black infidels), and another Speen Caufirs (white infidels). Both epithets are taken from their dress, for the whole of the Caufirs are remarkable for the fairness and beauty of their complexion, but those of the largest division wear a sort of vest of black goat-skin, while the others dress in white cotton.

"There are several languages among the Caufirs, but they have all many words in common, and all have a near connection with the Sanskrit. Their religion does not resemble any other with which I am acquainted. They believe in one God; but they also worship numerous idols, which, they say, represent great men of former days, who intercede with God in favour of their worshippers. These idols are of stone or wood, and always represent men or women, some mounted and some on foot.

"They have hereditary priests. They have also persons who can procure an inspiration of some superior being by holding their heads over the smoke of a sacrifice. Their festivals are often accompanied with a sacrifice, and always with a feast. They have no titles of their own, but they have borrowed that of Khaun from the Afghans for their rich men. Their property chiefly consists in cattle and slaves.

"The houses of the Caufirs are often of wood, and they have generally cellars where they keep their cheeses, clarified butter, wine, and vinegar. In every house there is a wooden bench fixed to the wall, with a low back to it. There are also stools shaped like drums, but smaller in the middle than at the ends, and tables of the same sort, but larger.

The Caufirs, partly from their dress and partly from habit, cannot sit like the other Asiatics; and if forced to sit down on the ground, stretch out their legs like Europeans. They have also beds made of wood and thongs of neats' leather: the stools are made of wicker-work.

"They celebrate a sacrifice at a particular place near the village where there was a stone post; a fire was kindled before it, through which flour, butter, and water were thrown on the stone. At length an animal was sacrificed, and the flesh was burned, and part eaten by the assistants, who were numerous, and who accompanied the priest in prayers and devout gesticulations."*

Their neighbours, the dwellers in the beautiful vale of Cashmere, also claim descent from the Jews, " a claim† borne out by the personal appearance of the race, their garb, the cast of their countenance, and the form of their beards. There is a belief, too, among them that Moses died in the capital of Cashmere, and that he is buried near it." (This belief is erroneous, as that Lawgiver ended his days very far away from Cashmere.)

"There is no doubt that they were originally of Brahmin (Hebrew) origin; and prosperous must have been the people—wise, beneficent, and energetic the rulers, in those old days, if tradition and legend are to be believed, and the mighty monuments of a past grandeur, long anterior to the days when Mogul wealth and taste embellished the valley, are to be

---

* See Lev. vi. 14-18.—J. V. G.
† Lieut.-Colonel Torrens, *Travels in Ladâk, Tartary, and Kashmir.*

looked on as faithful witnesses; but to this golden age succeeded centuries of oppression.

"We must, therefore, not be too hard on the Kashmiri; his faults are those that oppression fosters, and his virtues, for he has some, are his industry, his religious toleration, his observance of family ties and obligations, while for qualities of head and hand he is second to no Eastern race. As artificers, the pale, slim, sneaking denizens of the crowded lanes of Sreenuggur will compete with any in the East, and the sturdy, broad-shouldered, large-limbed peasant is a painstaking and successful husbandman.

"Among the many changes of masters which Cashmere has undergone, one class of men appear not only to have retained the religion of their Brahmin (Hebrew) forefathers, but also a high position among their fellows. I allude to the Kashmiri Pundits—men of lengthy pedigree, of wealth and influence, who, thanks to their superior education and fitness for business, were largely employed by their successive conquerors, placed in posts of trust, and seemingly exempted from the forcible conversion to the creed of Mahommed, which was universally imposed on their countrymen."

From Cashmere the invading host of Moses entered Hindostan, known at that period under the name of Ind, from the river Indus. The natives of the country were a variety of barbarous tribes, who resisted the entry of Moses and his followers, and many sanguinary battles were fought before they were subdued, and the conquerors permitted to take possession of the whole peninsula. Here Moses assumed the name of Manu, and called his Hebrew nationality Brahmin.

The language he employed while in Hindostan was Sanscrit; all his laws and ordinances were written in this sacred language. He established classes or castes. The Brahmins in India occupied the same position as the Levites in Judea, and were the priests, the instructors, and the philosophers of the nation.

The chronicles of this epoch record the wars and the brave exploits of heroes, and the wisdom and learning of the conquerors. The first mention made of this invading nation gives as their residence a tract of country between the rivers Sersooty and Caggar, distant from Delhi about one hundred miles to the north-west. It then bore the name of Bramhaverta, as being the haunt of gods; and although it was but about sixty-five miles long by forty broad, it was the scene of the adventures of the first princes, and the residence of the most famous sages. They extended their territory, which seems to have included at that time the districts of Oude, Agra, Allahabad, Lahore, and Delhi. The city of Oude, then termed Ayodha, was the capital. In course of time they moved down the peninsula, and subdued the Deccan and the whole of the south. The celebrated rock temples of Ellora, and the sculptured cave of Elephanta, are some of the many monuments left by these Brahmins, the descendants of Abraham the Hebrew. Every traveller, in viewing these wonderful remains is forcibly reminded of similar remains in Egypt and Nubia — unmistakable proof of the works having been executed under the guidance of the same inspired intellect.

The colonies left by Moses or Manu in the peninsula of India within the Ganges were distinctly traceable in the days of Alexander the Great, the southern colonists being swarthy, tall, and handsome, not unlike Ethiopians, whilst those of the northern latitudes were much fairer, and not unlike the Egyptians, and those still farther south were Jews. Of such as these were the forces and followers of Moses in his progress over the earth.

After conquering the whole peninsula he left the mainland and went over to the island of Ceylon. The Cingalese are well versed in biblical history; and they even believe that Adam and Eve came to Ceylon after their expulsion from the garden of Eden. There are remains of former grandeur and colossal statues to mark the presence of the god-like Lawyer in the island.

From the island of Ceylon he went by sea and landed on the opposite peninsula, or India beyond the Ganges. The neighbourhood of Siam has splendid ruins of most noble buildings and statuary. In Bangkok, the capital of Siam, the temples and all other religious buildings are evidently of Egyptian origin. The Siamese of the present time, from the King to the peasant, live in poor houses of wood or bamboo; and they frankly admit that they did not build those ancient monuments, and do not even know who were the builders of them.

Recent travellers in Chin-India speak in rapturous terms of the ruins of Angkor, the great temple in Siam. One writer says: "The ruins of Angkor are as imposing as the ruins of Thebes or Memphis, and more mysterious"; while another thinks that "one of these temples, a rival to that of Solomon, and erected by some ancient Michael Angelo, might take an honourable place beside our most beautiful buildings. It is grander than anything left to us by Greece or Rome."

The following description of these wonderful ruins is taken from the work of a recent traveller who visited them:—*

"The ruins of Angkor are situated in the province of Siamrap, eastern Siam, in about lat. 13° 30' N. and long. 104° E. We entered upon an immense causeway, the stairs of which were flanked with six huge griffins, each carved from a single block of stone. This causeway, which leads directly to the main entrance of the temple, is 725 feet in length, and is paved with stones, each of which measures four feet in length by two in breadth. On either side of it are artificial lakes fed by springs, and each covering about five acres of ground. We passed through one of the side gates and crossed the square to a *sala* situated at the very entrance of the temple. Embosomed in the midst of a perfect forest of cocoa, betel-nut, and toddy palms, and with no village in sight, excepting a dozen or more huts, the abodes of priests having the charge of it; the general appearance of the wonderful temple is beautiful and romantic as well as impressive and grand. A just idea of it can hardly be conveyed by writing; it must be seen to be understood and appreciated. Still, perhaps, a detailed description might assist the imagination somewhat in forming a proper estimate of the grand genius which planned, and the skill and

* Frank Vincent, Jun., *The Land of the White Elephant.*

patience which executed, such a masterpiece of architecture.

"The outer wall of Nagkon Wat—which words signify a city or assemblage of temples or monasteries—about half a mile square, is built of sandstone, with gateways on each side, which are handsomely carved with figures of gods and dragons, arabesques, and intricate scrolls. Upon the western side is the main gateway, and passing through this and up a causeway (paved with slabs of stone three feet in length by two in breadth) for a distance of a thousand feet, you arrive at the central main entrance of the temple. About the middle of the causeway, on either side, are image-houses, much decayed and overgrown with rank parasitic plants; and a little farther on are two small ponds, with carved stone copings, which in most places are thrown down.

"The foundations of Nagkon Wat are as much as ten feet in height, and are very massively built of the same volcanic rock as that used in the construction of the 'Angels' Bridge.' The entire edifice, which is raised on three terraces, the one about thirty feet above the other, including the roof, is of stone, but without cement; and so closely fitting are the joints as even now to be scarcely discernible. The quarry where the stone was hewn is about two days' travel—thirty miles—distant; and it is supposed the transportation of the immense boulders could only have been effected by means of a water communication—a canal or river, or when the country was submerged at the end of the rainy season. The shape of the building is oblong, being 796 feet in length and 588 feet in width, whilst the highest central pagoda rises some 250 odd feet above the ground, and four others, at the angles of the court, are each about 150 feet in height.

"Passing between low railings, we ascend a platform composed of boulders of stone four feet in length, one and a half feet in width, and six inches in thickness, and enter the temple itself through a columned portico, the façade of which is beautifully carved in basso-relievo with ancient mythological subjects. From this doorway, on either side, runs a corridor, with a double row of columns, cut—base and capital—from single blocks, with a double, oval-shaped roof covered with carving and consecutive sculptures upon the outer wall.

"This gallery of sculptures, which forms the exterior of the temple, consists of over half a mile of continuous pictures, cut in basso-relievo upon sandstone slabs six feet in width, and represents subjects taken from Hindoo mythology—from Ramayana, the Sanscrit epic poem of India, with its 25,000 verses describing the exploits of the god Rama and the son of the King of Oudh. The contests of the King of Ceylon, and Hunaman, the monkey god, are graphically represented. There is no key-stone used in the arch of this corridor, and its ceiling is uncarved. On the walls are sculptured the immense number of 100,000 separate figures (or at least heads). Entire scenes from the Ramayana are pictured; one, I remember, occupies 240 feet of the wall.

"Weeks might be spent in studying, identifying, and classifying the varied subjects of this wonderful gallery. You see warriors riding upon elephants and in chariots, foot soldiers with shield and spear, boats, unshapely divinities, trees, monkeys, tigers, griffins, hippopotami, serpents, fishes, crocodiles, bullocks, tortoises, soldiers of immense physical development, with helmets, and some people with beards. The figures stand somewhat like those on the great Egyptian monuments, the side partly turned towards the front; in the case of the men, one foot and leg are always placed in advance of the other; and I noticed, besides, five horsemen, armed with spear and sword, riding abreast, like those seen upon the Assyrian tablets in the British Museum. In the procession several of the kings are preceded by musicians playing upon shells and long bamboo flutes. Some of the kings carry a sort of battle-axe, others a weapon which much resembles a golf-club, and others are represented as using the bow and arrow. In one place is a grotesque divinity, who sits elegantly dressed upon a throne surmounted by umbrellas; this figure, of peculiar sanctity, evidently, has been recently gilded, and before it, upon a small table, there were a dozen or more 'joss-sticks' kept constantly burning by the faithful.* But it is almost useless to particularise when the subjects and style of execution are so diverse. Each side of the long corridor seemed to display figures of distinct feature, dress, and character.

"'The most interesting sculptures,' says Dr. Adolf Bastian, the President of the Royal Geographical Society of Berlin, who explored these wonderful ruins in 1864, 'the most interesting sculptures at Nagkon Wat are in two compartments, called by the natives respectively the procession and the three

* A modern addition.—J. V. G.

stages (heaven, earth, and hell). What gives a peculiar interest to this section is the fact that the artist has represented the different nationalities in all their distinctive characteristic features, from the flat-nosed savage in the tasseled garb of the Pnom, and the short-haired Lao, to the straight-nosed Rajaput, with sword and shield, and the bearded Moor, giving a catalogue of nationalities, like another column of Trajan in the predominant physical conformation of each race. On the whole there is such a prevalence of Hellenic cast in the features and profiles, as well as in the elegant attitude of the horsemen, that one might suppose Xenocrates of old, after finishing his labours in Bombay, had made an excursion to the east.'

"There are figures sculptured in high relief (nearly life-size) upon the lower parts of the walls about the entrance ; all are females, and apparently of Hindoo origin. The interior of the quadrangle, bounded by the long corridor just described, is filled with galleries—halls, formed with huge columns, crossing one another at right angles. In the Nagkon Wat as many as 1,532 solid columns have been counted, and among the entire ruins of Angkor there are reported to be the immense number of 6,000, almost all of them hewn from single blocks and artistically carved. On the inner side of the corridor there are blank windows, each of which contains seven beautifully turned little columns. The ceilings of the galleries were hung with tens of thousands of bats and pigeons, and other birds had made themselves comfortable nests in out-of-the-way corners.

"We pass on up steep staircases, with steps not

more than four inches in width, to the centre of the galleries which here bisect one another. There are two detached buildings in this square. In one of the galleries we saw two or three hundred images—made of stone, wood, brass, clay—of all shapes and sizes and ages (some of the large stone idols are said to be 1,400 years old).

"We walk on across another causeway, with small image-houses* on either hand, and up a steep flight of steps, fully thirty feet in height, to other galleries crossing each other in the centre above which rises the grand central pagoda, 250 feet in height, and at the four corners of the court four smaller spires. These latter are much dilapidated and do not now display their full height; the porticoes also bear evidence of the presence of the 'heavy hand of time.'

"There is one more gallery, and then we come to the outer corridor, and pass through a magnificent doorway to the rear of the temple, and walk round to our *sala*, not knowing which to admire the most, the vastness of the plan or the propriety and grace of the performance.

"The principal ruins of Siam and Cambodia yet discovered lie in the province of Siamrap, as already stated. At about three miles north-east of Angkor, on the opposite side of the Siamrap river, are the ruins of a city called Pentaphrohm, the citadel of Taphrohm, and near it is a *wat* styled Phrakeoh, or the Gem Tower, presenting the same combination of a royal and priestly residence as Angkor and Nagkon Wat. Some of these temples and palaces, with their

* Out-offices for the servants of the palace.—J. V. G.

columns, sculptures, and statues, are quite as interesting, though not so well-preserved, as those at Angkor. About four miles east of Nagkon Wat are two other remains of antiquity, Bakong and Lailan.

"In the province of Battambong, forty or fifty miles south-west from Siamrap town, there are also ruins, temples, monasteries, and palaces, and indeed the whole valley of the Makong river to the very borders of China is spread with ruins of more or less magnitude, beauty, and interest. Near the monastery of Phrakeoh is an artificial lake called Sasong (the royal lake), built by the kings of Pentaphrohm, and surrounded with pleasure-houses for their recreation. Dr. Bastian thinks that it must have been a work of immense labour, and the whole population of Cambodia of to-day would scarcely be able to raise such a gigantic structure.

"The lake of Sasong he describes as being 'of oblong shape, about 2,000 feet broad and 4,000 feet long, and surrounded by a high embankment of solid masonry. Some of the blocks are fourteen to sixteen feet long and highly finished. In convenient places square platforms were built overhanging the water, with broad flights of steps leading down to it, and in such places the huge masses of stone laid on each other are embellished by delicate chisellings, bearing the figures of serpents, eagles, lions (in their fabulous shapes as Naga, Kruth, Sinto) on the ends. In the middle of the lake is a small island with the remains of a former palace upon it. Of all the figures used for ornaments, that which recurs most frequently is that of the Naga ; and the Chinese officer who visited Cambodia in 1295 describes already 'the pillars of the stone bridges adorned with serpents, each of which had nine heads.'

"About half a mile north-west of Nagkon Wat there are the ruins of an observatory, built upon the summit of a hill perhaps 500 feet in height. A foot-path leads up this hill through the thick jungle. The first indication of any antiquities thereabouts is two immense stone griffins, one standing on each side of the path; and next we pass a small image with the head of an elephant and the body of a human being; it is the elephant-headed Ganesh—the god of wisdom of the Hindoo mythology. This hill is cut in five terraces paved with stone, and having staircases, each about twelve feet in height, ornamented with stone lions upon their balusters; and at the corners of each terrace are small image-houses.

"The building is quadrilateral, and covers the entire crest of the hill, there being four entrances; the central spire is now an unshapely mass of large boulders, all overgrown with trees, shrubs, and vines. From the summit we obtained an extensive view of the surrounding country. To the north there extended from east to west a range of low blue hills; to the south-east we could just discern the placid waters of Lake Thalaysap; to the south lay the quaint old town of Siamrap, and to the south-west there was another large lake of bright, clear water."

On his arrival in the southern portion of the peninsula beyond the Ganges, the great Lawgiver evidently set his followers to execute the wonderful monuments above described.

The sculptures on the walls of the palace of Angkor represent exploits of bravery and conquest, from the first invasion of Ind to the arrival of the invaders on the island of Ceylon, and to their landing in Siam.

The observatory shows that Moses loved astronomy, and pursued the study of that science in the distant east as he had done in Thebes.

When these noble undertakings were completed—which serve as *souvenirs* of his visit to the country—he, no doubt, left a colony to protect them, and proceeded northward, where there are ample traces which clearly indicate the route. The country he came to was like that which is on the other side of the Bay of Bengal, inhabited by various tribes of savages.

The empire he founded here was called the Empire of Brahma, and the people Brahmins. The scriptures were expounded, and the doctrine of the Lawgiver propagated, so that the natives of the country to this day relate the fall of Adam, and all the particulars regarding that memorable event. The following is a literal translation, by Dr. Mason, of some rude verses which the Karens have preserved:—

"Anciently, God commanded, but Satan appeared
    bringing destruction.
Formerly, God commanded, but Satan appeared
    deceiving unto death.
The woman Eu and the man Tha-nai pleased not
    the eye of the dragon.
The dragon looked on them, the dragon beguiled
    the woman and Tha-nai.
How is this said to have happened?
The great dragon succeeded in deceiving—de-
    ceiving unto death.

How do they say it was done?
A yellow fruit took the great dragon, and gave
to the children of God;
A white fruit took the great dragon, and gave
to the daughter and son of God.
They transgressed the commands of God, and
God turned His face from them.
They kept not all the words of God—were de-
ceived, deceived unto sickness.
They kept not all the law of God—were deceived,
deceived unto death."

It is evident that this tradition came from a written source, and there is no other source than the books of Moses.

There is in the Christian world an erroneous acceptation of the first and second chapters of the first book of Moses. Expounders of the Pentateuch, of our enlightened age, err with respect to these two chapters, and the consequence of this error is much confusion among believers. These expounders say that God created only one man at the creation of the world; and that when this man complained of *ennui* and loneliness, then the Almighty created the woman to keep him company. This account of the creation of man has been the cause of many controversies and divisions and secessions from the true faith.

In the first chapter of Genesis, Moses records the creation of heaven and earth with all the contents of each of them. Man, male and female, was created on the sixth day—not one couple, but many couples, as other animals were created; they were without number. And the Almighty blessed them, and told them to multiply and replenish the earth, and subdue it; to have dominion over the fish of the sea, and over the fowl of the air, and over every living thing that moveth upon the earth. He gave them every herb bearing seed, which is upon the face of all the earth, and every tree, in the which is the fruit of a tree yielding seed, for meat, &c.

This was accomplished on the sixth day; and "on the seventh day He rested from all His work which He had made. And God blessed the seventh day, and sanctified it: because that in it He had rested from all His work which God had created and made."

After this first seventh day, God created Adam, and the Lord God formed *this* man of the dust of the ground, and breathed into his nostrils the breath of life; and he became a living soul. "And the Lord God planted a garden eastward in Eden; and there he put *this* man whom he had formed. And out of the ground made the Lord God to grow every tree that is pleasant to the sight, and good for food; the tree of life also in the midst of the garden, and the tree of knowledge of good and evil. And a river went out of Eden to water the garden; and from thence it was parted, and became into four heads."

The man Adam was ruddy, for the earth or dust out of which he was formed was red. The rest of the men who were created on the sixth day were black, for the garden of Eden was divided from the rest of negroland by the river Nile, which surrounded it entirely. During the heavy rains in this portion of Africa, the waters of the lakes overflow, the Nile, passing in its course through the red soil of Ethiopia, gets tinged with that colour; and the waters, after entering Egypt, retain that hue for a long distance towards the Mediterranean Sea.

"And the Lord God took the man (Adam) and put him in the garden of Eden, to dress it and to keep it. And the Lord God commanded the man, saying, Of every tree of the garden thou mayest freely eat: but of the tree of the knowledge of good and evil, thou shalt not eat of it; for in the day that thou eatest thereof thou shalt surely die." So this man alone, of all the created human beings, received this commandment from God.

There is sculptured on the wall of a palace in Upper Egypt, which Norden, the Danish traveller saw and sketched, a group of three persons with a tree in the centre. The principal personage in this group is seated, and is addressing a man standing before him, as if giving the commandment above stated. The third figure is of a man standing behind the seated person, with a sarcastic expression of countenance. This sculpture no doubt represents the event in question.

After this, Eve was created. And it is recorded that "the serpent was more subtil than any beast of the field which the Lord God had made." He tempted the woman, and succeeded in making her break the commandment which God had given to Adam.

Now there is another sculpture in Upper Egypt, representing a man with a serpent's head. So that the creature that tempted and seduced Eve was a man; and he made her commit two sins: she broke the commandment of God, and her troth to her husband. When she had thus doubly sinned, she beguiled her husband, and persuaded him to disobey his Creator.

The Lord God visited the garden of Eden at certain hours of the day, and Adam and Eve attended as keepers of it. But when the time of the visit of the Lord God arrived, the man and his wife hid themselves, so that the Lord called for Adam, "and said unto him, Where art thou? And he said, I heard Thy voice in the garden, and I was afraid, because I was naked; and I hid myself. And He said, Who told thee that thou wast naked? Hast thou eaten of the tree, whereof I commanded thee that thou shouldest not eat? And the man said, The woman whom thou gavest to be with me, she gave me of the tree, and I did eat.

"And the Lord God said unto the woman, What is this that thou hast done? And the woman said, The serpent beguiled me, and I did eat. And the Lord God said unto the serpent, Because thou hast done this, thou art cursed above all cattle, and above every beast of the field ; *upon thy belly shalt thou go*, and dust shalt thou eat all the days of thy life ; and I will put enmity between thee and the woman, and between thy seed and her seed; it shall bruise thy head, and thou shalt bruise his heel."

From this it is evident that the serpent, before he was cursed by God, walked erect as a man, and it was only after the curse that he became the creeping animal that we see him now. The Almighty, in His pity, made coats of skins for Adam and Eve, and clothed them. This is another proof that this man and his wife were different from the rest of mankind, for these clothe themselves, whereas savages, to this day, go about without clothing of any kind—perfectly naked as in the day they were created.

Moses, in thus separating these two from other beings, gave a beginning to the Jewish nation, as descending from the children of God. He was the historian of this nation, and it was for these people that he wrote his laws and ordinances of religion. Other nations of the earth are only mentioned by him in his records incidentally, as coming in contact with his nation by chance or accident.

The confusion made by the seventy elders who translated the Pentateuch from the Hebrew into Greek, by having added six verses to the second chapter of the book of Genesis, has caused great mischief in the Church, resulting in disbelief of the Bible. If these first six verses were removed from the second chapter, the version would be quite correct, and as it was intended by Moses.

Adam and Eve were expelled from the garden of Eden, and, proceeding to the East along the Nile, they made the caves in the rocks their dwelling-place. In due time Eve gave birth to the child conceived in sin, and she called him Cain. She had another son after this, whom she called Abel. Cain had the vices of the serpent, and consequently hated this younger brother; and when they became old enough to offer sacrifices to God, he found that while his brother's offering was accepted, his was rejected. Thereupon high words were spoken, and, rising up in anger, he struck his brother and killed him.

"And the Lord said unto Cain, ' Where is Abel thy brother? And he said, I know not: Am I my brother's keeper? And He said, What hast thou done? the voice of thy brother's blood crieth unto me from the ground. And now art thou cursed from the earth, which hath opened her mouth to receive thy brother's blood from thy hand; when thou tillest the ground, it shall not henceforth yield unto thee her strength; a fugitive and a vagabond shalt thou be in the earth.

"And Cain said unto the Lord, My punishment is greater than I can bear. Behold, Thou hast driven me out this day from the face of the earth; and from Thy face shall I be hid; and I shall be a fugitive and a vagabond in the earth; and it shall come to pass, that every one that findeth me shall slay me.

"And the Lord said unto him, Therefore whosoever slayeth Cain, vengeance shall be taken on him sevenfold. And the Lord set a mark upon Cain, lest any finding him should kill him. And Cain went out from the presence of the Lord, and dwelt in the land of Nod, on the east of Eden."

Here we have the first mention of intercourse between the people that were created in the world on the sixth day, and a descendant of Adam and Eve, who were created by the Lord God in the second week, and placed by themselves in the garden of Eden. This land of Nod, on the east of Eden, where Cain took up his abode, and married a woman of the land, must have been near Noph in Egypt.

It is said Eve had another son, after the death of Abel and the departure of Cain; he was named Seth. In the Pentateuch the children of Adam and Eve are called the sons of God; and the descendants of the human family in the world at large were styled the sons and daughters of men.

In Munipúr snake-worship is still in existence. It is reported that :—" The Raja's peculiar god is a species of snake called Pakúng-ba, from which the royal family claim descent. When it appears it is coaxed on to a cushion by the priestess in attendance, who then performs certain ceremonies to please it.

" This snake appears, they say, sometimes of great size, and when he does so it is indicative of his being displeased with something. But as long as he remains of diminutive form it is a sign he is in good humour. Pakúng-ba is a snake by day, and by night assumes the human form. A house is prepared for it, and when it appears the priests give intimation of it, and all the head men and most orthodox Hindus, from the Raja downwards, do *poojah* (worship) before it."*

The colonists left by Moses in his progress through the different countries of Eastern Asia claim descent from celestial beings, especially in India beyond the Ganges, in China, and other kingdoms as far as the western shores of America. This claim originated from their being the direct descendants of Adam and Eve. The savages among whom they dwelt in bygone days admitted the claim, and, moreover, credited them with divine attributes.

The kings of Burmah consider the throne-room of their palace, where they receive homage from their subjects and strangers, as holy ground, and have made it a rule that all who seek the royal presence

* Lieut.-General Fytche, *Burmah Past and Present.*

shall put off their shoes. Embalming the dead is also practised in Burmah, the members of the royal family, when they die, being embalmed—a custom brought by Moses from Egypt. The title of Phra among the Siamese is also imported from Egypt, being used in both countries as a royal appellation.

The inspired Lawgiver proceeded eastward from the kingdom of Brahma, and entered China. The inhabitants of this immense tract of land lying along the sea-shore were savages, ignorant of the arts and comforts of civilized life. He imparted to them the knowledge of agriculture and astronomy, arithmetic and navigation, and all the useful arts and sciences. He reclaimed them from the darkness of profound ignorance, and gave them laws for guidance in their duties towards God and their fellow-beings.

Moses also taught these people to read and write; the writing being in hieroglyphics, similar to that of Egypt. He established here a form of government resembling that of the other kingdoms he had founded on his route. And when he had reclaimed these savages and raised them to a height of civilization equal to that of Egypt, he departed, leaving a colony to continue the good work which he had begun.

It is remarked by Dr. Mason, that "there have been Jews in China from time immemorial, and that ancient copies of the Pentateuch, written on sheep-skins, have been found in their possession."

Since the departure of Moses the kingdom of China, which he founded, has many times been invaded by different nations of Western Asia; and has had conquerors so savage that they ordered all the books to be burnt, and compelled the people to adopt many strange customs, which prevail in China even to this day. So that the Chinese were more civilized in the days immediately succeeding Moses' time than they are in this century.

The country along the sea-board adjoining China is Corea; and the Lawgiver visited this country also before he crossed over to the island of Japan. The original Coreans were savages, like all their primitive neighbours; and here the god-like Lawgiver imparted to the ignorant men the same lessons he had given in all the countries along his route. He formed the peninsula of Corea into a dependency of China; so that its annals are included in the History of China.

The Coreans have a knowledge of the writings of Moses; and a system of caste prevails as in the Eastern parts of India. The colonists were, of course, the nobles of the land. A traveller states:—*

"The features of a very considerable portion of the natives I had an opportunity to see during my travels in the country bore an expression so noble and so marked, that they might have passed for Europeans, had they been dressed after our fashion. This was also most strikingly observable in a great number of children, whose handsome, regular features, rosy skin, blue eyes, and auburn hair really made it so difficult to distinguish them from European children that at first I could not account for their looks but by believing them to be of European descent—an impression which had, of course, to be abandoned as altogether false and erroneous after

* Ernest Oppert, *A Forbidden Land.*

penetrating further into the interior, when appearances of the same nature became of daily occurrence."

From the peninsula of Corea Moses and his followers crossed over to the beautiful island of Japan, in the North Pacific Ocean, not far distant from the continent of Asia. The people inhabiting the numerous isles which compose the kingdom of Japan were savages—ignorant and superstitious, like the rest of the children of Nature, whom the Lawgiver had met in his journey, and whom he reclaimed from the darkness of ignorance to the knowledge of God and His commandments.

Here he taught the Japanese as he had other people; and after giving laws and ordinances for their guidance, he departed, leaving a colony to govern the country.

CHAPTER VIII.

MISSION OF MOSES IN THE WEST.

PROCEEDING still further eastward Moses landed on the western coast of North America. He found the natives inhabiting this vast tract of land as savage as those he had left on the continent and the adjacent islands of Asia—profoundly ignorant of God, living like the animals around them, and going about as nude as in the day when they were first created. The god-like Lawgiver founded an extensive empire in this wilderness, and brought these savages under subjection, and taught them all things necessary for their happiness and well-being. This empire was Mexico.

In this new empire he constructed monuments resembling those of Upper and Lower Egypt, Nubia and Ethiopia ; he set up statues, built pyramids, aqueducts, palaces, and bridges. His works he embellished with sculpture portraying the battles his forces had fought with the different nations that opposed their landing to occupy the country. And he brought his new subjects to the same state of civilization as the ancient Egyptians of his time. The following extracts are from the work of a modern traveller, concerning the pyramids and other ruins of Mexico:—*

"We arrived at Chollula after a pleasant ride over plains covered with corn-fields, interspersed with plantations of the *Agava Americana*. This city was, before the conquest, one of the most considerable belonging to the ancient Mexicans. It was famed for its idols, its sanctity, and its pagan worship.

"The Teocalli or temple is composed of alternate layers of clay and sun-burnt brick, forming an immense pyramid, divided into regular stages, or platforms; but time, and the growth of the prickly pear, the tuna, or nopal, and other vegetables, have left but little of its original form visible, and it now resembles a natural hill; the high road from Puebla is cut through a part of it, which serves to show its internal structure.

"We ascended by a steep winding road, partly cut into steps, to a level area of 140 (one hundred and forty) feet long, on which stands a very neat church, ninety feet in length, with two towers and a dome; from this exalted platform the spectator enjoys a most lovely landscape. We descended with reluctance the side of this pyramid, whose base is more extensive than that of the Great Pyramid of Egypt. It is covered with trees of great variety, some species of which I had never before seen; but they had evidently been planted there.

"On our descent to the plains we visited two detached masses, constructed, like the great pyramid, of unburnt brick and clay. The one to the northeast had been cut or taken away; its broken sides

* W. Bullock, *Six Months' Residence and Travels in Mexico.*

were so perpendicular as to prevent access to its summit. The other detached piece has been engraved by Humbolt, whose figure of the great pyramid conveys an idea of its ancient rather than its present state, nor is the church on its summit like the original.

"The corner-stone of the building now occupied by the lottery-office, and fronting the market for shoes, is the head of the serpent-idol, of great magnitude, which I should judge was not, when entire, less than seventy-feet in length. Under the gateway of the house, nearly opposite the entrance to the mint, is a fine statue, in a recumbent posture, of a deity, bearing the human form, and ornamented with various symbols; it is about the size of life, and was found a few years since in digging a well.

"The house at the corner of a street at the south-east of the great square is built upon and in part supported by a fine circular altar of black basalt, ornamented with the tail and claws of a gigantic reptile. In the cloisters behind the Dominican Convent is a noble specimen of the great serpent idol, almost perfect, and of fine workmanship; this monstrous divinity is represented in the act of swallowing a human victim, which is seen crushed and struggling in its horrid jaws.

"The only works of art of the inhabitants of the city of Mexico before the conquest, then called Tenochtitlan, now publicly seen, are the great Calendar Stone, popularly called Montezuma's watch, and the Sacrificial Stone, or the grand altar, once standing in the great temple before the principal idol. The former measures twelve feet in diameter, and is cut from one large block of porous basaltic stone. It is supposed to have been placed in the roof of the great temple in the same manner as the Zodiac was in the temple of Tentyra in Upper Egypt.* It now stands against the north-west wall of the cathedral, and is an attractive object of antiquarian research, and a striking proof of the perfection the nation to which it belonged had attained in some of the sciences; few persons, even of the most enlightened cities of Europe, of the present day, would be capable of executing such a work.

"From the first moment I beheld it I determined, if possible, to convey to Europe a fac-simile of so fine a specimen of Aztec skill. Through the influence of Don Lucas Alarman, the prime minister, I obtained permission of the clergy to erect a scaffold against the cathedral, and took an impression of it in plaster, which was afterwards carefully packed up, and with some difficulty conveyed to Vera Cruz. It has fortunately arrived safely in England, and now forms one of the subjects of the exhibition of Ancient Mexico to be seen in the Egyptian Hall.

"The Sacrificial Stone, or altar, is buried in the square of the cathedral, within a hundred yards of the Calendar Stone. The upper surface only is exposed to view, which seems to have been done designedly. As I had been informed that the sides were covered with historical sculpture, I applied to the clergy for the further permission of having the earth removed from around it, which they not only

---

* And the Zodiac in the Hindoo Temple at Benares in India.—J. V. G.

granted, but moreover had it performed for me at their own expense.

"I then took casts of the whole. It is twenty-five feet in circumference, and consists of fifteen groups of figures, representing the conquests of the warriors of Mexico over different cities, the names of which are written over them.

"After a pleasant ride over a country not very fertile, we reached the gates of Tescuco. Some time before approaching the immediate vicinity of the city, you are apprised that you are near a place of great antiquity. You pass the large aqueduct for the supply of the town, which is still in use, and you also pass the ruins of several stone buildings of great strength.

"On entering the gates, to the right are seen those artificial tumuli, the teocalli of unburnt brick so common in most Indian towns, supposed to be temples, tombs, or places of defence, or perhaps serving for all these purposes. The foundations and ruins of temples, fortresses, palaces, and other extensive buildings, are alone sufficient to attest its former consequence and splendour; but it is likewise well known to have been in earlier times the seat of Mexican literature and art. It was the Athens of America, and the residence of historians, orators, poets, artists, and the great men of every department of the sciences who existed in those days.

"What a subject for contemplation does this collection of ruins present to the reflecting mind! The seat of a powerful monarch, whose subjects (if we may judge from their works) were probably an enlightened people, existing and flourishing long before the continent of America was known to Europe, and yet a people whose customs, costume, religion, and architecture strongly resembled those of an enlightened nation of Africa."

Mr. Bullock continues:—

"We soon arrived at the foot of the largest pyramid (at Otumba), and began to ascend. It was less difficult than we expected, although, the whole way up, lime and cement are mixed with fallen stones.* The terraces are perfectly visible, particularly the second, which is about thirty-eight feet wide, covered with a coat of red cement eight or ten inches thick, composed of small pebble-stones and lime. In many places, as you ascend, the nopal trees have destroyed the regularity of the steps, but nowhere injured the general figure of the square, which is as perfect in this respect as the Great Pyramid of Egypt.

"We everywhere observed broken pieces of instruments like knives, arrow and spear-heads, &c. composed of obsidian, the same as those found on the small hills of Chollula; and, on reaching the summit, we found a flat surface of considerable size, but which has been much broken and disturbed. On the northeast side, about half-way down, at some remote period, an opening has been attempted.

"Dr. Oteyza, who has given us the measure of these Pyramids, makes the base of the largest six hundred and forty-five feet in length, and one hundred and seventy-one in perpendicular height. I should certainly consider that the latter measurement is considerably under the mark, and that its altitude must be half its breadth."

* These must have been fallen casing-stones.—J. V. G.

There is no doubt that these Mexican pyramids were built by Moses for the same purpose as those in Egypt; and that these were similarly finished off with casing-stones, to preserve the corn from the effects of the elements, like their prototypes throughout Egypt. Dr. Robertson in his *History of North and South America*, says:—

" As far as one can gather from their obscure and inaccurate descriptions, the great temple of Mexico, the most famous in New Spain, which has been represented as a magnificent building, raised to such a height that the ascent to it was by a flight of a hundred and fourteen steps, was a solid mass of earth of a square form, faced partly with stone. Its base on each side extended ninety feet, and decreasing gradually as it advanced in height, it terminated in a quadrangle of about thirty feet."

In its original state this building would have terminated in a sharp point, instead of a quadrangle of such extent; and have been faced entirely with stone, smoothly polished, from base to summit—resembling the Egyptian pyramids.

When the Spaniards under Cortes, visited Mexico, "the Empire* was at a pitch of grandeur to which no society ever attained in so short a period. Its dominion extended from the North to the South sea, over territories stretching, with some small interruption, above five hundred leagues from east to west, and more than two hundred from north to south, comprehending provinces, not inferior in fertility, population, and opulence, to any in the torrid zone.

* Dr. Robertson.

"The people were warlike and enterprising, the authority of the monarch unbounded, and his revenues considerable. If, with the forces which might have been suddenly assembled in such an empire, Montezuma had fallen upon the Spaniards whilst encamped on a barren unhealthy coast, unsupported by any ally, without a place of retreat, and destitute of provisions, it seems to be impossible, even with all the advantages of their superior discipline and arms, that they could have stood the shock, and they must either have perished in such an unequal contest, or have abandoned the enterprise."

The Spaniards were received by Montezuma in the city of Mexico, and Dr. Robertson goes on to say:—

"When they drew near the city, about a thousand persons, who appeared to be of distinction, came forth to meet them, adorned with plumes and clad in mantles of fine cotton. Each of these, in his order, passed by Cortes, and saluted him according to the mode deemed most respectful and submissive in their country. They announced the approach of Montezuma himself, and soon after his harbingers came in sight.

"There appeared first two hundred persons in an uniform dress, with large plumes of feathers, alike in fashion, marching two and two, in deep silence, bare-footed, with their eyes fixed on the ground. These were followed by a company of higher rank, in their most showy apparel, in the midst of whom was Montezuma, in a chair or litter richly ornamented with gold and feathers of various colours.

"Four of his principal favourites carried him on their shoulders, others supported a canopy of curious workmanship over his head. Before him marched three officers with rods of gold in their hands, which they lifted up on high at certain intervals, and at that signal all the people bowed their heads, and hid their faces, as unworthy to look on so great a monarch.

"When he drew near, Cortes dismounted, advancing towards him with officious haste, and in a respectful posture. At the same time Montezuma alighted from his chair, and leaning on the arms of two of his near relations, approached with a slow and stately pace, his attendants covering the street with cotton cloths, that he might not touch the ground.

"Cortes accosted him with profound reverence, after the European fashion. He returned the salutation, according to the mode of his country, by touching the earth with his hand, and then kissing it. This ceremony, the customary expression of veneration from inferiors towards those who were above them in rank, appeared such amazing condescension in a proud monarch, who scarcely deigned to consider the rest of mankind as of the same species with himself, that all his subjects firmly believed those persons, before whom he humbled himself in this manner, to be something more than human.

"Montezuma conducted Cortes to the quarters which he had prepared for his reception, and immediately took leave of him, with a politeness not unworthy of a court more refined. 'You are now,' says he, 'with your brothers in your own house; refresh yourselves after your fatigue, and be happy until I return.'

"The place allotted to the Spaniards for their lodging was a house built by the father of Montezuma. It was surrounded by a stone wall, with towers at proper distances, which served for defence as well as for ornament, and its apartments and courts were so large as to accommodate both the Spaniards and their Indian allies.

"In the evening, Montezuma returned to visit his guests with the same pomp as in their first interview, and brought presents of such value, not only to Cortes and to his officers, but even to the private men, as proved the liberality of the monarch to be suitable to the opulence of his kingdom. A long conference ensued, in which Cortes learned what was the opinion of Montezuma with respect to the Spaniards.

"It was an established tradition, he told him, among the Mexicans, that their ancestors came originally from a remote region, and conquered the provinces now subject to his dominion : that after they were settled there, the great captain who conducted this colony returned to his own country, promising that at some future period his descendants should visit them, assume the government, and reform their constitution and laws ; that from what he had heard and seen of Cortes and his followers he was convinced they were the very persons whose appearance the Mexican traditions and prophecies taught them to expect ; that accordingly he had received them, not as strangers, but as relations of the same blood and parentage, and desired that they might consider themselves as masters in his dominions, for both himself and his subjects should be ready to comply with their will, and even to prevent their wishes.

"Cortes made a reply in his usual style, with respect to the dignity and power of his sovereign, and his intention in sending him into that country; artfully endeavouring so to frame his discourse that it might coincide as much as possible with the idea which Montezuma had formed concerning the origin of the Spaniards.

"Mexico, or Tenuchtitlan, as it was anciently called by the natives, is situated in a large plain, environed by mountains of such height, that, though within the torrid zone, the temperature of its climate is mild and healthful. All the moisture which descends from the high grounds is collected in several lakes, the two largest of which, of about ninety miles in circuit, communicate with each other. The waters of the one are fresh, those of the others brackish. On the banks of the latter, and on some small islands adjoining to them, the capital of Montezuma's empire was built.

"The access to the city was by artificial causeways or streets formed of stones and earth, about thirty feet in breadth. As the waters of the lake during the rainy season overflowed the flat country, these causeways were of considerable length. That of Tacuba, on the west, extended a mile and a half; that of Tepeaca, on the north-west, three miles; that of Cuoyacan, towards the south, six miles.

"On the east there was no causeway, and they could be approached only by canoes. In each of these causeways were openings at proper intervals, through which the waters flowed, and over these beams of timber were laid, which, being covered with earth, the causeway or street had everywhere an uniform appearance.

"As the approaches to the city were singular, its construction was remarkable. Not only the temples of their gods, but the houses belonging to the monarch, and to persons of distinction, were of such dimensions, that, in comparison with any other buildings which had been hitherto discovered in America, they might be termed magnificent. The habitations of the common people were mean, resembling the huts of other Indians. But they were all placed in a regular manner, on the banks of the canals which passed through the city in some of its districts, or in the sides of the streets which intersected it in other quarters.

"In several places were large openings or squares, one of which, allotted for the great market, is said to have been so spacious that forty or fifty thousand persons carried on traffic there. In this city, the pride of the New World, and the noblest monument of the industry and art of man, the Spaniards reckon that there were at least sixty thousand inhabitants."

The explanation given to the Spaniards by the King of Mexico of his conduct in receiving them in the manner he did—humbling himself in the presence of his European visitors—proves that the founders of the Mexican Empire were white men, similar to the Spaniards; and, in firm belief in the promise of the great chief—that at some future time his descendants would visit the Mexicans—the king made up his mind to deliver the empire into the hands of Cortes, as the representative of that chief.

So that, even when Montezuma was kept a prisoner, and ill-treated by these Spaniards, he submitted with the utmost humility to every indignity without offering the slightest opposition. He only discovered his mistake regarding the identity of these men when Cortes tried to impose the forms of the Roman Catholic religion, and placed the image of the Virgin Mary in their great temple in Mexico. Then, and only then, did he resent, and allow the Mexican nobles to assert their liberty, and to take up arms against their cruel invaders, who had broken every international law, and usurped the power of their kingdom.

The cruelty and the superstition of the Spaniards in New Spain are well known throughout the civilized world, so that it is needless to recount them here. These usurpers did all in their power to destroy every monument of the ancient Mexicans, under the ignorant impression that every building was a heathen temple, and every statue the image of a pagan god, to whom prayers and sacrifices were offered. They even built churches on the tops of some of the large Pyramids, thinking that these were temples, erected for the performance of idolatrous worship!

The inspired Law-giver, after establishing a firm government, with good laws and regulations for its continuance, left a colony in power over the conquered natives of the soil, and, departing from Mexico, landed on the shores of the southern continent of America, where he founded the extensive Empire of Peru.

At the time of Pizarro's arrival in Peru the

dominion of its sovereign extended in length, from north to south, above fifteen hundred miles along the Pacific Ocean; its breadth from east to west was much less, it being uniformly bounded by the vast ridge of the Andes, stretching from one extremity of the country to the other.

When Moses and his followers landed, the country was inhabited, like the rest of the primitive world, by independent tribes of savages, differing from each other in manners, and in their rude forms of polity. He, however, brought them all under his government; imparted to them the knowledge of God; gave them laws; and instructed the men in agriculture and other useful arts, while the women were taught to spin and weave, as in China and other kingdoms and empires that he had already founded. So that, as by the labour of the one sex subsistence became less precarious, by that of the other life was rendered more comfortable.

There is a tradition preserved among the Peruvians, that when their ancestors were mere savages roaming the woods, without clothing, or any settled place of residence, their condition became changed under the following circumstances:—

" After they had struggled for several ages with the hardships and calamities which are inevitable in such a state, and when no circumstance seemed to indicate the approach of any uncommon effort towards improvement, we are told that there appeared, on the banks of the Lake Titiaca, a man and a woman of majestic form, clothed in decent garments.

" They declared themselves to be children of the

sun, sent by their beneficent parent, who beheld with pity the miseries of the human race, to instruct and to reclaim them. At their persuasion, enforced by reverence for the divinity in whose name they were supposed to speak, several of the dispersed savages united together, received their commands as heavenly injunctions, and followed them to Cuzco, where they settled and began to lay the foundations of a city.

"Manco Capac and Mama Ocollo, for such were the names of these extraordinary personages, having thus collected some wandering tribes, formed that social union which, by multiplying the desires and uniting the efforts of the human species, excites industry, and leads to improvement.

"After securing the objects of first necessity in an infant state, by providing food, raiment, and habitations for the rude people of whom he took charge, Manco Capac turned his attention towards introducing such laws and policy as might perpetuate their happiness. By his institutions the various relations in private life were established, and the duties resulting from them prescribed with such propriety, as gradually formed a barbarous people to decency of manners.

"In public administration, the functions of persons in authority were so precisely defined, and the subordination of those under their jurisdiction maintained with such a steady hand, that the society in which he presided soon assumed the aspect of a regular and well governed state.

"Thus, according to the Indian tradition, was founded the empire of the Incas, or Lords of Peru. At first its extent was small. The territory of Manco

Capac did not reach above eight leagues from Cuzco. But within its narrow precincts he exercised absolute and uncontrolled authority. His successors, as their dominions extended, arrogated a similar jurisdiction over the new subjects which they acquired; the despotism of Asia was not more complete.

"The Incas were not only obeyed as monarchs, but revered as divinities. Their blood was held to be sacred, and, by prohibiting intermarriages with the people, was never contaminated by mixing with that of any other race. The family, thus separated from the rest of the nation, was distinguished by peculiarities in dress and ornaments, which it was unlawful for others to assume. The monarch himself appeared with ensigns of royalty reserved for him alone; and received from his subjects marks of obsequious homage and respect, which approached almost to adoration.

"But, among the Peruvians, this unbounded power of their monarchs seems to have been uniformly accompanied with attention to the good of their subjects. It was not the rage of conquest, if we may believe the accounts of their countrymen, that prompted the Incas to extend their dominions, but the desire of diffusing the blessings of civilization, and the knowledge of the arts which they possessed, among the barbarous people whom they reduced. During a succession of twelve monarchs, it is said that not one deviated from this beneficent character."*

At the time Pizarro arrived in Peru there was a civil war between two Incas; and he was invited by

* Dr. Robertson.

one of these to visit Caxamalca as a friend and ally. The following is an account of his visit:—

"On entering Caxamalca, Pizarro took possession of a large court, on one side of which was a house which the Spanish historians call a palace of the Inca, and on the other a temple of the sun, the whole surrounded with a strong rampart or wall of earth. When he had posted his troops in this advantageous station, he dispatched his brother Ferdinand and Hernando Soto to the camp of Atahualpa, which was about a league distant from the town.

"He instructed them to confirm the declaration which he had formerly made of his pacific disposition, and to desire an interview with the Inca, that he might explain more fully the intention of the Spaniards in visiting his country. They were treated with all the respectful hospitality usual among the Peruvians in the reception of their most cordial friends, and Atahualpa promised to visit the Spanish commander next day in his quarters.

"The decent deportment of the Peruvian monarch, the order of his court, and the reverence with which his subjects approached his person and obeyed his commands, astonished those Spaniards who had never met in America with anything more dignified than the petty cazique of a barbarous tribe. But their eyes were still more powerfully attracted by the vast profusion of wealth which they observed in the Inca's camp.

"The rich ornaments worn by him and his attendants, the vessels of gold and silver in which the repast offered to them was served up, the multitude of utensils of every kind formed of those precious metals, opened prospects far exceeding any idea of opulence that a European of the sixteenth century could form.

"Early in the morning the Peruvian camp was all in motion. But as Atahualpa was so solicitous to appear with the greatest splendour and magnificence in his first interview with the strangers, the preparations for this were so tedious, that the day was far advanced before he began his march. Even then, lest the order of the procession should be deranged, he moved so slowly, that the Spaniards became impatient, and apprehensive that some suspicion of their intention might be the cause of this delay. In order to remove this, Pizarro despatched one of his officers with fresh assurances of his friendly disposition.

"At length the Inca approached. First of all appeared four hundred men, in a uniform dress, as harbingers to clear the way before him. He himself, sitting on a throne or couch adorned with plumes of various colours, and almost covered with plates of gold and silver enriched with precious stones, was carried on the shoulders of his principal attendants.

"Behind him came some chief officers of his court, carried in the same manner. Several bands of singers and dancers accompanied the cavalcade, and the whole plain was covered with troops, amounting to more than thirty thousand men.

"As the Inca drew near the Spanish quarters, Father Vincent Valverde, chaplain to the expedition, advanced, with a crucifix in one hand and a breviary in the other, and in a long discourse explained to him the doctrine of the Creation, the fall of Adam, the incarnation, the sufferings and resurrection of Jesus Christ, the appointment of St. Peter as God's vicegerent on earth, the transmission of his apostolic power by succession to the popes, the donation made to the King of Castile, by Pope Alexander, of all the regions of the New World.

"In consequence of all this, he required Atahualpa to embrace the Christian faith, to acknowledge the supreme jurisdiction of the Pope, and to submit to the King of Castile as his lawful sovereign; promising, if he complied instantly with this requisition, that the Castilian monarch would protect his dominions, and permit him to continue in the exercise of his royal authority; but if he should impiously refuse to obey this summons, he denounced war against him in his master's name, and threatened him with the most dreadful effects of his vengeance.

"This strange harangue, unfolding deep mysteries, and alluding to unknown facts, of which no power of eloquence could have conveyed at once a distinct idea to an American, was so lamely translated by an unskilful interpreter, little acquainted with the idiom of the Spanish tongue, and incapable of expressing himself with propriety in the language of the Inca, that its general tenor was altogether incomprehensible to Atahualpa. Some parts in it, of more obvious meaning, filled him with astonishment and indignation.

"His reply, however, was temperate. He began with observing that he was lord of the dominions over which he reigned by hereditary succession; and added, that he could not conceive how a foreign priest should pretend to dispose of territories which did not belong to him; that if such a preposterous grant had been made, he, who was the rightful possessor, refused to confirm it; that he had no inclination to renounce the religious institutions established by his ancestors; nor would he forsake the service of the sun, the immortal divinity whom he and his people revered, in order to worship the god of the Spaniards, who was subject to death; that with respect to other matters contained in his discourse, as he had never heard of them before, and did not understand their meaning, he desired to know where the priest had learned things so extraordinary.

"'In this book,' answered Valverde, reaching out to him his breviary. The Inca opened it eagerly, and turning over the leaves, lifted it to his ear. 'This,' says he, 'is silent; it tells me nothing'; and threw it with disdain to the ground. The enraged monk, running towards his countrymen, cried out, 'To arms, Christians! to arms! the word of God is insulted; avenge this profanation on those impious dogs!'

"Pizarro, who, during this long conference, had with difficulty restrained his soldiers, eager to seize the rich spoils of which they had now so near a view, immediately gave the signal of assault. At once the martial music struck up, the cannon and muskets began to fire, the horse sallied out fiercely to the charge, the infantry rushed on sword in hand.

"The Peruvians, astonished at the suddenness of

an attack which they did not expect, and dismayed with the destructive effect of the fire-arms, and the irresistible impression of the cavalry, fled with universal consternation on every side, without attempting either to annoy the enemy or to defend themselves.

"Pizarro, at the head of his chosen band, advanced directly towards the Inca; and though his nobles crowded around him with officious zeal, and fell in numbers at his feet, while they vied one with another in sacrificing their own lives, that they might cover the sacred person of their sovereign, the Spaniards soon penetrated to the royal seat; and Pizarro, seizing the Inca by the arm, dragged him to the ground, and carried him as a prisoner to his quarters.

"The fate of the monarch increased the precipitate flight of his followers. The Spaniards pursued them towards every quarter, and with deliberate and unrelenting barbarity continued to slaughter wretched fugitives who never once offered to resist. The carnage did not cease until the close of the day. About four thousand Peruvians were killed. Not a single Spaniard fell, nor was one wounded but Pizarro himself, whose hand was slightly hurt by one of his own soldiers, while struggling eagerly to lay hold on the Inca.

"The plunder of the field was rich beyond any idea which the Spaniards had yet formed concerning the wealth of Peru, and they were so transported with the value of the acquisition, as well as the greatness of their success, that they passed the night in the extravagant exultation natural to indigent adventurers on such an extraordinary change of fortune.

"At first the captive monarch could hardly believe a calamity, which he so little expected, to be real. But he soon felt all the misery of his fate, and the dejection into which he sank was in proportion to the height of grandeur from which he had fallen. Pizarro, afraid of losing all the advantages which he hoped to derive from the possession of such a prisoner, laboured to console him with professions of kindness and respect, that corresponded ill with his actions.

"By residing among the Spaniards, the Inca quickly discovered their ruling passion, which, indeed, they were nowise solicitous to conceal, and, by applying to that, made an attempt to recover his liberty. He offered as a ransom what astonished the Spaniards, even after all they now knew concerning the opulence of his kingdom. The apartment in which he was confined was twenty-two feet in length and sixteen in breadth; he undertook to fill it with vessels of gold as high as he could reach.

"Pizarro closed eagerly with the tempting proposal, and a line was drawn upon the walls of the chamber, to mark the stipulated height to which the treasure was to rise. Atahualpa, transported with having obtained some prospect of liberty, took measures instantly for fulfilling his part of the agreement, by sending messengers to Cuzco, Quito, and other places, where gold had been amassed in largest quantities, either for adorning the temples, or the houses of the Inca, to bring what was necessary for completing his ransom directly to Caxamalca. Though Atahualpa was now in the custody of his enemies, yet so much were the Peruvians accustomed to respect every mandate issued by their sovereign, that his orders were executed with the greatest alacrity.

" Soothed with hopes of recovering his liberty by this means, the subjects of the Inca were afraid of endangering his life by forming any other scheme for his relief ; and though the force of the empire was still entire, no preparations were made and no army assembled to avenge their own wrongs or those of their monarch. The Spaniards remained in Caxamalca tranquil and unmolested. Small detachments of their number marched into remote provinces of the empire, and instead of meeting with any opposition, were everywhere received with marks of the most submissive respect.

" The Indians daily arrived at Caxamalca from different parts of the kingdom, loaded with treasure. A great part of the stipulated quantity was now amassed, and Atahualpa assured the Spaniards that the only thing which prevented the whole from being brought in was the remoteness of the provinces where it was deposited.

" But such vast piles of gold presented continually to the view of needy soldiers, had so inflamed their avarice, that it was impossible any longer to restrain their impatience to obtain possession of this rich booty. Orders were given for melting down the whole, except some pieces of curious fabric, reserved as a present for the Emperor. After setting apart the fifth due to the crown, and a hundred thousand pesos as a donation to the soldiers which arrived with Almagro, there remained one million five hundred and twenty-eight thousand five hundred pesos to Pizarro and his followers.

"The festival of St. James, the patron saint of Spain, was the day (July 25, A.D. 1533) chosen for the partition of this enormous sum, and the manner of conducting it strongly marks the strange alliance of fanaticism and avarice, which I have more than once had occasion to point out as a striking feature in the character of the conquerors of the New World. Though assembled to divide the spoils of an innocent people, procured by deceit, extortion, and cruelty, the transaction began with a solemn invocation of the name of God, as if they could have expected the guidance of Heaven in distributing those wages of iniquity.

"In this division above eight thousand pesos, at that time not inferior in effective value to as many pounds sterling in the present century, fell to the share of each horseman, and half that sum to each foot-soldier. Pizarro himself, and his officers, received dividends in proportion to the dignity of their rank.

"The Spaniards having divided among them the treasure amassed for the Inca's ransom, he insisted with them to fulfil their promise of setting him at liberty. But nothing was further from Pizarro's thoughts. During his long service in the New World, he had imbibed those ideas and maxims of his fellow soldiers, which led them to consider its inhabitants as an inferior race, neither worthy of the name nor entitled to the rights of men. In his compact with Atahualpa, he had no other object than to amuse his captive with such a prospect of recovering his liberty as might induce him to lend all the aid of his authority towards collecting the wealth of his kingdom. Having now accomplished this, he no longer regarded his plighted faith; and at the very time when the credulous prince hoped to be replaced on his throne, he had secretly resolved to bereave him of life.

"Many circumstances seemed to have concurred in prompting him to this action, the most criminal and atrocious that stains the Spanish name, amidst all the deeds of violence committed in carrying on the conquest of the New World. Though Pizarro had seized the Inca, in imitation of Cortes's conduct towards the Mexican monarch, he did not possess talents for carrying on the same artful plan of policy. Destitute of the temper and address requisite for gaining the confidence of his prisoner, he never reaped all the advantages which might have been derived from being master of his person and authority.

"Atahualpa was, indeed, a prince of greater abilities and discernment than Montezuma, and seems to have penetrated more thoroughly into the character and intentions of the Spaniards. Mutual suspicion and distrust accordingly took place between them. The strict attention with which it was necessary to guard a captive of such importance, greatly increased the fatigue of military duty. The utility of keeping him appeared inconsiderable ; and Pizarro felt him as an encumbrance from which he wished to be delivered.

"But in order to give some colour of justice to this violent action, and that he himself might be exempted from standing singly responsible for the commission of it, Pizarro resolved to try the Inca with all the formalities observed in the criminal courts of Spain. Pizarro himself, and Almagro, with two assistants, were appointed judges, with full power to acquit or to condemn; an attorney-general was named to carry on the prosecution in the King's name; counsellors were chosen to assist the prisoner in his defence, and clerks were ordered to record the proceedings of court.

"Before this strange tribunal, a charge was exhibited still more amazing. It consisted of various articles: that Atahualpa, though a bastard, had dispossessed the rightful owner of the throne, and usurped the regal power; that he had put his brother and lawful sovereign to death; that he was an idolater, and had not only permitted, but commanded the offering of human sacrifices; that he had a great number of concubines; that since his imprisonment he had wasted and embezzled the treasures which now belonged of right to the conquerors; that he had incited his subjects to take arms against the Spaniards.

"On these heads of accusation, some of which are so ludicrous, others so absurd, that the effrontery of Pizarro in making them the foundation of a serious procedure is not less surprising than his injustice, did this strange court go on to try the sovereign of a great empire, over whom he had no jurisdiction. With respect to each of the articles, witnesses were examined; but as they delivered their evidence in their native tongue, Philippillo had it in his power to give their words whatever turn best suited his malevolent intentions. To judges predetermined in their opinion, this evidence appeared sufficient. They pronounced Atahualpa guilty, and condemned him to be burnt alive. Friar Valverde prostituted the authority of his sacred function to confirm this sentence, and by his signature warranted it to be just.

" Astonished at his fate, Atahualpa endeavoured to avert it by tears, by promises, and by entreaties that he might be sent to Spain, where a monarch would be the arbiter of his lot. But pity never touched the unfeeling heart of Pizarro. He ordered him to be led instantly to execution; and, what added to the bitterness of his last moments, the same monk who had just ratified his doom offered to console, and attempted to convert him. The most powerful argument Valverde employed to prevail with him to embrace the Christian faith, was a promise of mitigation in his punishment. The dread of a cruel death extorted from the trembling victim a desire of receiving baptism. The ceremony was performed; and Atahualpa, instead of being burnt, was strangled at the stake!

" On the death of Atahualpa, Pizarro invested one of his sons with the ensigns of royalty, hoping that a young man without experience might prove a more passive instrument in his hands than an ambitious monarch, who had been accustomed to independent command."

These accounts of the wealth and the fate of these two monarchs—the one of the extensive empire of Mexico, and the other of the equally powerful dominions of Peru—recall to mind the power and wealth of Solomon, the King of Israel. These three kingdoms were founded by Moses, and peopled and ruled by the descendants of Abraham. The wealth of Solomon was so great that it is recorded in the Bible that "he made silver and gold at Jerusalem as plenteous as stones, and cedar trees made he as the sycamore trees that are in the vale for abundance."

The display made by the two American sovereigns of their grandeur and riches before foreigners, and the consequences of their pride and ostentation, have a parallel in the scriptures.

"At that time Berodach-baladan, the son of Baladan, King of Babylon, sent letters and a present unto Hezekiah; for he had heard that Hezekiah had been sick. And Hezekiah hearkened unto them, and shewed them all the house of his precious things, the silver and the gold, and the spices, and the precious ointment, and all the house of his armour, and all that was found in his treasures; there was nothing in his house, nor in all his dominion, that Hezekiah shewed them not.

"Then came Isaiah the prophet unto King Hezekiah, and said unto him, What said these men? and from whence came they unto thee? And Hezekiah said, They are come from a far country, even from Babylon. And he said, What have they seen in thine house? And Hezekiah answered, All the things that are in mine house have they seen; there is nothing among my treasures that I have not shewed them. And Isaiah said unto Hezekiah, Hear the word of the Lord. Behold, the days come that all that is in thine house, and all that which thy fathers have laid up in store unto this day, shall be carried into Babylon; nothing shall be left, saith the Lord."*

The words of Isaiah the prophet, addressed to King Hezekiah, could have been as appositely addressed to King Montezuma and to his neighbour and kinsman Atahualpa; for they were equally applicable, and the words came true in all three cases. As the Babylonians conquered and took possession of Judea, so did the Spaniards in Mexico and Peru.

Moses, the founder of these several empires in different parts of the earth, foresaw the power and opulence to which they would attain in the course of time, and forbade the colonists from having intercourse with the outer world, who were strangers to them, knowing that they would be envied by them. For wherever indigent adventurers have been admitted by the rulers of these empires, they have been deceived, and their possessions carried away, as the prophet so graphically described to King Hezekiah.

The historian of North and South America continues:—

"The violent convulsions into which the empire had been thrown, first by the civil war between the two brothers, and then by the invasion of the Spaniards, had not only deranged the order of the Peruvian Government, but almost dissolved its frame. When they beheld their monarch a captive in the power of strangers, and at last suffering an ignominious death, the people in several provinces, as if they had been set free from every restraint of law and decency, broke out in the most licentious excesses.

* 2 Kings xx.

"So many descendants of the sun, after being treated with the utmost indignity, had been cut off by Atahualpa that not only their influence in the state diminished with their number, but the accustomed reverence for that sacred race sensibly decreased. In consequence of this state of things, ambitious men in different parts of the empire aspired to independent authority, and usurped jurisdiction to which they had no title. The general who commanded for Atahualpa in Quito, seized the brother and children of his master, put them to a cruel death, and, disclaiming any connection with either Inca, endeavoured to establish a separate kingdom for himself."[*]

The Spaniards eventually became masters of the whole empire, and in their endeavours to obliterate every record of its past history they burned everything they found which had any hieroglyphics or painting on it. Though only the ruins of monuments remain, yet these attest the superior ingenuity of the Peruvians. Ruins of sacred or royal buildings are found in every province of the empire, and by their great number demonstrate that they are monuments of a powerful people. They appear to have been edifices of various dimensions; some of a moderate size, many of immense extent, but all remarkable for solidity, and resembling each other in style of architecture.

"The temple of Pachacamac, together with a palace of the Inca, and a fortress, were so connected together as to form one great structure, above half a league in circuit. In this prodigious pile the same

[*] Dr. Robertson.

singular taste in building is conspicuous as in other works of the Peruvians."

The land of the Peruvians and the Mexicans contained the precious metals in greater abundance than any other part of America; and Moses taught them to obtain gold by searching in the channels of rivers, or washing the earth in which particles of it were contained. But in order to procure silver, under his instruction, they exerted no inconsiderable degree of skill and invention. They hollowed deep caverns in the banks of rivers, and the sides of mountains, and exhausted such veins as did not dip suddenly beyond their reach. In other places, where the vein lay near the surface, they dug pits to such a depth that the person who worked below could throw out the ore, or hand it up in baskets. Moses taught them, moreover, the art of smelting and refining, either by the simple application of fire, or, where the ore was more stubborn, and impregnated with foreign substances, by placing it in small ovens or furnaces, so constructed on high ground that the draught of air performed the functions of a bellows. By this simple device the purer ores were smelted with facility; and the quantity of silver in Peru was so considerable that many of the utensils commonly employed were made of it.

In the land of Midian, where the Law-giver dwelt for many years, there are remains of similar caverns and pits where mines of the precious metal have been worked, which attest his ingenuity and skill.

"In the armoury* of the royal palace at Madrid are shown suits of armour, which are called Montezuma's.

* Dr. Robertson, *History of North and South America.*

They are composed of thin lacquered copper-plates. In the opinion of very intelligent judges, they are evidently eastern. The forms of the silver ornaments upon them, representing dragons, &c., may be considered as confirmation of this.

"The only unquestionable specimen of Mexican art that I know of in Great Britain, is a cup of very fine gold, which is said to have belonged to Montezuma. It weighs 5 oz. 12 dwt. Three drawings of it were exhibited to the Society of Antiquaries, June 10, 1765. A man's head is represented on the cup. On one side the full face, on the other the profile, on the third the back parts of the head. The relievo is said to have been produced by pinching the inside of the cup, so as to make the representation of a face on the outside. The features are gross, but represented with some degree of art. This cup was purchased by Edward, Earl of Orford, while he lay in the harbour of Cadiz with the fleet under his command, and is now in the possession of his grandson, Lord Archer. I am indebted for this information to my respectable and ingenious friend Mr. Barrington.

"As the Mexican paintings are the most curious monument extant of the earliest mode of writing, it will not be improper to give some account of the means by which they were preserved from the general wreck of every work of art in America, and communicated to the public. For the most early and complete collection of these published by Purchas, we are indebted to the attention of that curious inquirer, Hakluyt.

"Don Antonio Mendoza, viceroy of New Spain,

having deemed those paintings a proper present for Charles V., the ship in which they were sent to Spain was taken by a French cruiser, and they came into the possession of Thevet, the King's geographer, who, having travelled himself into the New World, and described one of its provinces, was a curious observer of whatever tended to illustrate the manners of the Americans.

" On his death they were purchased by Hakluyt, at that time chaplain of the English ambassador to the French court; and being left by him to Purchas, were published at the desire of the learned antiquary Sir Henry Spelman. They were translated from English into French by Melchizedeck Thevenot, and published in his collection of voyages, A.D. 1683.

" The second specimen of Mexican picture-writing was published by Dr. Francis Gemelli Carreri, in two copper-plates. The first is a map, or representation of the progress of the ancient Mexicans* on their first arrival in the country, and of the various stations in which they settled, before they founded the capital of their empire in the lake of Mexico. The second is a chronological wheel, or circle, representing the manner in which they computed and marked their cycle of fifty-two years. He received both from Don Carlos de Siguenza y Congorra, a diligent collector of ancient Mexican documents.

" But as it seems now to be a received opinion (founded, as far as I know, on no good evidence) that Carreri was never out of Italy, and that his famous *Giro del Mundo* is an account of a fictitious voyage, I have not mentioned these paintings in the

* Moses and his followers, from Japan.—J. V. G.

text. They have, however, manifestly the appearance of being Mexican productions, and are allowed to be so by Boturini, who was well qualified to determine whether they were genuine or supposititious. Mr. Clavigero likewise admits them to be genuine paintings of the ancient Mexicans. To me they always appeared to be so, though, from my desire to rest no part of my narrative upon questionable authority, I did not refer to them.

"The style of painting in the former is considerably more perfect than any other specimen of Mexican design; but as the original is said to have been much defaced by time, I suspect that it has been improved by some touches from the hand of an European artist. The chronological wheel is a just delineation of the Mexican mode of computing time, as described by Acosta. It seems to resemble one which that learned Jesuit had seen; and if it be admitted as a genuine monument, it proves that the Mexicans had artificial or arbitrary characters, which represented several things besides numbers. Each month is there represented by a symbol expressive of some work or rite peculiar to it.

"The third specimen of Mexican painting was discovered by another Italian. In 1736, Lorenzo Boturini Benaduci set out for New Spain, and was led by several incidents to study the language of the Mexicans, and to collect the remains of their historical monuments. He persisted nine years in his researches, with the enthusiasm of a projector and the patience of an antiquary.

"In 1746 he published, at Madrid, *Ida de una Nueva Historia General de la America Septentrional*, containing an account of the result of his inquiries; and he added to it a catalogue of his American historical Museum, arranged under thirty-six different heads. His idea of a New History appears to me the work of a whimsical, credulous man. But his catalogue of Mexican maps, paintings, tribute-rolls, calendars, &c., is much larger than one could have expected. Unfortunately a ship, in which he had sent a considerable part of them to Europe, was taken by an English privateer during the war between Great Britain and Spain, which commenced in the year 1739; and it is probable that they perished by falling into the hands of ignorant captors.

"Boturini himself incurred the displeasure of the Spanish court, and died in an hospital in Madrid. The history, of which the *Idea, &c.*, was only a prospectus, was never published. The remainder of his Museum seems to have been dispersed. Some part of it came into the possession of the present Archbishop of Toledo, when he was primate of New Spain; and he published from it that curious tribute-roll which I have mentioned.

"The only other collection of Mexican paintings, as far as I can learn, is in the Imperial Library at Vienna. By order of their imperial majesties, I have obtained such a specimen of these as I desired, in eight paintings made with so much fidelity that I am informed the copies could hardly be distinguished from the originals. According to a note in this Codex Mexicanus, it appears to have been a present from Emanuel, King of Portugal, to Pope Clement VII., who died A.D. 1533. After passing through the hands of several illustrious proprietors, it fell into those of Cardinal of Saxe-Eisenach, who presented it to the Emperor Leopold. These paintings are manifestly Mexican, but they are in a style very different from any of the former. An engraving has been made of one of them. Were it an object of sufficient importance, it might, perhaps, be possible, by recourse to the plates of Purchas, and the Archbishop of Toledo, as a key, to form plausible conjectures concerning the meaning of this picture. Many of the figures are evidently similar. The targets and darts, are almost in the same form with those published by Purchas. The figures of temples, nearly resemble those in Purchas and in Lorenzana. A bale of mantles, or cotton cloths, is also shown, the figure of which occurs almost in every plate of Purchas and Lorenzana; and there appear to be Mexican captains in their war-dress, the fantastic ornaments of which resemble the figures in Purchas. I should suppose this picture to be a tribute-roll, as the mode of noting numbers occurs frequently.

"According to Boturini the mode of computation by the number of knots was known to the Mexicans as well as to the Peruvians, and the manner in which the number of units is represented in the Mexican paintings in my possession seems to confirm this opinion. They plainly resemble a string of knots on a cord or slender rope.

"Since I published the former edition, Mr. Waddilove, who is still pleased to continue his friendly attention to procure me information, has discovered, in the library of the Escurial, a volume in folio, consisting of forty sheets of a kind of paste-board, each the size of a common sheet of writing-paper, with great variety of uncouth and whimsical figures of Mexican painting, in very fresh colours, and with an explanation in Spanish to most of them. The first twenty-two sheets are the signs of the months, days, &c. About the middle of each sheet are two or more large figures for the month, surrounded by the signs of the days. The last eighteen sheets are not so filled with figures. They seem to be signs of deities, and images of various objects.

" According to this Calendar in the Escurial, the Mexican year contained 286 days, divided into 22 months of 13 days. Each day is represented by a different sign, taken from some natural object, a serpent, a dog, a lizard, a reed, a house, &c. The signs of days in the Calendar of the Escurial are precisely the same with those mentioned by Boturini, *Idea, &c.*, p. 45.

" But, if we may give credit to that author, the Mexican year contained 360 days, divided into 18 months of 20 days. The order of days in every month was computed, according to him, first by what he calls a tridecenary progression of days from one to thirteen, in the same manner as in the Calendar of the Escurial, and then by a septenary progression of days from one to seven, making in all twenty. In this Calendar not only the signs which distinguish each day, but the qualities supposed to be peculiar to each month, are marked.

" The paste-board, or whatever substance it may be on which the Calendar in the Escurial is painted, seems, by Mr. Waddilove's description of it, to resemble nearly that in the Imperial Library in Vienna. In several particulars the figures bear some likeness to those in the plate which I have published. The figures . . . which induced me to conjecture that this painting might be a tribute-roll similar to those published by Purchas and the Archbishop of Toledo, Mr. Waddilove supposed to be signs of days; and I have such confidence in the accuracy of his observations as to conclude his opinion to be well founded.

"It appears, from the characters in which the explanations of the figures are written, that this curious monument of Mexican art had been obtained soon after the conquest of the Empire. It is singular that it should never have been mentioned by any Spanish author."

The following are the various modes in which the Mexicans contributed towards the support of government, modes resembling the revenue system of Egypt in ancient times. Some persons of the first order were exempted from payment of tribute, but at the same time were bound to personal service in war, and to follow the banner of their sovereign with their vassals. The immediate vassals of the crown not only contributed by personal military service, but also paid a certain proportion of the produce of their lands in kind. Those who held offices of honour or trust paid a certain share of the emoluments derived therefrom.

Each "association" cultivated some part of the common field allotted to it, for the behoof of the crown, and deposited the produce in the royal granaries. Some part of whatever was brought to the public markets, whether fruits of the earth or the various productions of artists and manufacturers, was demanded for the public use, and the merchants who paid this tax were exempted from every other. The peasants were bound to cultivate certain districts in every province, which may be considered as crown lands, and brought the increase into public storehouses.

Thus the sovereign received some part of whatever was useful or valuable in the country, whether it was the natural production of the soil, or the result of the industry of the people. Yet what each contributed towards the support of government was inconsiderable, the value of it in money being not more than about eighteen-pence or two shillings per head.

CHAPTER IX.

GRANARIES OF THE ANCIENT WORLD.

The storehouses or granaries now in use in Mexico, Peru, and other empires, are not the Pyramids which were built and used in the time of Joseph and Moses. A recent traveller gives the following description of a modern granary situated near Canton, in China:—

"Here we saw a large magazine for grain; it was a quadrangular building about 350 feet each way, lined on the outside with plank, and on the whole appeared well adapted for the intended purpose. Such depôts for corn, they (the Chinese) tell us, are very common everywhere, yet, except in this instance, they have hitherto escaped our notice."

From what the same traveller says about some remarkable rocks that he saw in China, there appears to be every likelihood of finding pyramids in that country which, built by Moses and his followers during their sojourn there, still remain unopened after all these ages, even by the present generation of the Chinese, who conquered the country from the colonists left in the empire by the Law-giver. These solitary rocks were situated in plains surrounded by corn-fields, similar to the situation and position of the Pyramids of Egypt and Mexico. The traveller says:—

"In the course of the day we passed by one town and three villages (proceeding towards Canton from the south), likewise several remarkable rocks, nearly perpendicular on all sides, and about two hundred feet high, perfectly isolated, and unconnected with any elevated ground whatsoever; besides, the circumjacent country is low, level, alluvial soil, *well cultivated*.

"All these circumstances considered, it is rather difficult to account for the existence of such a phenomenon as these solitary rocks, so remote, too, from any mountain, unless, perhaps, those prodigious masses of solid stone have been, at some very remote period of time, each the nucleus of a hill, in which case they must have been below the surface of the soil, which, being gradually washed down and carried away by the floods, these rocks became denuded, and left exposed in their present situation.

"Another conjecture may be offered on this subject, that probably they have been placed, as now seen, by the operation of the same causes that effected the general deluge, when the globe suffered such dreadful disruptions and convulsions as, according to the Mosaic relation, to shake the very pillars of the earth, and to break up the fountains of the great deep; the truth of this will appear obvious when we consider the nature of that powerful agent which occasioned this memorable catastrophe."*

The Pyramids of Mexico are termed by the learned

* *Voyages and Travels*, vol. vi.

Dr. Robinson temples and mounds of earth; and the Pyramids of Egypt have been mentioned by Bruce and other travellers as natural rocks and mounds. So that it is not extraordinary that a shipwrecked seaman, travelling on foot along the coast of China towards Canton, should call these unexplored pyramids solitary rocks. There are such mounds or rocks in Ireland. Now that country was visited in ancient times by the Phenicians, who were originally a colony of Egyptians, and who must have witnessed the construction, or perhaps even assisted in the building of the Pyramids of Egypt, by command of Joseph, or Zaphnath-paaneah; they also assisted King Solomon in building the Temple in Jerusalem. These Phenicians, then, built pyramids in Ireland, which, though a fertile island, has been subject to frequent visitations of famine. The learned traveller Kohl speaks of these erections, in his work on Ireland, as follows:—

"The Moate of Lisserdowling is a round conical hill, about forty feet high, and almost five hundred feet in circumference. It stands in a plain, and is surrounded by *corn-fields*, and, being planted with trees and white-thorn bushes, presents a stately object on the naked level. On the summit the Moate was flat, with an indentation in the middle, leaving a few stones bare, that seemed to form part of some masonry concealed under the turf, by which the whole of the artificial hill was covered.

"The popular tradition, I was told, assigned the moat as a dwelling-place to an ancient Irish chief of the name of Naghten O'Donnell, and a small by-road in the neighbourhood is still called, after him, Naghten's Lane. The hill stands in high repute throughout the country, and is a favourite resort on fine afternoons, when hundreds may be seen sitting and lying on its sides ; but not one of these visitors remains after dark, when the Moate of Lisserdowling, and the lane leading to it, are abandoned to the fairies, or 'good people,' as they are called in Ireland. Nor will anyone touch a stone or a stick on the hill, 'unless they have had a dream,' as my farmer expressed himself, 'and have had a commission from the good people.'

"I observed on the side of the mount the stump of an old thorn-bush. My guide informed me that the bush itself had been blown down one windy night, many years ago, and had been left to rot on the ground where it fell, no one daring to touch it, though in general the poor people are ready enough to appropriate to themselves anything burnable that they may find by the wayside. Young trees they will steal with very little remorse, but wood growing on one of these fairy mounts is almost always secure from their depredations.

"On the following day I visited a similar hill, the Moate-o'-Ward, which was likewise covered with white thorns, and in the sequel I met with great numbers of these artificial hillocks, of which Ireland contains many more than England or Scotland. The people call them moats, a word used in English to designate the ditch of a fortress. In Irish they are called 'raths,' a word bearing precisely the same signification. They are also sometimes called 'Dane's Mounts'; for in Ireland, as every art of destruction is charitably set down to Cromwell's account, so every erection of a remote date is attributed to the Danes.

"The popular belief is quite unanimous, therefore, in giving the Danes the credit of having erected these tumuli, as fortresses whence they might hold the country in subjection; and when the Danes had been expelled, an Irish chief here and there chose the deserted fastness for his dwelling-place. The learned are not quite so unanimous in their views as to the origin of these erections. Some go with the stream, and set them down to Danish account; others believe the hillocks to be of a much more ancient date, and to have formed the strongholds of the ancient native kings. In the north of Ireland is a mound of enormous size, said to have been the seat of the kings of Ulster.

"Probably this earthy architecture, which appears to have been so widely diffused over Ireland, was the work of different ages, of various races, and had more objects than one in view. Nearly all the nations of Europe, in the infancy of their civilization, seem to have delighted in the erection of these artificial hills. The whole of Southern Russia is full of them, and we meet with them in Hungary, Turkey, Scandinavia, and Denmark, as well as in England and Ireland; but nowhere in such numbers as in Ireland, whence we may conclude that the ancient Irish must have built many of their raths long before the Danes arrived among them.

"It is also probable that they were erected with different objects in view. Some, we know, were intended as boundary marks, and some, we know, were raised over the remains of distinguished heroes and chiefs. From some it was customary for the law-givers and judges to announce their decisions to the assembled multitude, and on others kings were anointed and crowned. The Druids required sacred hills to offer their sacrifices on, and where a natural hill was not to be had an artificial one, no doubt, was often formed.

"Others, again, may have been intended as fortresses on which the people might seek refuge from an enemy. Many, no doubt, remain that are quite enigmatical. Several, when opened, are found to contain passages and cells, of which it is difficult to guess what use they were intended for. They are too small for storehouses, and can scarcely have served as tombs, or bones and other remains would have been found there.

"Lisserdowling, a high pyramid surrounded by a low rampart and ditch, is more likely, in my opinion, to have been erected as a religious monument than as a fortress. Had it been intended for a fortress, why should so much labour have been expended in giving it a conical form, and why not have bestowed more pains on the circumvallation. As a fortress it would have been the strangest and most ineligible that could have been built. The space on the summit would scarcely afford room for two huts, and when the ramparts had once been stormed by the enemy, the defenders would have been at the greatest disadvantage on the sides of the cone.

"Probably the circumvallation has led to the belief that this, and many other tumuli, were intended for fortresses; but Stonehenge, which nobody ever took to be a fortress, is also surrounded by rampart and ditch. The circumvallation may have been intended simply to mark the boundary of the holy place, and to cut off all connection with the profane part of the world."

These ruins which Mr. Kohl has described, and respecting which he has given his opinion, are simply the remains of ancient granaries or pyramids, erected by the Phenicians, who left them standing when they returned to their own country. After the departure of these Phenicians, Ireland was visited by the Moors, who were masters of Spain and Portugal. These Moors coming from the coast of Africa, opposite Spain, were a colony formerly from the heart of Negroland, whence they reached the coast by way of the great desert called the Sahara, and joined their cuuntrymen who had already settled in the new empire called Mauritana, which comprised Morocco and Tunis, &c., of our time.

These new visitors erected the round towers, in which to stack corn, just as their predecessors had constructed the Pyramids for a like purpose. There are round granaries in Africa, constructed with materials procurable in the place; but in Ireland they used stone instead, which was more durable, although retaining the same form as in the prototypes. The following is what Kohl says about the round towers:—

"On leaving Kilrush I entrusted my person and my portmanteau to a small boat which I had engaged to carry me over to Scattery Island, and thence to the coast of Kerry. The morning was warm, and not a breath of wind disturbed the surface of the water, but the sun was completely concealed by a thick yellow fog, which scarcely allowed us to see beyond the length of our boat. Nevertheless, my boatman brought me in safety to the little green island, which I was about to visit for the sake of its interesting ruins, and by the time we reached its shore the fog had sufficiently dispersed to allow us to distinguish the remains of its 'Seven Churches,' while the lofty column of the round towers presented itself at first as a dark line, and then gradually broke with more distinctness through the turbid atmosphere.

"These Round Towers are the most interesting remains of antiquity that Ireland possesses. Like most travellers in Ireland, I was soon infected with a passion for round towers; but as this passion is one of which few of my friends in Germany are likely to have a distinct idea, I believe that some introductory remarks on these venerable buildings will not be out of place here.

"These Round Towers are built of large stones, and when seen at a distance look rather like lofty columns than towers, being from the base to the top of nearly the same thickness. They are now, indeed, by no means all of the same height, many of them having fallen into ruins; but those which remain tolerably complete are all from 100 to 120 feet high, from forty to fifty in circumference, and from thirteen to sixteen in diameter. At the base the wall is always very thick and strong, but becomes slighter towards the top. Within, the tower is hollow, without any opening but a door, generally eight or ten feet from the ground, and some very narrow apertures or windows, mostly four in number, near the top.* These windows are usually turned towards the four cardinal points of the compass.

"In all parts of Ireland these singular buildings are found scattered about, all resembling each other like the obelisks of Egypt. Sometimes round towers are found in solitary islands, sometimes on the side of a river, or a plain, or some secluded corner of a valley. The whole number of them, according to the map of Ireland published by the Society for the Diffusion of Useful Knowledge, is, at present, 118; of these fifteen are in a perfect state of preservation, and of thirty-six little more than the foundation remains.

"The general name of 'Round Towers' is very little characteristic of these remarkable buildings, for towers are seldom otherwise than round. Some writers have called them 'pillar temples,' but this name assigns to them a designation which it is by no means certain that they bore. The characteristic peculiarity of these towers consists in their resemblance to mighty pillars, and the most appropriate name for them would, in my opinion, be 'pillar towers.'

"In no part of Europe do we find any similar building of antiquity. In Scotland, it is said, two or three pillar towers exist, and these, it may be inferred, were reared by Irish colonists. In the far east only we come to erections of the same character and dimension; the first thing that a traveller is reminded of on seeing an Irish round tower, is a Turkish minaret.

* In the Pyramids these apertures are called by Egyptologists "air channels"; they were for throwing the corn into the body of the granary.—J.V.G.

"No authentic records exist to guide us to a knowledge of the time when these towers were built, or of the use for which they were intended. Everything proves that they have existed from a very remote antiquity, and the most opposite conclusions have been adopted with respect to the period and object of their erection; none of these hypotheses carry conviction with them, but of many, at least, the absurdity can be shown with little trouble.

"Some, for instance, have maintained that these towers were built by the Danes; but these sages appear to have forgotten that round towers are found in parts of the island where the Danes never set foot, as, for instance, in Donegal and the remote counties of Connaught. Besides, had these been Danish erections, how came the Danes not to leave any of them in England?

"Popular tradition assigns them to the Phœnicians, and learned antiquarians ought not too hastily to reject popular tradition, for often the memory of a people undergoes less corruption and change in the course of a thousand years than do the records preserved in books. There is nothing very improbable in the hypothesis that these towers were built by the Phœnicians, who are known to have visited the island and to have exercised power there.

"Travellers have recently discovered in the Persian province of Masanderan towers precisely similar to those of Ireland, and in India erections of a similar kind, dedicated to religious purposes, have also been met with. This, taken in connection with the shape of the Turkish minaret, makes it extremely probable that the round towers have had an Oriental origin. Many have been staggered by the great antiquity which such an hypothesis would assign to the Irish towers, but they are buildings of wonderful solidity, and there is nothing at all extraordinary in the supposition that these stones may have remained in their present position for some thousands of years. Have we not even brick buildings of Roman erection, that are known to have been built before the Christian era?

"No less diversified have been the opinions respecting the use for which the round towers were intended, and on this subject some strangely absurd doctrines have been advanced. Some people have supposed them to have formed chains of telegraph stations spread out over the whole island; but the absurdity of this notion is sufficiently shown by the position of some of the towers upon low ground, in the corners of valleys, and on remote and solitary islands, whence nothing could well be seen, and nothing, therefore, made known. This opinion is, nevertheless, still entertained by many.

"Others suppose the towers to have been fortresses, erected in the early ages of Christianity as places of refuge, in case of danger, for the priests and their church treasures. I can hardly think, however, that any people could have selected such a style of architecture for places of defence. The defenders within would have had to stand upon each other's heads, and their only means of annoying their enemies would have been the four small openings at the top, eighty or a hundred feet from the ground. Besides, had the round towers been military places of defence, they would probably have all been destroyed in the course of the constant wars by which the island has been afflicted, whereas the round towers have evidently been preserved by the people with great care, and have ever been looked on by them with the greatest veneration.

"The notion that the round towers were built by the early Christians as steeples to hang their bells in is equally untenable, for, though they are frequently found in close vicinity to the ruins of churches, yet no kind of steeple could be worse constructed for such a purpose, as the sound of the bells would scarcely have been heard through the small apertures at the top, except by those who had already assembled around the tower.

"Many other opinions have been hazarded, but all at variance with the popular tradition, which represents the round towers to have been the temples of the old fire-worshippers from the East, who came over with the Phœnicians. The poet Moore and other Irish antiquarians are disposed to adopt this tradition, the more so as the pyreas of the Ghebers, according to the account of several travellers, bear the closest similitude to the Irish towers, and because the worship of fire is known to have been at one time the prevailing religion of Ireland. The dark interiors of these towers have been well calculated to show the sacred fire preserved there to the greatest advantage, and the height of the entrance-door from the ground would be explained by the sanctity of the place, to which only a few were probably allowed to have access.

"The great height of the towers has been objected to as entirely superfluous, supposing them to have been applied to such a use ; but it may have been customary to place the sacred fire in an elevated position, as an additional mark of respect, and then the towers may have answered more purposes than one ; from the windows at the top signals may have been made to summon the faithful to prayer, or the apertures may have been used for astronomical observations, intended to fix the time of the religious feasts.

"Christian emblems have been discovered in some of these towers. On the summit of that near Swords, in the county of Dublin, is a small stone cross, and in others even representations of the Virgin have been found ; but these, there cannot be a doubt, are of modern addition. That churches and cemeteries should so often be found in the vicinity of these towers is nothing surprising, for a building that has once become sacred in the eyes of a people, generally retains a portion of its sanctity, even though the original religion may be utterly swept away. Most of the early Christian churches were erected on the foundations of heathen temples, and a large portion of the Turkish mosques were formerly Christian churches.

"Generally, where in the vicinity of a round tower there occur the ruins of churches, these are in number seven. This has been explained by supposing that, previously to the appearance of St. Patrick, Christianity—but not Roman Catholic Christianity—had been introduced into Ireland. This ante-patrician Christianity is said to have been introduced by the Apostle James, who first preached the gospel in Ireland, and established the Eastern Church there, with the rites of the Eastern

Œcumenic Synods; and the frequent appearance of seven churches close to each other is accounted for as a reference to the seven celebrated churches of the East.

"In this hypothesis, though stoutly denied by the Roman Catholics, there is nothing improbable, and, if true, it affords another remarkable proof of the early connection between Ireland and the East. In no other Christian land in Europe do we constantly find the ruins of ancient churches in groups of seven.

"We effected a landing on Scattery Island, called in ancient times Inniscattery, and at present occupied by a few tenants of a Mr. M'Kean, who graze their cattle there. 'It is a very old ancient place,' said one of the boatmen, as he was carrying me through the water on his shoulders, for we had come to a landing-place where the tide had left one foot of water over a large extent of coast. This pleonasm of 'old ancient' might be applied to many parts of Ireland, where old and older ruins are constantly found in close contiguity.

"In general, where there are seven churches, in Ireland, some ancient saint is named as having lived and died there, and as having belonged to the first preachers of Christianity in the country. At Scattery it is Saint Senanus, whose grave is still shown amid one of the ruins, and whose fame has been extended far beyond his native isle by one of Moore's melodies. These ancient ruins, however, have many graves of a more modern date; for bodies are still brought over from the mainland to be interred at Scattery. On the occasion of such a funeral, one boat serves generally as a hearse, and the mourners follow in other boats.

"I saw many tomb-stones only a few years old, with new inscriptions, from which the gilding had scarcely begun to fade, and their effect upon the solitary and remote island was peculiar and by no means unpleasing. Among them were the tombs of several captains of ships, and it would have been difficult to suggest a more appropriate place of interment for such men than this little island cemetery at the mouth of a great river, with the wide ocean rolling in front. Indeed, there is no other country in Europe where there are such interesting cemeteries, or such picturesque tombs, as in Ireland, partly on account of the abundance of ivy with which they are hung, and partly on account of the practice that still prevails of burying the dead among ruins.

"Of some of the seven churches on Scattery isle, scarcely a trace remained; but three of them were in tolerable preservation. Their walls, covered with ivy, remained, and into the wall of one of them, that nearest the round tower, a stone strangely sculptured into the form of a human face had been introduced. Strange to say, it has completely the stiff, mask-like features and projecting ears of the Egyptian statue, whence I conclude it must have belonged originally to some other building. On the opposite wall is a stone with evident traces of an ancient inscription.

"The round tower stands a little to the side. Although not perfect, it belongs to the most picturesque in Ireland, for it has been struck by lightning, and has received a split on one side from top to bottom. On the south side it is covered completely with mosses and creeping plants; on the north and west side it is bare, the heavy winds, as the sailors told me, making all vegetation impossible there. Lightning and vegetation are the worst enemies the round towers have to contend with, and it is strange that such active foes should not have been able to overturn the whole of them in a space of two thousand years.

"All the land upon the little island, except the cemetery, is pasturage. A small battery has been erected here to protect the mouth of the Shannon, the entrance to which river is defended by no less than six batteries and forts, while at the mouth of the Thames there is not one.

"On leaving Inniscattery, to repair to the kingdom of Kerry, we had work enough before us, for the tide was against us, besides which we had to contend with such a variety of currents, that the boatmen required all their skill and experience to carry their slight skiff in safety to the little port of Tarbert, whither we were bound. The mouth of the Shannon has rather the character of an arm of the sea, but to consider it as such would be in violation of the principles of Irish geography.

"The waves, now of a very respectable size, were rolling out towards the ocean; but the fog was completely gone, and we had the most beautiful sunshine. With the exception of our own little bark, which seemed to crest the waves like a bird, neither ship nor boat was to be seen upon the noble estuary, and, without passing a human creature with whom we could have exchanged a salutation, we arrived at length in safety at our destined harbour.

"There I learned, when it was too late, that without any additional expenditure of time or trouble, I might have effected a landing at Ballybunian, whose marine caverns, at the mouth of the Shannon, are reckoned among the wonders of Ireland. These caverns stretch more than a mile from the sea into the land. Ireland, indeed, is rich in remarkable caverns, many of which are but little known to the scientific world."

The original models from which the Round Towers of Ireland were taken are still to be found in the Soudan of Africa; and the people whose ancestors erected buildings after this fashion, as they migrated from their native country to the seaboard, and crossed over to Spain—whence they visited Ireland—are to this day as savage in manners and customs as their forefathers were before they left Africa. The following description of the round conical granaries, the country where they are situated, and the builders of them, is taken from a work called *Egypt, the Soudan, and Central Africa*, by John Petherick, F.R.G.S., Her Britannic Majesty's Consul for the Soudan:—

"Those of my men who had wintered with the Djour had procured from the negroes a large quantity of tusks, the accumulation of several years' hunting. Their journeys had extended to the confines of the Rohl, in the east, and in the territory of the Djour westwards beyond the large stream which, on reference to the map, will be seen as the largest feeder of the lake. I had discovered southwards they had penetrated the Dôr territory; and as they had succeeded in gaining the good-will of the Dôr chief Djau, I despatched a party to invite him to meet me.

"The porters who had accompanied me from the Raik, on learning my intention to proceed south amongst tribes unknown to them, and dreaded in consequence of the difference of weapons and savage habits, refused to proceed; and, consigning loads of ivory to them, in charge of a detachment of my Khartoumers, I sent them back to their own country. Levying in their stead a party of Djour for the transport of my stock in trade, I took the advantage of a moonlight night to perform the journey to the Dôr to Fan-Djau (the country of Djau), so named after my chief Djau, situated in about six degrees north latitude.

"Our reception amongst them was most hospitable, and in the vicinity of the chief's huts we were accommodated with strong wooden sheds, about six feet high, upon which their corn, divested of its reeds, was prettily stacked, consisting of different kinds of dourra of different colours—white, grey, and red—in separate batches. The stacks were formed with much taste, the sides being perpendicular, terminating in a cone. The precaution of raising their stacks so high from the ground was to preserve it from vermin and the white ants.

"The Dôr surpass the Djour in industry, a proof of which existed in their extensive fields and granaries. Prior to the rainy season, their grain was threshed and preserved in large cylindrical receptacles, constructed of reeds and clay, from twelve to fifteen feet in diameter, and four feet in height, supported upon a strong wood framework some four feet from the ground. To preserve its contents from the rain, it was covered by a large thatched framework, not unlike an extinguisher in shape, and was so light in substance, that when the grain was required, one side of it could be lifted and supported by a pole, and the granary entered.*

"Their huts were constructed of a beautiful basket-work of cane. The perpendicular walls were six feet high, and were surmounted with a pretty cupola-shaped reed roof, topped with wood carvings of birds. A wooden bedstead occupied its centre, and an oval-shaped hole, two and a half feet high, barely sufficient to admit a man in a stooping posture, formed the doorway. At night this was barricaded with logs of wood laid horizontally upon each other, between perpendicular posts.

"Cooking was carried on in a separate hut, and in lieu of the stone-mill in use in the Soudan, a large wooden mortar, the pestle some four or five feet in length, by three inches diameter, served as their flour-mill. Their food consisted principally of a thick porridge, and a sauce flavoured with herbs and red pepper; but beef, whenever they could obtain it by barter for grain with the Djour, or meat from the chase, was preferred. Rats, mice, and snakes were highly esteemed, and of these the children were continually in search. Fowls were reared to a great extent, but from some unaccountable superstition they were only considered proper

---

* In the Round Tower there is a door by which it can be entered.—J. V. G.

food for women: if eaten by men, it was a proof of effeminacy.

"The Dôr territories are more considerable than any I had yet traversed; and their language, the nouns of which generally terminated in *o* or *a*, was entirely different from any that I had heard. The men were shorter in stature than the tall Dinka Shillooks, but broader in the chest and stouter-limbed.

"Total nudity was held in contempt by them, although their covering was reduced to the smallest possible amount; and when the Djour entered their village, the little hide ornament worn by them in common with the Dinka tribes, as a mark of respect was turned round to the front.

"Of a dark brown colour, they further differed from the negroes hitherto described, in the preservation of their teeth and the difference of their weapons: these consisted of bows and arrows, fearfully-barbed lances, and a variety of clubs. Some resembled the mace of the Middle Ages, whilst others, made of hard wood, were like the mushroom. The edges were firm and sharp, and when employed against an enemy would cleave the skull. The points of their arrows, made of iron, are also numerously barbed; the workmanship, in a variety of patterns, is admirable.

"The Dôr perhaps excel the Djour in smithery; and, possessing no cattle, their valuables consist in objects of iron, mostly in circular plates from nine inches to one foot in diameter, and long ornamented lance-like articles. For a certain number of these they intermarry.

"Goats and fowls are their only domestic animals; the former a short-legged and smooth-haired variety. The coat is fine, and coloured frequently with large round spots of black, yellow, or brown upon white: they are not milked, although, when taken to Khartoum and crossed with the native race, they become excellent milkers.

"The women would be handsome were it not for a disfiguration of the under lip, in which circular pieces of wood are inserted, varying in size, according to age, from a sixpence to a florin. The young women are naked, but the married women wear large clusters of green leaves in front and behind, which, attached by a belt to the waist, reach to the ankles. Clean in their habits, they are particular in the daily renewal of their costume from the bush, the numerous evergreens and creeping plants affording them an abundant material for that purpose.

"Their ears, necks, and waists are profusely adorned with beads, and on their wrists they wear numerous iron bracelets. The ankles are encumbered with bright heavy iron rings, fully one inch thick; and these tinkling together as they dance produce a peculiarly fascinating sound.

"In the centre of the village is a large circus, where, on a tree, their war-trophies, the skulls of the slain, are suspended. Beneath it large tom-toms, made of hollowed trunks of trees, well finished, and strung with dressed buffalo-hides, were used only on occasions of universal rejoicing, or to sound the alarm in time of war. The sound could be heard miles distant. At ordinary times smaller instruments of the same kind were employed. This large circus was carefully swept and watered; and under the shade of the tree the men met during the day, and in the evenings, more especially on moonlight nights, it was the scene of great conviviality.

"The several approaches to it were narrow footpaths, and both sides were ornamented with rough wooden posts, carved into semblances of human figures, four feet apart; the first were largest in size, the others had on their heads wooden bowls. These figures were said to represent the chief proceeding to a festival, and followed by his retainers bearing viands and *mau* to the feast.

"The village was prettily situated at the foot of a hill, around which were two or three other villages, this forming the entire community of a large district. From its summit a beautiful view of the surrounding country was obtained. Surrounding the village, at a moderate distance, were the unfenced gardens of the villagers, in which cucurbits, vegetables, and seeds were grown; and beyond, to the eastward, was a large plain of cultivated dourra fields; southward, at about one mile distant, a winding brook was to be seen, bordered with superb trees and flourishing canes.

"The bush supplied a variety of game, consisting of partridges, guinea-fowl, a large white boar, gazelles, antelopes, and giraffes. Elephants and buffalo I did not encounter, and I was told they only frequented the locality during the rainy season.

"The Dôr acknowledge no superior chief, and the tribe is divided into separate communities; and these, although living, as in this instance, in close proximity, look upon each other as almost separate tribes, holding little or no communication. They live in a state of continual feud, attributable to encroachments on hunting-grounds. Their battues consist in driving the game into strong nets, which, suspended to the trunks of trees at right angles, cover a space of several miles.

"During my stay at Djau, a hunt of this description, in which the inhabitants of a village some miles distant joined, took place, and, as usual, ended in a quarrel. Sitting under my habitation at noon, several boys returned to the village for extra weapons for the use of their fathers. The alarm spread instantly that a fight was taking place, and the women *en masse* proceeded to the scene with yellings and shrieks indescribable. Seizing my rifle, and accompanied by four of my followers, curiosity to see a negro fight tempted me to accompany them.

"After a stiff march of a couple of hours through bush and glade, covered with waving grass reaching nearly to our waists, the return of several boys warned us of the proximity of the fight, and of their fear of its turning against them—the opposing party being the most numerous. Many of the women hurried back to their homes, to prepare, in case of emergency, for flight and safety in the bush. For such an occurrence, to a certain extent, they are always prepared; several parcels of grain, and provisions neatly packed up in spherical forms, in leaves surrounded by network, being generally kept ready in every hut for a sudden start.

"Accelerating our pace, and climbing up a steep hill, as we reached the summit and were proceeding down a gentle slope, I came in contact with Djau and his party in full retreat, and leaping like greyhounds over the low underwood and high grass. On perceiving me they halted, and rent the air with shouts of 'The white chief! the white chief!' and I was almost suffocated by the embraces of the chief. My presence gave them courage to face the enemy again; a loud peculiar shrill whoop from the grey-headed but still robust chief was the signal for attack, and, bounding forward, they were soon out of sight. To keep up with them would have been an impossibility; but, marching at the top of our pace, we followed them as best we could.

"After a long march down a gentle declivity, at the bottom of which was a beautiful glade, we again came up with them, drawn up in line in pairs, some yards apart from each other, within the confines of the bush, not a sound indicating their presence. Joining them, and inquiring what had become of the enemy, the men whom I addressed silently pointed to the bush on the opposite side of the glade, some three hundred yards across.

"Notwithstanding my intention of being a mere spectator, I now felt myself compromised in the fight; and although unwilling to shed blood, I could not resist my aid to the friends who afforded me an asylum amongst them. Marching accordingly into the open with my force of four men, I resolved that we would act as skirmishers on the side of our hosts, who retained their position in the bush.

"We had proceeded about a third of the way across the glade, when the enemy advanced out of the wood and formed a long line of two or three deep, on its confines opposite to us. I also drew up my force, and for an instant we stood looking at each other. Although within range, at about two hundred yards' distance, I did not like to fire upon them; but in preference continued advancing, thinking the prestige of my fire-arms would be sufficient. I was right. We had scarcely marched fifty yards, when a general flight took place, and in an instant Djau and his host, amounting to some three or four hundred men, passed us in hot pursuit.

"After reflection on the rashness of exposing myself with so few men to the hostility of some six hundred negroes, and in self-congratulation on the effect my appearance in the fight had produced, I awaited the return of my hosts. In the course of an hour this took place; and as they advanced I shall never forget the impression they made upon me. A more complete picture of savage life I could not have imagined. A large host of naked negroes came trooping on, grasping in their hands bow and arrow, lances and clubs, with wild gesticulations and frightful yells proclaiming their victory, whilst one displayed the reeking head of a victim.

"I refused to join them in following up the defeat of their enemies by a descent on their villages. With some difficulty they were persuaded to be content with the success already achieved—that of having beaten off a numerically superior force—and return to their homes. Their compliance was only obtained by an actual refusal of further co-operation; but in the event of a renewed attack upon their villages, the probability of which was suggested, I promised them my willing support.

"We had not gone fifty paces, when I beheld the form of a young man prostrate, apparently lifeless;

and seeing only a deep incision across his wrist, nearly severing the hand from the arm, and a lance-thrust that had penetrated the shoulder between the muscle and the flesh, his open eyes suggested that life might not be extinct. I felt his pulse, but it was imperceptible. At the same time a negro with his lance coolly severed the muscle, and extricated the barbed projectile. I looked upon the man with disgust; but, with a laugh, taking the body by the hand, he rolled it over on the chest, and then two open lance-wounds between the shoulders plainly showed the cause of death.

"On our way home the body was drawn by the legs for a considerable distance, and finally carried on the shoulders of some of the party to conceal the trail. It was secreted in the bush in the hope of its eluding the search of the enemy, leaving it to be devoured by beasts of prey; but the head, severed from the body, was secured and destined, with four others, to be suspended on the tree in the centre of the village circus.

"At night great rejoicings took place, commencing with a war-dance by the women, who, in pairs, closely following each other to the sound of the tom-tom, and chanting a war-song, moved in measured steps round the tree. At each time, as the procession approached the heads of the victims, a halt took place, and insulting epithets addressed to the fallen were followed by the clanking of their anklets and shrieks of applause. Sickened with the exhibition, I retired from the scene.

"The day following, after a night's conviviality, the heads were secreted in the bush in order to bleach the skulls. Another feast celebrated their suspension on the tree."

These are the descendants of the Moors who built the Round Towers in Ireland, when they became masters of Spain!

CHAPTER X.

DEATH OF MOSES.

THE Law-giver, when he had firmly established the two extensive empires of Mexico and Peru, had it in his mind to found another kingdom in the north of Mexico, which should include King George's Sound, in the Pacific Ocean, and stretch across the continent of North America till it reached the Atlantic Ocean.

This immense tract of country was inhabited by savages, living like the wild animals by whom they were surrounded. They knew not God, nor had they any idea of religion, having no greater intelligence than that possessed by the brute creation. It was, however, the intention of Moses to visit these people, to teach them the knowledge of civilised life, and to impart to them the blessings of religion and industry.

This, indeed, was the mission on which Moses was sent over the different quarters of the habitable globe by his God, who spoke to him on Mount Sinai, and who took him away from the camp of the children of Israel at the ford of the river Jordan, viz. that he (Moses) might carry the glorious tidings of salvation to nations that were living in ignorance and superstition. He obeyed the sacred behest, and there are ample proofs which attest the success of his mission and labour of love.

The route he took is marked by signs of flourishing empires, with religion, learning, and laws, as far as the spot where the servant of God was killed by savages—the very people whom he came to reclaim. He visited the coast of North America in a boat made of copper, everything on board of which was made of that metal. Of this the Indians are passionately fond, and for the sake of it they killed the inspired missionary.

But the sequel proves that they repented of their wicked deed—when it was too late. In the hope of obtaining forgiveness from the murdered old man, they paid him divine worship, and carved an image to represent the visitant whom they so cruelly deprived of life. The memory of this remarkable event was handed down to posterity from generation to generation, even to the time when Captain Meares visited that coast in his ship; and the story was related to him by one of the descendants of those who committed the horrid crime. Captain Meares gives the following narrative of what he heard :—*

"For a long time the English thought the inhabitants had no religious belief whatever. To the huge mis-shapen images seen in their houses they addressed no homage; they had neither priests nor temples, nor did they offer any sacrifices ; but an accidental circumstance led to the discovery that, though devoid of all superstitious observances, and wholly ignorant of the true God, they were not without a certain

* Meare, *Voyages*, vol. ii. pp. 70-71.

species of mythology, including a belief of an existence after death. This discovery arose from our inquiries on a very different subject.

"On expressing our wish to be informed by what means they became acquainted with copper, and why it was such a peculiar object of their admiration, a son of Hannapa, one of the Nootkan chiefs, a youth of uncommon sagacity, informed us of all he knew on the subject; and we found, to our surprise, that his story involved a little sketch of their religion. When words were wanting he supplied the deficiency by those expressive actions which nature or necessity seems to communicate to people whose language is imperfect ; and the young Nootkan conveyed his ideas by signs so skilfully as to render them perfectly intelligible. He related his story in the following manner :—

"He first placed a certain number of sticks on the ground, at small distances from each other, to which he gave separate names. Thus, he called the first his father, and the next his grandfather : he then took what remained and threw them all into confusion together, as much as to say that they were the general heap of his ancestors, whom he could not individually reckon.

"He then, pointing to this bundle, said, when they lived an old man entered the sound* in a copper canoe, with copper paddles, and everything else in his possession of the same metal ; that he paddled along the shore, on which all the people were assembled to contemplate so strange a sight, and that, having thrown one of his copper paddles on shore, he himself

* Nootka Sound.—J. V. G.

landed. The extraordinary stranger then told the natives that he came from the sky, to which the boy pointed with his hand; that their country would one day be destroyed, when they would all be killed, and rise again to live in the place from whence he came.

"Our young interpreter explained this circumstance of his narrative by lying down as if he were dead, and then, rising up suddenly, he imitated the action as if he were soaring through the air. He continued to inform us that the people killed the old man, and took his canoe, from which event they derived their fondness for copper; and he added that the images in their houses were intended to represent the form, and perpetuate the mission, of this supernatural person who came from the sky."

Thus ended the glorious life of the man of God. His death was as mysterious to his followers in America, as was his disappearance and supposed death to the Israelites in Asia. He was the first missionary who carried the glad tidings of God's good-will towards an erring world; and he died the death of a martyr at the hands of the very world that he came to enlighten.

At the time of his death Moses must have been very old, for he was already one hundred and twenty years old when he left the Israelites. To arrive at the exact age to which he attained, an acquaintance with the chronicles of many kingdoms would be necessary, in order to know the date at which he arrived, and what length of time he sojourned, in each. But as most of the empires which Moses founded are now under the government of various nations, who have wantonly destroyed every vestige of the history and traditions of their former kings, this knowledge cannot be attained in this age of the world.

When Moses commenced his missionary life he was accompanied by his Ethiopian consort,* and a son, by her, as there is evidence to prove in the painting at Thebes, where there is a representation of the Ethiopian princess with a boy on her lap.† There also went with him Zipporah and her two sons, Gershom and Eliezer,‡ and their sons,§ and a large company of Jews, Egyptians, and Ethiopians.‖

The doctrine that Moses preached everywhere was the same as that he wrote and left among the Jews. It will, therefore, not be out of place to rehearse it here, as he rehearsed it before the Israelites previous to his departure from their midst:—

"Give ear, O ye heavens, and I will speak; and hear, O earth, the words of my mouth. My doctrine shall drop as the rain, my speech shall distil as the dew, as the small rain upon the tender herb, and as the showers upon the grass: Because I will publish the name of the Lord: ascribe ye greatness unto our God. He is the Rock, his work is perfect: for all his ways are judgment: a God of truth and without iniquity, just and right is he.

"They have corrupted themselves, their spot is not the spot of his children. Do ye thus requite the Lord, O foolish people and unwise? Is not he thy

---

* Numbers, xii. 1.
† See Wilkinson, *Manners and Customs of the Ancient Egyptians*, illustration facing p. 222.
‡ Exodus, xviii.
§ 1 Chronicles, xxiii. 15–17.
‖ Exodus, xii. 37, 38.

father that hath bought thee? hath he not made thee, and established thee?

"Remember the days of old, consider the years of many generations: ask thy father, and he will shew thee; thy elders, and they will tell thee. When the Most High divided to the nations the inheritance, when he separated the sons of Adam, he set the bounds of the people according to the number of the children of Israel. For the Lord's portion is his people; Jacob is the lot of his inheritance. He found him in a desert land, and in the waste howling wilderness; he led him about, he instructed him, he kept him as the apple of his eye.

"As an eagle stirreth up her nest, fluttereth over her young, spreadeth abroad her wings, taketh them, beareth them on her wings: so the Lord alone did lead him, and there was no strange god with him. He made him ride on the high places of the earth, that he might eat the increase of the fields, and he made him to suck honey out of the rock, and oil out of the flinty rock; butter of kine, and milk of sheep, with fat of lambs, and rams of the breed of Bashan, and goats, with the fat of kidneys of wheat; and thou didst drink the pure blood of the grape.

"But Jeshurun waxed fat, and kicked: thou art waxed fat, thou art grown thick, thou art covered with fatness; then he forsook God which made him, and lightly esteemed the Rock of his salvation. They provoked him to jealousy with strange gods, with abominations provoked they him to anger. They sacrificed unto devils, not to God; to gods whom they knew not, to new gods that came newly up, whom your fathers feared not. Of the Rock that begat thee thou art unmindful, and hast forgotten God that formed thee.

"And when the Lord saw it, he abhorred them, because of the provoking of his sons, and of his daughters. And he said, I will hide my face from them, I will see what their end shall be: for they are a very froward generation, children in whom is no faith. They have moved me to jealousy with that which is not God; they have provoked me to anger with their vanities: and I will move them to jealousy with those which are not a people; I will provoke them to anger with a foolish nation. For a fire is kindled in mine anger, and shall burn unto the lowest hell, and shall consume the earth with her increase, and set on fire the foundations of the mountains.

"I will heap mischiefs upon them; I will spend mine arrows upon them. They shall be burnt with hunger, and devoured with burning heat, and with bitter destruction: I will also send the teeth of beasts upon them, with the poison of serpents of the dust. The sword without, and terror within, shall destroy both the young man and the virgin, the suckling also with the man of gray hairs.

"I said, I would scatter them into corners, I would make the remembrance of them to cease from among men: Were it not that I feared the wrath of the enemy, lest their adversaries should behave themselves strangely, and lest they should say, Our hand is high, and the Lord hath not done all this. For they are a nation void of counsel, neither is there any understanding in them.

"O that they were wise, that they understood

this, that they would consider their latter end! How should one chase a thousand, and two put ten thousand to flight, except their Rock had sold them, and the Lord had shut them up? For their Rock is not as our Rock, even our enemies themselves being judges. For their vine is of the vine of Sodom, and of the fields of Gomorrah : their grapes are grapes of gall, their clusters are bitter. Their wine is the poison of dragons, and the cruel venom of asps. Is not this laid up in store with me, and sealed up among my treasures?

"To me belongeth vengeance, and recompence ; their foot shall slide in due time : for the day of their calamity is at hand, and the things that shall come upon them make haste. For the Lord shall judge his people, and repent himself for his servants, when he seeth that their power is gone, and there is none shut up or left. And he shall say, Where are their gods, their rock in whom they trusted, which did eat the fat of their sacrifices, and drank the wine of their drink offerings? let them rise up and help you, and be your protection.

"See now that I, even I, am he, and there is no god with me : I kill, and I make alive ; I wound; and I heal : neither is there any that can deliver out of my hand. For I lift up my hand to heaven, and say I live for ever. If I whet my glittering sword, and mine hand take hold on judgment; I will render vengeance to mine enemies, and will reward them that hate me. I will make mine arrows drunk with blood, and my sword shall devour flesh : and that with the blood of the slain and of the captives, from the beginning of revenges upon the enemy.

"Rejoice, O ye nations, with his people: for he will avenge the blood of his servants, and will render vengeance to his adversaries, and will be merciful unto his land, and to his people.

"And Moses came and spake all the words of this song in the ears of the people, he, and Hoshea the son of Nun. And Moses made an end of speaking all these words to all Israel.

"And he said unto them, Set your hearts unto all the words which I testify among you this day, which ye shall command your children to observe to do, all the words of this law. For it is not a vain thing for you; because it is your life: and through this thing ye shall prolong your days in the land, whither ye go over Jordan to possess it."*

* Deut. xxxii. v. 1 to 47.

CHAPTER XI.

RECORD OF FAMINES.

It appears from the numerous ruins of Pyramids (and Round Towers), that the ancients, such as Zaphnath-paaneah and Moses—the latter under a great many different names—in their wisdom and forethought erected them as granaries, so that, notwithstanding the various causes of famine, their territories might be always well provisioned and able to withstand the attack of the dire enemy.

The Famine Statistics of modern times show how necessary those precautions were. If the Round Towers of Ireland had still been used in the Christian Era as granaries, and well stored with corn, instead of being turned into towers for hanging church bells in, how many precious lives would have been saved during all those famines which devastated that beautiful island!

The following is a Chronological Table of Famines[*] that visited Ireland within the Christian Era.

A.D.	
10–15	A general fruitlessness, giving rise to famine and great mortality.
76	Great scarcity.

[*] Walford, *On the Famines of the World: Past and Present.*

RECORD OF FAMINES.

A.D.	
192	General scarcity; bad harvest; mortality and emigration, "so that lands and houses, territories and tribes, were emptied."—First notice of emigration.
535	Destruction of food and scarcity, lasted four years.
664	Great famine.
669	Great scarcity; and in following year.
695–700	Famine and pestilence during three years, "so that men ate each other."
759	Great famine throughout the kingdom; and more or less for several years.
768	Famine and an earthquake.
772	Famine from drought.
824–25	Great dearth.
895–97	Famine from invasion of locusts.
963–64	An intolerable famine, "so that parents sold their children for food."
1047	Great famine and snow.
1116	Great famine, "during which the people even ate each other."
1153	Great famine in Munster, and spread all over Ireland.
1188	Great scarcity of food in north of Ireland.
1200	"A cold, foodless year."
1203	A great famine, "so that priests ate flesh in Lent."
1227	A great famine throughout the country.
1262	Great destruction of people from plague and hunger.
1271	Pestilence and famine in the whole of Ireland.
1295	Great dearth during this and the previous and following years.
1302	Famine.
1314	Famine and various distempers.

A.D.	
1316	Great dearth. Eight captured Scots eaten at siege of Carrickfergus.
1317	A great famine throughout the country in consequence of Bruce's invasion.
1332	A peck of wheat sold for 22 shillings.
1339	A general famine.
1410	"A great famine."
1433	Famine of great severity.
1447	Great famine in the Spring.
1491	Such a famine that it was called, "The Dismal Year."
1497	"Intolerable famine throughout all Ireland—many perished."
1522	A great famine.
1586	Extreme famine consequent on the wars of Desmond. Human flesh said to have been eaten.
1588–89	Great famine, "when one did eate another for hunger."
1601–03	Great scarcity and want. Cannibalism again reported.
1650–51	A famine throughout the country. Sieges of Limerick and Galway.
1690	Famine and disease.
1727–29	Corn very dear. "Many hundreds perished." Emigration.
1739–40	Potatoes destroyed by frost; wheat 42 shillings per kilderkin.
1765	Great scarcity; distilling and exportation of corn prohibited by Act of Parliament.
1822	Dreadful famine, produced by failure of potato crop. "While, however, the agriculturists of the continent were suffering from an abundance, a grievous famine arose in Ireland, showing the anomalies of her situation, resulting

A.D.	
	either from the staple food of her population differing from that of surrounding nations, or the limitation of her commercial exchanges with her neighbours. Her distresses from scarcity were aggravated by the agrarian outrages, originating in the pressure of tythes and rack-rents on the peasantry and small farmers. Several of the ringleaders of these disorders were apprehended by the civil and military power, and great numbers executed or transported."—Wade's *Brit. Hist.*
1831	Famine; Parliament granted £40,000 for relief; £74,410 subscriptions in England.
1845	Famine; the Government expended £850,000 in relief of sufferers.
1846–47	Great potato famine; Parliament advanced nearly £10,000,000; about 275,000 persons are supposed to have perished. The famine in the whole lasted over nearly six years; the population became reduced by about 2,500,000. The emigration to America was 1,180,409, and 1,029,552 are said to have died from starvation and pestilence consequent upon it. This is probably over-stated. It is further said that about 25 per cent. of the emigrants died within twelve months of leaving. The Commerce and Navigation Laws were repealed.

The above table shows how terribly the Irish people have suffered from want of food, and how in their hunger they have been compelled to have recourse to cannibalism in order to save themselves from death by starvation. This sad picture should be a lesson to fanatics like those who, in their misdirected zeal to serve their Master in heaven, destroyed the granaries of the ancient people, mistaking them to be temples dedicated to heathen gods. For, had the pyramids, which appear to have existed in large numbers all over Ireland, been filled during the years of plenty, and the grain kept in reserve until the time of scarcity, there would then have been sufficient food not only for the inhabitants of Ireland, but also for the wants of the sister islands.

The following chronological table of the famines that have devastated England, Scotland and Wales, is taken from Walford's *Famines of the World*. It presents a sad picture of human misery and wretchedness, which might have been prevented by wisdom and forethought.

TABLE OF FAMINES IN ENGLAND, SCOTLAND, AND WALES.

A.D.	
54	England. Grievous famine.
104	England and Scotland. Famine.
107	Britain. From long rains.
119	,, "After a pillar of fire seen several nights in the air."
151	Wales. Grievous.
160	England. Multitudes starved.
173	,, After severe frost and snow.
228	Scotland. "Thousands were starved."
238	,, "Most grievous."
259	Wales. Thousands were "pined to death."
272	Britain. People ate the bark of trees and roots.

A.D.	
288	Britain. Famine all through.
298	Wales. After a comet.
306	Scotland. Thousands died ; most grievous and fatal for four years.—Short.
310	England. 40,000 perished.
325	Britain. Generally, severe famine.
439	,, After a comet.
466	,, "And bad fatal air."—Short.
480	Scotland. After a comet.
515	Britain. "Most afflictive."
523	Scotland. "Terrible."
527	North Wales. Famine.
531	South Wales. And a small plague.
537	Scotland. Dearth ; also in Wales.
576	,, "Fatal."
590	England. From a tempest that raised a great flood.
592	,, Drought from 10th January to September ; and locusts.
605	,, From heat and drought.
625	Britain. Grievous.
667	Scotland. Grievous.
680	Britain. From three years' drought.
695–700	England. Famine and pestilence during three years, " so that men ate each other."
712	Wales. Famine.
730	England, Wales and Scotland. Great famine.
746	Wales. Dearth.
748	Scotland. Famine.
774	,, "With plague."
791	Wales. Grievous.
792	Scotland. Dearth.
793	England. "After many meteors"; and in other parts of the world.
803	Scotland. "Terrible."

A.D.	
822–23	England. "Thousands starve"; also in Scotland, according to Short.
836	Wales. "The ground covered with dead bodies of men and beasts."—Short.
856	Scotland. A four years' famine began.
863	Scotland. With a plague.
872	England. "From ugly locusts."
887	,, "Grievous two years."
890	Scotland. Great dearth.
900	England. Famine.
931	Wales. Famine.
936	Scotland. After a comet; four years, "till people began to devour one another."—Short.
954	England, Wales, and Scotland. Great famine, which lasts four years.
962	England. Famine caused by frost.
969	,, "All grain burnt by the winds."—Short.
975	,, Famine scoured the hills.
976	,, This was the "great famine," *micla hungor*.—John of Brompton.
988	,, From rains and barren land.
989	,, "Grievous, from a rainy winter; bad spring; neither ploughing nor sowing; snowy harvest."
1004	England. "Such a famine prevailed as no man could remember."
1005	,, "This year was the great famine in England." Sweyn the Dane quits in consequence.
1008	Wales. Attended with plague.
1012	England. Endless multitudes died of famine.
1025	,, From rains, and plague.
1031	,, From great rains and locusts.—Short.

A.D.	
1042	England. About this time such a famine came on that a sextarius of wheat, which is usually a load for one horse, sold for five solidi and more. —Henry of Huntingdon. Lasted seven years.
1047	,, From snow and frost.
1047–48	Scotland. Famine extending over two years.
1050	England. Great famine and mortality; from barrenness of the land.
1053	,, Famine after a comet; lasted two years.
1068	,, Famine and plague after a severe winter.
1069	,, Normans desolated England, and in the following year famine spread over the northern counties of England, "so that man, driven by hunger, ate human, dog, and horse flesh"; some to sustain a miserable life sold themselves for slaves. All land lying "between Durham and Yorke lay waste, without inhabitants or people to till the ground, for the space of nine years, except only the territory of St. John of Bewlake."—(Beverley.) "Divers other parts of his realm were so wasted with his wars that, for want both of husbandry and habitation, a great dearth did ensue, whereby many were forced to eat horses, dogs, cats, rats, and other loathsome and vile vermin; yea, some abstained not from the flesh of men. This famine and desolation

A.D.	
	did specially rage in the north parts of the realm."—*Harleian Miscellany*, III. p. 151.
1073	England. Famine, followed by mortality so fierce that "the living could take no care of the sick, nor bury the dead."—Henry of Huntingdon.
1086	,, A great murrain of animals, and such intemperate weather that many died of fever and famine.—Henry de Knyghton. Excessive rains.—Short.
1087	,, Pestilence followed by famine; great suffering.
1093	,, Great famine and mortality.—Stow.
1096	,, "Heavy-timed hunger that severely oppressed the earth."—*Saxon Chronicle*. "Summer rain, tempests, and bad air."—Short.
1099	,, Famine from rains and floods.
1106	,, From barren land; then plague.
1111	,, Winter long and very severe; great scarcity followed.
1117	,, From tempest, hail, and a year's incessant rains.
1121–22	,, "Great famine from long and cruel frosts."
1124	,, "Such a famine prevailed that everywhere in cities, villages, and cross-roads lifeless bodies lie unburied."
	"By means of changing the coine all things became very deere, whereof an extreame famine did arise, and afflict the multitude of the people, even to death."—Penkethman.

A.D.	
1125	England. Great flood on St. Lawrence's Day; famine in consequence of destruction of crops, &c.
1126	,, "Incessant rains during the summer, when followed in all England a most unheard-of scarcity. A sextarius of wheat sold for 20 shillings."
1135–37	England. Great drought and famine.
1141	,, Famine, said to have lasted twelve years.—Short.
1154	,, From rains, frost, tempest, thunder, and lightning.
1175	,, Pestilence, followed by great dearth.
1176	Wales. A great famine and mortality.
1183	England and Wales. A great famine severely afflicted both England and Wales.
1193–96	England. Famine occasioned by incessant rains. "The common people (*Vulgus pauperum*) perished everywhere for lack of food; and on the footsteps of famine the fiercest pestilence followed, in the form of an acute fever."—Walter Hemingford.
1203	,, A great mortality and famine, from long rains.
1209	,, Famine from a rainy summer and severe winter.
1224	,, A very dry winter and bad seed-time, whence followed a great famine.
1235	,, Famine and plague; 20,000 persons die in London; people eat horseflesh, bark of trees, grass, &c.—Short.

A.D.	
1239	England. Great famine, "people eat their children."—Short.
1248	,, "By reason of embasing the coin a great penury followed."
1252	,, No rain from Whitsuntide to autumn; no grass; hence arose a severe famine; great mortality of man and cattle; dearness of grain and scarcity of fruit.
1257	,, The inundations of autumn destroyed the grain and fruit, and pestilence followed.
1258	,, North winds in spring destroyed vegetation; food failed, the preceding harvest having been small, and innumerable multitudes of poor people died. Fifty shiploads of wheat, barley, and bread were procured from Germany; but citizens of London were forbidden by proclamation against dealing in same. "A great dearth followed this wet year pest, for a quarter of wheat was sold for 15 and 20 shillings, but the worst was in the end; there could be none found for money when—though many poor people were constrained to eat barks of trees and horseflesh, but many starved for want of food—20,000 (as it was said) in London."—Penkethman.
1271	,, A violent tempest and inundation, followed by a severe famine in the entire district of Canterbury.
1286	,, Short speaks of a twenty-three years' famine commencing this year.

A.D.	
1289	England. A tempest destroyed the seed, and corn rose to a great price.
1294	,, Severe famine; many thousands of the poor died.
1295	,, No grain or fruits, "so that the poor died of hunger."—Camden. Hail, great concussion of elements.—Short.
1297	Scotland. "Calamitous" famine and pestilence.
1298	England. 26 Edward I. "A great famine in England, chiefly want of wine; so that the same could scarcely be had to minister the communion in the churches."—Penkethman.
1302	England and Scotland. Famine.
1314	England. Grains spoiled by the rains. Famine "so dreadful that the people devoured the flesh of horses, dogs, cats, and vermin." Parliament passed a measure limiting the price of provisions.
1316	,, Universal dearth, and such a mortality, particularly of the poor, followed, that the living could scarcely bury the dead. Royal proclamation: no more beer to be made.
1321	,, Famine again; this is regarded by some writers as the last serious famine in this country.
1335	,, Famine occasioned by long rains.
1336	Scotland. Desolated by a famine.
1341	England, Scotland. Great dearth in this and following year. People ate

A.D.	
	horses, dogs, cats, &c., to sustain life.—Holinshed.
1353	England. Great famine.—Rapin.
1355	,, Great scarcity; grain brought from Ireland afforded much relief.
1358	,, "A great dearth and pestilence happened in England, which was called the second pestilence."—Penkethman.
1369	,, Great pestilence among men and larger animals; followed by inundations and extensive destruction of grain. Grain very dear.
1390	,, Great famine arising from scarcity of money to buy food.
1392	,, Great scarcity for two years; people ate unripe fruit, and suffered greatly from "Flux." The Corporation of London advanced money and corn to the poor at easy rates.—Stow.

Short attributes the famine of these three years to the "hoarding of corn."

Penkethman gives further details regarding the assistance rendered by the Corporation of London, as follows: "The Mayor and Citizens of London took out of the Orphans'-chest in their Guildhall, 2,000 marks to buy corn and other victualls from beyond the sea; and the Aldermen each of them layd out twenty pound to the like purpose of buying corn; which was bestowed in divers places, where the poore might buy at an appointed price, and such as lacked

A.D.	
	money to pay doune, did put in surity to pay in the yeare following: in which yeare, when Harvest came, the fields yielded plentifull increase, and so the price of Corne began to decrease," p. 68.
1427	England. Famine from great rains.
1429	Scotland. Dearth.
1437–38	England. Wheat rose from its ordinary price of 4s. to 4s. 6d. per quarter to 26s. 8d.
	Bread was made from fern-roots. —Stow.
	Rains and tempests.—Short.
1438	„ "In the 17th yeere of Henry the Sixt, by meanes of great tempests, immeasurable windes and raines, there arose such a scarcitie that wheat was sold in some places for 2 shillings 6 pence the bushell." —Penkethman.
1439	„ (18 Hen. VI.). "Wheat was sold at London for 3s. the bushell, mault at 13s. the quarter, and oates at 8d. the bushell, which caused men to eat beanes, peas, and barley, more than in an hundred years before : wherefore Stephen Browne, then maior, sent into Pruse (Prussia), and caused to be brought to London many ships laden with rye, which did much good ; for bread-corne was so scarce in England that poor people made their breade of ferne rootes."—Penkethman.
1440	„ A scarcity. Scotland.—A famine.

A.D.	
1486	England. "Famine sore."
1491	,, Considerable scarcity.
1494	,, Great scarcity and high prices.
1521	,, Famine and mortality. "Wheat sold in London for 20s. a quarter."
1523	,, Severe famine.
1527	,, (19 Hen. VIII.). "Such scarcitie of bread was at London and throughout England that many dyed for want thereof. The King sent to the Citie, of his owne provision, 600 quarters: the bread carts then coming from Stratford (where nearly all the bakings were, probably on account of proximity to Epping Forest) towards London, were met at the Mile End by a great number of citizens, so that the maior and sheriffes were forced to goe and rescue the same, and see them brought to the markets appointed, wheat being then at 15s. the quarter. But shortly after the merchants of the Stiliard (Steelyard) brought from Danske (Danzic) such store of wheat and rye, that it was better cheape at London than in any other part of the Realme."—Penkethman.
1545	,, A wonderful dearth and extreme prices.
1549	,, Famine from neglect of agriculture.
1556–58	,, Famine from great rains, bad and inconstant seasons; heat and long south winds.—Short.

A.D.	
1563	London. Famine and pestilence, said to have carried off 20,000 people.
1565	British Isles. Extended famine. £2,000,000 said to have been expended in importation of grain.
1586	England. "In the 29th yeare of Queen Elizabeth, about January, Her Majesty observing the general Dearthe of Corne, and other Victual, growne partly through the unseasonablenesse of the year then passed, and partly through the uncharitable greediness of the Corne-masters, but especially through the unlawful and overmuch transporting of graine in forreine parts; by the advice of Her most Hon. Privy Council, published a Proclamation, and a Booke of Orders, to be taken by the Justices for reliefe of the Poore [commencement of the poor law], notwithstanding all which the excessive prices of graine still encreased: so that Wheat in meale, was sold at London for 8s. the Bushel, and in some other parts of the Realme above that price."—Penkethman.
1594	,, Famine. During the siege of Paris by Henry IV. this year, owing to famine, bread which had been sold, while any remained, for a crown a-pound, was at last made from the bones of the charnel-house of the Holy Innocents.—Hinault.
1595	,, (36 Elizabeth.) "By the late Transportations of graine into forreine parts, the same was here

A.D.	
	grown of an excessive price, as in some parts of this Realme, from 14s. to 4 markes the quarter, and more, as the Poore did feele; and all other things whatsoever were made to sustain man, were likewise raysed, without all conscience and reason. For remedie whereof our Merchants brought back from Danske (Danzic) much rye and wheat, but passing deere; though not of the best, yet serving the turn in such extremities. Some 'Prentices and other young people about the Citie of London, being pinched of their Victuals, more than they had beene accustomed, tooke Butter from the market folkes in Southwarke, paying but 3d. where the owners would not afford it under 5d. by the pound. For which disorder the said young men were punished on the 27th June, by whipping, setting on the Pillorie, and long imprisonment."—Penkethman.
1630	England. Dearth; bread made of turnips, &c.
1649	Scotland and North of England. "From rains and wars"; also following year.
1649	Lancashire. Occasioned by the ravages of the armies; and the plague follows it.—Salmon's *Chronological Historian*.
1694–99	Scotland. Famine; England, great dearth, "from rains, colds, frosts, snows; all bad weathers."—Short.
1700	England. From rain and cold of previous year.

A.D.	
1709	Scotland. From rain and cold; also in England.
1740–41	England. "From frost, cold, exporting and hoarding up corn."—Short.
1741	Scotland. From "terrible shake-winds when corn was ready for reaping."—Short.
1748	England. Extended famine.
1766	Scotland. "The magistrates of Edinburgh and Glasgow have put a stop to the exportation of grain, tallow, and butter, in their respective jurisdictions; a power which the magistrates of London do not seem to possess."—*Gentleman's Magazine*, February.
1795	England. Scarcity of food severely felt.
1801	United Kingdom. Great scarcity; flour obtained from America; Committees of both Houses of Parliament were appointed to inquire into means of supplying food.
1812	United Kingdom. Great scarcity in England and Ireland.

To this list of heart-rending desolation caused by famine, may be added many other cases which have occurred more recently, and among them the appalling famine in China—a kingdom well provided with granaries constructed by the ancient founder, Moses. From the account given by a traveller, who marvelled at such solitary hills standing in plains surrounded by fertile corn-fields, it may safely be inferred that these Pyramids or Storehouses still remain unopened, and, consequently, are stored with the produce of the fields that surround them. So that had the Emperors of China been aware of the existence of such treasure-houses in their extensive dominions, peopled by innumerable millions of human beings, they would never have had the sorrow of reading such a harrowing account of misery suffered by their subjects, arising from want of food, which was so near at hand! This severe famine visited China in A.D. 1877-78, and is thus chronicled by Walford:—

"North China.—A telegram dated 26th January 1878, says : 'Appalling famine raging throughout four provinces North China. Nine million people reported destitute. Children daily sold in markets for (raising means to procure) food. Foreign Relief Committee appeal to England and America for assistance.' Total population of districts affected, seventy millions. Mr. Fredk. H. Balfour, of Shanghai, said : ' The people's faces are black with hunger ; they are dying by thousands upon thousands. Women and girls and boys are openly offered for sale to any chance wayfarer. When I left the country, a respectable married woman could be easily bought for six dollars, and a little girl for two. In cases, however, where it was found impossible to dispose of their children, parents have been known to kill them sooner than witness their prolonged sufferings, in many instances throwing themselves afterwards down wells, or committing suicide by arsenic.'

"'Lord Derby received a report drawn up by Mr. Mayers, Chinese Secretary of the Legation at Pekin, upon the distress which the drought of the last two years has caused in the northern and central provinces of China. This famine, it seems, has been most severely felt in the district furthest from the coast. With the exception of Chefoo, and, in a lesser degree, Tien-tsin, no foreign settlement has come directly into contact with the misery which has been described as existing in the interior, nor are any immediate traces of it visible in the neighbourhood of the capital. The apparent cause was disturbance in the usually unfailing regularity of the summer monsoons. The spring and summer of 1876 were marked in the southern maritime provinces, Kwangtung and Fuhkien, and in a less degree also along the coast as far north as Ningpo, by an excessive rain-fall, causing in the two provinces above-named disastrous floods and much destruction of crops. In the north, on the contrary, from the Yangtsze to the neighbourhood of Pekin and thence eastward to the borders of Corea, an unusual drought was experienced.'—*Times*, 13th March 1878.

"Further papers on this famine were presented to Parliament, 2nd July 1878. The number of souls for whom relief is required is said to be between three and four millions. One point brought out is the enormous cost of transporting supplies to the province of Shansi, where a mountain range has to be crossed and a distance of some hundreds of miles to be traversed by carts. Mr. Mayers says the reported cost of transporting these supplies to Shansi would be about four taels per picul, or, say, £12 sterling per ton. Mr. Hugh Fraser sends from Pekin, 18th January, the translation of a memorial addressed to the throne by Yen King-Ming, 'Special High Commissioner for the Superintendence of the Arrangements for Famine Relief in Shansi. The commissioner dwells upon the painful scenes he has witnessed at every stage of his journey, in the course of which his chair has continually been surrounded by crowds of the famine-stricken population imploring relief, to whom he has administered comfort in soothing words, assuring them of the Imperial sympathy. The roads are lined with corpses in such numbers as to distance all efforts for their interment, while women and children, starving and in rags, know not where to look for the means of keeping body and soul together. The memorialist, his heart wrung with despairing pity, cannot but ask, why has a calamity so awful as this been visited upon the people. He can only ascribe it to his own failure in the due discharge of his duty, and he feels that his short-coming admits of no excuse. In reply, the Grand Council has received a rescript expressing profound sympathy with the sufferings of the people as reported in this memorial, and directing that all that is possible for their relief be done, in consultation with the governor of the province.'

" Note.—The Empire of China has long been subject to the most serious famines; but of these we have found no details available."

It is sad to know that famines will occur, as long as man exists on the earth at enmity with his Creator. The ground was cursed on man's account, and therefore it is man's duty to appease the anger of his offended God. As man was taught by the Lord God to plough, and to sow, to reap and to garner up for the winter; so is it incumbent on those who govern nations to exercise their benevolence and make provision of food in granaries and storehouses against the recurrence of famines.

In the olden times, there were constructed near corn-fields, in all the countries over which the descendants of Israel ruled, most noble, solid granaries in rocks, as well as aqueducts and canals throughout their dominions. In the present age not a single civilized nation is prepared for a calamity which is sure to visit every country under heaven, sooner or later.

Of all countries, India is the one where famines recur most frequently, as the following table attests.

CHRONOLOGICAL LIST OF FAMINES IN INDIA.*

B.C.	
503–443	India. During the reign of the Emperor Jei-chund; extending over this period, there was a great pestilence and famine.
A.D.	
1022	Hindoostan (reign of Musaood I). Great drought followed by famine; whole countries entirely depopulated. This year was remarkable for drought and famines in many parts of the world.—Dow's *Hindustan*.
1052–60	Hindustan. There was seven years' drought in Ghor (? Ghore, supposed to be one of the earliest seats of the Afghan race), so that the earth was burned up, and thousands of men and animals perished with heat and famine.—Dow's *Hindustan*.
1291	India. No rain fell in the provinces

* Walford, *Famines of the World, Past and Present*.

A.D.		
		about Delhi, and there was in consequence a most terrible famine.—*Vide* Birni's *History of Feroze*.
1342	India.	Famine in Delhi, very severe; few of the inhabitants could obtain the necessaries of life.
1344–45	,,	A famine, supposed to have extended more or less over the whole of Hindustan. Very severe in the Deccan. The Emperor Mahommed, it is said, was unable to procure the necessaries for his household.—Dow's *Hindustan*.
1412–13	,,	Great drought, followed by famine, occurred in the Ganges-Jumna delta.
1471	,,	A famine in Orissa.
1495	,,	A great dearth occurred about this date in Hindustan.
1521	,,	A very general famine in Sind.
1540–43	,,	A general famine in Sind during these years.
1631	,,	A general famine caused by drought and war; and throughout Asia.
1661	,,	Famine caused by drought, and supposed to be confined to the Punjab.
1703	,,	Famine in Thar and Parkar districts of Sind.
1733	,,	Famine; appears to have been confined to North Western Provinces.
1739	,,	Famine in Delhi and its neighbourhood.
1745–52	,,	Famine in Nara districts of Sind, and Thar and Parkar.

| A.D. 1769-70 | Hindustan. First great Indian famine of which we have record. It was estimated that 3,000,000 of people perished. The air was so infected by the noxious effluvia of dead bodies, that it was scarcely possible to stir abroad without perceiving it; and without hearing also the frantic cries of the victims of famine who were seen at every stage of suffering and death. Whole families expired, and villages were desolated. When the new crop came forward in August it had in many cases no owners.—*Encyclopædia Britannica,* Art. Hindustan. Other estimates have been that one-third of the population perished.

"Alarming want of rain was also reported throughout all the upper parts of Bengal. Madras was also suffering from drought, and from the ravages of the enemy, and the demands for grain caused a scarcity also in Calcutta. During September, October, and November, the drought continued nearly all over Bengal, the calamity being most severely felt in Behar and the Bengal districts north of the Ganges. A plentiful rain fell in June 1770; but the hopes of relief from the next crop which were thereby raised, ere disappointed by the overflowing of the rivers in the eastern provinces; but the new crops in all the districts not greatly injured by floods were

A.D.		
1781–83	India.	good." The famine ceased by the end of the year.—Danvers, 1877. Famine in the Carnatic and the Madras Settlement. "The Carnatic had been devastated by Hyder Ali's incursions in 1780–81, and the settlement of Madras was reduced to great straits for food, as the whole country in its vicinity was suffering from a general scarcity. Early in 1781 the Government of Madras took steps to regulate the supply of grain; and the distress continuing, in January 1782 a public subscription was raised for the relief of the poor, to which the Government contributed. This was the origin of the institution for the relief of the native poor, known as the Monegar Choultry. Early in October the Government deemed it necessary to take the supply of rice and food-grain into their own hands. The scarcity seems to have come to an end in the early months of 1783."—Danvers, 1877.
1782–84	,,	Famine in province of Sind, including Thar and Parkar. "When the Kulhora dynasty ceased in 1782, and that of the Talpors commenced, a very severe famine occurred, which lasted for two and a half years. During four months of this time not a grain of corn was procurable. This famine was caused by the burning of crops, and the suspension of cultivation during a period of

A.D.	
	hostilities. There was also no rainfall for two years."—Danvers, 1877.
1783-84	India. Famine in the north-west provinces of the Punjab. "The disturbance of the season of 1783 seems to have been general; but as the countries most affected were not then subject to British rule, very little information therein is obtainable. There are reasons for believing that the upper parts of Hindustan had been visited with extraordinary drought during the two previous years. In September and October 1783 there was an abnormal cessation of rain and extreme drought, and in the latter month a terrible famine was reported in all the countries from beyond Zahore to Karumnasa (the western boundary of Behar) .... and the famine had been already felt in all the western districts towards Delhi. To the northward of Calcutta, the crops upon the ground had been scorched, and nearly destroyed."—Danvers, 1877. By the middle of 1784 the famine had abated.
1787-88	India. Famine prospects in Behar and north-west provinces of Punjab, consequent upon excess of rain and floods. The Government laid an embargo on the exportation of grain.
1790-91	,, Famine in district of Baroda, and in many adjoining districts, in some of which, however, it was

only partial and local. " Very little is known concerning the famine in many of the districts named, beyond the fact that in 1790 tradition records the occurrence of a very severe famine. An almost total failure of rain was the immediate cause, apparently, of the calamity ; and sufficient information exists to prove that it was one of the most remarkable on record. So great was the distress that many people fled to other districts in search of food ; while others destroyed themselves, and some killed their children, and lived on their flesh. In Belgaum the scarcity was aggravated by people flocking into the district boarding on the Godavery."—Danvers, 1877.

In Kach, in 1791, a famine was caused by innumerable black ants which swarmed in almost all parts of the country, and destroyed vegetation. [This Kach, formerly Cutch, is in Bombay Presidency, situated south-east of the mouths of the Indus, and appears in later times to have become a terribly Godforsaken place : famines and plagues constantly !]

1790–92   India. Serious dearth in the northern districts of the Madras Presidency, and the pressure continued for about two years, from November 1790 to November 1792. "Many deaths from starvation occurred. At an

A.D.		
		early period Government suspended the import and transit duties on all kinds of grain and provisions, and themselves imported grain from Bengal. In the latter part of 1791 the export of rice from Tanjore was prohibited, except to the distressed districts. Rice was distributed by Government, and relief was afforded by employing the poor on public works."—Danvers, 1877.
This was the first occasion of the poor being employed on public works by the Government in India.
1802–4	India.	Famine in the Nizam's dominions (Bombay Presidency). "This famine was caused in the several districts affected by it by four distinct causes, which operated apparently about the same time. In Kach the crops are said to have been destroyed by locusts. In Pahlumpur, Rerva Kanta, Surat, Guzerat, Hyderabad, Belgaum, and Rutnagherry, the famine is stated to have been caused by want of rain. Candeish was overrun by the armies of Holkar; and the Pindaree bands sacked and burnt villages in every direction, even destroying the grain standing in the fields; and the same fate attended the districts of Ahmednagar, Poona, and Sholapur: whilst the influx of starving people from other districts into Sattara, Kolapur, Dharwar, and Colaba, caused a

A.D.	
	scarcity of food in those districts."—Danvers, 1877.
1804–7	India. Scarcity in the Bombay Presidency, following the unfavourable season of 1804; severe pressure on the poorer classes. "In the latter part of the following year a general failure of crops appears to have occurred in most parts of the presidency, and the scarcity caused thereby had not passed over until October 1807."— Danvers, 1877.
1812–13	,, Famine in parts of Sind and other neighbouring districts, attributed to failure of rain. "In Kach and Pahlunpore the loss was aggravated by locusts; and in Kattywar it was followed by a plague of rats. Guzerat suffered most from scarcity caused by export of grain to the famine districts; and Ahmedabad was overrun with starving immigrants. In Mahee Kanta the distress was caused by internal disturbances; whilst in Broach there was no failure of rain, but the crops, before they were reaped, were entirely devoured by locusts, which came in very large numbers, and spread all over the country."—Danvers, 1877.
1812–14	,, Scarcity in Madras Presidency, following unfavourable season of 1811; "but no serious distress appears to have been generally experienced throughout the presidency on this occasion, although the district of

A.D.		
		Madras suffered considerably."—Danvers, 1877.
1813–14	India.	Partial famine in many parts of the Agra district; the autumn crop of 1812 failed, and the harvest of the following spring was indifferent. In 1813 the rains set in late, and were then only partial.
1819	,,	Great scarcity in the Allahabad and neighbouring districts, under the following circumstances:— "The rains set in late, but when they did come they appear to have fallen in abundance. The land which had hitherto been so dried up by the heat that sowing had to be undertaken twice without any effect, became so drenched that a third sowing was not possible till the middle of September. In Bundelkhand the kharif of 1819 failed extensively, and frost nipped the spring crops in the beginning of 1820."—Danvers, 1877.
1820–22	,,	Famine in Upper Sind and neighbouring provinces, caused only partially by drought. "In 1819 there was a failure of crops in Ahmedabad, caused by unseasonable weather after the monsoon; whilst in Sawunt Warru it was occasioned by a sudden and unusual fall of rain, accompanied by a terrific storm—the former destroying the ground crops, and the latter the bagayut produce."—Danvers, 1877.
1824–25	,,	Famine in several districts. In

A.D.		
		Delhi and neighbouring provinces it was due to severe drought; in the Madras Presidency, and more particularly in the Carnatic and Western districts, the cause was failure of rains at the usual season. In Hindustan the same.
1825-26	India.	Famine in the north-west provinces, occasioned by failure of rains; and scarcity in Saugor and Nerbada territories caused by blight, and a succession of heavy thunderstorms.
1827-28	,,	Famine in parts of Hindustan. "The autumn of 1827 and the following spring were marked by drought across the Jumna. In Pergunnahs, Raneea, and Sirsa, the rains commenced auspiciously, but stopped abruptly early in July, and did not begin again till the 22nd September. It was then too late to retrieve the mischief which the drought had already caused; and to add to the general distress, there was every chance of a failure in the wheat. This was the staple rubbee crop in these regions, and its success was mainly dependent on the river Ganges overflowing its banks, but on this occasion the usual inundations did not occur."—Danvers, 1877.
1831-32	,,	Scarcity in Poona and the Mahratta country, producing considerable distress, but hardly a famine.
1832-34	,,	Famine in some of the north-west

A.D.		
		provinces. "It is said that not a single shower of rain fell in Ajmir in 1832. In the following year the drought was most severely felt in Bundelkhand, and in the southern pergunnahs of Cawnpore; but in the pergunnahs bordering on the Ganges, the rubbee was good owing to the facilities for irrigation."—Danvers, 1877.
1833	India.	Famine in the Guntoor and other districts in the Madras Presidency; about 200,000 perished. Mr. Danvers says, "this was the most serious famine which has occurred since the British occupation, and from the fearful loss of life which took place in the Guntoor district on this occasion, the scarcity became generally known as the 'Guntoor Famine.'"
1833–35	,,	Famine in Madras Presidency. "In 1834 rain fell copiously in Kach; grain was sown and came up well; but locusts appeared and destroyed all the crops and grass as well as the trees. In Ahmedabad there was excessive rain the same year, which rendered cultivation impossible, and locusts also appeared in great quantities. In Broach the famine of 1835 was also caused by excessive rain, which destroyed the spring crops, whilst the winter crops were also burnt up by intense cold. In the other districts named, the scarcity ap-

A.D.	
	pears to have been caused by failure of crops owing to drought."—Danvers, 1877.
1837–38	India. Famine in north-west provinces, resulting from a general failure of rain. This was also felt in the lower provinces: for in Calcutta it is said the tanks were empty. Lord Auckland wrote in January 1838: "The fall in the usual season of the rains last year was unusually late and scanty; and an absolute drought has followed up to the present time."
1838–39	,, Great scarcity and considerable distress, caused by failure of rains in Surat and other districts in the Bombay Presidency. Large numbers of people left these provinces in search of food elsewhere.
1853–54	,, Great scarcity in the Bellary district (Madras Presidency). "The rains which usually fall in the months of October and November, ceased at an unusually early period in the year 1853; and the showers which usually fall in June and July had been scanty. The grain harvests were consequently almost universally deficient, and considerable distress occurred in several parts of this presidency. In Bellary district the season had been exceptionally unfavourable: an average fall of only $9\frac{1}{2}$ inches of rain having taken place during the year, against an average of about double that quantity in

A.D.		
		previous years. The stocks of grain on hand were small : for serious damage had been occasioned by a storm in 1851 to several of the irrigation works of the district ; and in 1852 the falls of rain had been unseasonable, and the crops short."—Danvers.
1860-61	India.	" In 1859-60 the Delhi territory suffered from want of rain. The great Nujjufghar Jheel became entirely dry—a thing never before known within the memory of man. The rains of 1860 completely failed in the country between the Jumna and the Sutlej ; and except where irrigation was available, no autumn or spring crop could be sown."—Danvers, 1877.
1861-62	,,	Considerable scarcity of food in Kach and various other districts of the Bombay Presidency, owing to scanty and unseasonable rains in 1861, and to short fall in the early part of 1862.
1866	,,	Awful famine in the Lower Provinces of Bengal, Orissa, Behar, &c. ; 1,500,000 persons reported to have perished. "The total quantity of rainfall for the year (1865) was not unusually small in most of the districts of Bengal, but it fell abnormally and out of time. Much rain fell early in the season, before the usual time for sowing, while the later rains, which are usually

A.D.	
	expected in the end of September and October, failed."—Danvers, 1877.
	Great scarcity also in Madras Presidency, through many districts.
1868–70	India. Famine and scarcity in a considerable number of the north-west provinces, including Delhi, Meerut, &c. This was occasioned by failure of the harvest of 1868, following upon the inferior crop of 1867.
1874	„ Bengal; famine arising from drought. The Government took early measures, and at a cost of £6,500,000 organised a system of relief. About 1,000,000 tons of rice were carried into the distressed districts, and about 100,000 remained after relief concluded. Mr. Danvers gives us the following details respecting this famine :—
	"During three successive years the weather in Bengal had been abnormal. In 1871 the rain was excessive, but the crops were good. In 1872 the rain was deficient, but although extraordinarily scanty, it was happily distributed both in time and place, and the crops were good in Bengal, and not bad in Behar. The year 1873 was again dry, almost beyond precedent, and what rain there was was unfortunately distributed. South of the Ganges it was excessive; but in North Behar, and almost the whole of Bengal, the rain was below the average. Coupled with deficient

A.D.		
		rainfall, the monsoon of 1873 was abnormally hot .... In January 1874 it was reported that the frost and west winds were drying up the crops in Patna. The famine reached its culminating point in April and May."
1877	India.	Madras Presidency. One of the most extended famines on record. The cost to the Government of India, in remedial measures and loss of revenue, is estimated at £10,000,000. The actual amount of mortality occasioned is difficult to determine, the estimates vary so much. Cholera prevailed in some of the famine districts, and added greatly to the number of deaths. The Mansion House Relief Fund, instituted by the Lord Mayor (Sir Thomas White), exceeded half a million sterling. Mr. Danvers gives the following details regarding the meteorological incidents associated with this famine :—

"The season of 1874 was generally good, but in parts it was unfavourable. In 1875 the season was in many places unpropitious. In 1876 the south-west monsoon, or summer rains, were deficient throughout the greater part of the Madras Presidency, and in the Bombay district of Poona. In the northern portions only of the Madras Presidency .... was the rainfall ordinarily propitious. The northeast monsoon, or autumn rains, failed still more disastrously. In October the whole of the nine districts of the Bombay Deccan were threatened with a serious famine, nearly all the monsoon crops having perished, and there having been no later rains to admit of sowing the rabi . . . . The spring and summer rains again failed in 1877 . . . . and added to this, the rainfall was short almost all over Northern India."

"Famines in India have arisen from several different causes; but the most general cause has not been failure of the usual rains. Distress has also, however, been caused by hostile invasions; by swarms of rats and locusts; by storms and floods; and not unfrequently by the immigration of the starving people from distant distressed parts into districts otherwise well provided with food supplies; and occasionally by excessive exports of grain into famine-stricken districts; or by combinations of two or more of the above-named circumstances."—Report 1878, p. 2, Mr. F. C. Danvers.

These stern facts prove that, in times of plenty, grain should be garnered in each district, and held in reserve till the time of famine, when, food being found at hand, the people would have no need to migrate into neighbouring provinces. The finest example set for the imitation of those who have the destiny of nations in their hands, is that precaution adopted by Joseph, when he expected the visitation of the seven years' famine.

This memorable famine took place in the year B.C. 1708. But the land of Egypt had corn in her granaries—the Pyramids of our time ; therefore none of the Egyptians died from starvation. Egypt even supplied food to other famine-stricken countries; for the Bible says, " the famine was over all the face of the earth; and all countries came into Egypt to Joseph for to buy corn, because that the famine was so sore in all lands."

In the year A.D. 1064 there was another seven years' famine in Egypt, but the land was governed by a people ignorant of what the Pyramids were, and how their contents had once saved the world from a cruel death. The following account shows the consequences of their ignorance :—

" Egypt.* For seven successive years the overflow of the Nile failed, and with it almost the entire subsistence of the country ; while the rebels interrupted supplies of grain from the north. Two provinces were entirely depopulated ; in another half the inhabitants perished; while in Cairo city (El-Káhireh) the people were reduced to the direst straits. Bread was sold for 14 dirhems to the loaf ; and all provisions being exhausted, the worst horrors of famine followed. The wretched resorted to cannibalism, and organised bands kidnapped the unwary passenger in the desolate streets, principally by means of ropes furnished with hooks and let down from the latticed windows.

" In the year 1072 the famine reached its height.

---

* Walford, *Famines of the World*.

It was followed by a pestilence, and this again was succeeded by an invading army."

And again in "1877, short rainfall and low Nile; great scarcity."

These calamities have occurred hitherto, and so long as the world exists they will occur again. It therefore behoves all monarchs and governors to adopt measures similar to those employed by Joseph, the first Viceroy of Egypt; that, wherever and whenever the enemy may appear, every nation may be found so well provided against it as to escape its dire consequences.

CHAPTER XII.

APOTHEOSIS OF MOSES.

DURING the period when the Shepherd Kings ruled the land of Egypt famine was not allowed to depopulate the world. After these Kings came their descendant Moses, the mortal to whom the Almighty spoke from the top of Mount Sinai, in the presence of a multitude of witnesses, and gave laws by which man must defend himself from an enemy more cruel than famine ; for those who die from famine may still rise to enjoy life eternal, whereas death brought into the world by sin, through the instigation of Satan, is death eternal, from which there is no resurrection.

This inspired Moses taught the Israelites how to serve God, the only way by which they can secure themselves from eternal death. And when he considered them capable of continuing in the way he set them, he went to other nations, and everywhere instructed the people, that they might live for ever.

One of the moral precepts he taught in the Far East, in Hindustan, is still revered by the Hindoos to this day. In that country he assumed the name of Manu, so that the children of Israel who were in

Palestine might not recognise him and claim him as their sovereign. The precept is this :—

> Daily* perform thine own appointed work
> Unweariedly; and to obtain a friend—
> A sure companion to the future world—
> Collect a store of virtue like the ants
> Who garner up their treasures into heaps;
> For neither father, mother, wife, nor son,
> Nor kinsman, will remain beside thee then,
> When thou art passing to that other home—
> Thy virtue will thy only comrade be.
>
> Single is every living creature born,
> Single he passes to another world,
> Single he eats the fruits of evil deeds,
> Single, the fruit of good; and when he leaves
> His body like a log or heap of clay
> Upon the ground, his kinsmen walk away;
> Virtue alone stays by him at the tomb,
> And bears him through dreary trackless gloom.
>
> Depend not on another, rather lean
> Upon thyself; trust to thine own exertions.
> Subjection to another's will gives pain;
> True happiness consists in self-reliance.
> Strive to complete the task thou hast commenced;
> Wearied, renew thy efforts once again;
> Again fatigued, once more the work begin;
> So shalt thou earn success and fortune win.

This Law-giver's moral teaching extended all over the Eastern world, including Corea and Japan, and thence to the western shores of the American continent; so that when his earthly course was finished, the dwellers in all these countries founded religions based on his precepts, making his memory the object of their worship.

* Monier Williams, *Hinduism*.

THE APOTHEOSIS OF MOSES.

The Mexicans and Peruvians held him and his followers in such reverence, and were so confident that some day he would revisit them, that, when the Spaniards appeared among them, they mistook them for the expected visitors, and were ready to worship them.

It is related that "Viracocho, the eighth Inca, beheld in a vision a man of majestic form, with a long beard, and garments reaching to the ground, who declared that he was a child of the sun. That monarch built a temple in honour of this person, and erected an image of him, resembling as nearly as possible the singular form in which he had appeared to him. In this temple divine honours were paid to him under the name of Viracocho."

"When the Spaniards first appeared in Peru, the length of their beards, and the dress they wore, struck everybody as so like to the image of Viracocho, that they supposed them to be children of the sun, who had descended from heaven to earth. All concluded that the last days of the Peruvian Empire were at hand, and that the throne would be occupied by new rulers. Atahualpa himself, considering the Spaniards as messengers from heaven, was so far from entertaining any thoughts of resisting them, that he determined to yield implicit obedience to their commands. From these sentiments flowed his professions of love and respect; to these were owing the cordial reception of Soto and Ferdinand Pizarro in his camp, and the submissive reverence with which he himself advanced to visit the Spanish general in his quarters."*

* Dr. Robertson, *History of America.*

The same idolatrous worship is paid in Japan and China to the memory of the Law-giver Moses, who was the founder and sovereign of these Empires. In Japan this mode of worship is called Shintoism, and in China Confucianism. The institutor of the latter was Confucius. After him came his disciple Laou-tsze, who wrote a book containing five thousand characters; on this he constructed the modern Chinese religion. The book is called Taou-tih-King; the religion, Taouism.

"The first chapter of the Taou-tih-King tells us that, 'that which is nameless is the beginning of heaven and earth,' and elsewhere we are let into the secret of the processes which led up to this creation. Taou produced one, the first great cause; one produced two, the male and female principles of nature; two produced three; and three produced all things, beginning with heaven and earth.

"Heaven is treated by Laou-tsze much in the same way as by Confucius, but with far more reserve. In the utterances of both teachers we find the word used to designate the material heaven as well as a personified heaven. Just as Confucius speaks of the Sage as being the equal of heaven, Laou-tsze says that he is the associate of heaven, and that he is heaven itself.

"Heaven, also according to him, gives laws to the earth, just as it takes its laws from Taou. It has no special love, but regards all existing beings as grass-dogs made for sacrificial rites, *i.e.* for temporary purposes. It is as unselfish as it is impartial, and because it does not aim at life it lasts long. It is great and compassionate, and is ever ready to become the saviour of men. But it is also the material heaven, and maintains its existence by the 'clearness' which is imparted to it by its unity with Taou."*

These religious systems are at the present time to a great extent superseded by Buddhism. This religion has many followers, and its tenets are known throughout the East, in Thibet, Central Asia, Siberia, and even as far west as Swedish Lapland.

The founder of Buddhism was born on the borders of Nepaul about B.C. 620, and was heir to the throne of Kapilavastu. Renouncing his claim, he made himself known to the world as the Buddha Gautama, whose advent was foretold by the Brahmans. It had been predicted that either he would live among men and become a Chacawati, or mighty ruler, whose sway all the human race would acknowledge; or, withdrawing from the world, he would become a recluse, and in that condition, after disentangling himself from the miseries of existence, would become a Buddha, and remove the veils of ignorance and sin from the world.

The tribe to which belonged the father of Gautama, whose name was Suddhódana, was called Sākya. His mother's name was Māya, "daughter of Suprabuddha, chief of the neighbouring and kindred tribe of Kolyans. Both tribes were of pure Aryan race, and branches of the Suryavansi, or line of the Sun."†

All statues of Guatama represent him with short

* Douglas, *Confucianism and Taouism.*
† Fytche, *Burmah, Past and Present.*

points of hair on the top of the head; in some the hair has a curled or woolly appearance. This, together with other circumstances, proves that the Sage descended from the Ethiopian Colonisers who entered India with Moses. Some of the precepts of the Buddha resemble those of Our Lord and Saviour Jesus Christ, who preached six hundred years later, though there are some differences of doctrine. Gautama abolished sacrifices, and taught the law of Love and Charity, and the reward of obedience; also the liberation of the soul from self, with its absorption into the Infinite, or the Finite lost in the Infinite and the Mortal in the Immortal.

The invocation which he taught his disciples was addressed to the Spirit in the Lotus, a mystical reference to the preservation of the Founder of his tribe—the Hebrew infant cast on the bosom of the sacred Nile in a cradle of bulrushes. The Trinity of the Buddhists, also, is analogous to the Trinity of the Egyptians—the Osiris, Isis, and their son Horus, signifying Moses (rescued from the water) and his Ethiopian consort Tharbis, and their son (represented in paintings in Thebes).

About six hundred years after Gautama's death Our Lord Jesus Christ entered the world. His coming was expected by the followers of the last Buddha, insomuch that the Brahmans came to Judea in search of the Infant, whose birth was made known to them by a bright, extraordinary star.

The mission of the Saviour was to fulfil the predictions of the Hebrew Scriptures, that, by His death, the world might be restored to the favour of God. And the reward of His Sacrifice of Himself on man's behalf will be the restoration of God's favour to His erring creatures, so that, in the fulness of time, the Lord God will again walk with man on earth, in the cool of the day, as He did in the days of Adam's innocency in the Garden of Eden.

APPENDICES.

APPENDICES.

APPENDIX I.

A Narrative of the Great Famine in the Land of Egypt, as recorded in the Talmud.*

PHARAOH the King issued a proclamation throughout the whole land of Egypt to the wise men thereof. And he called upon all the wise men to seek his presence and listen to the dreams which troubled him.

"He who can properly interpret to me the meaning of these visions shall have his dearest wishes granted as they issue from his lips; but he who is able to read dreams and neglects my bidding shall surely be put to death."

Then the wise men, and the soothsayers, and the magicians of the land of Egypt, came and stood before the King.

---

* From *The Talmud: Selections, &c.*, by H. Polano, pp. 85–112.

And the King related to them his dream, and though many interpreted, no two agreed as to its meaning. They contradicted one another, and they served but to confuse the King. Many were the interpretations.

"The seven fat cows," said one, "are seven kings who will arise over Egypt from royal families, and the seven lean cows are seven princes who will arise from them, and in the end of days destroy the seven kings. The seven rank ears are seven great princes of this land who shall in a coming time of war fall into the power of seven princes, now weak and in no wise to be feared."

"The seven fat cows," said another, "are seven queens whom thou shalt marry in the coming days, and the seven lean cows declare that these queens shall die during thy life, O King! The seven rank ears and the seven lean ears are fourteen children whom thou shalt beget, and they will fight among themselves, and the seven weaker ones shall conquer their stronger brethren."

But the King was not satisfied with these interpretations. His mind was still unquiet, for the Lord had ordained that Joseph was to be released from his prison and elevated to a princely position; therefore did Pharaoh remain unsatisfied with the words of his wise men.

And the King was wroth, and he dismissed the wise men from his presence; and all the wise men and the soothsayers and magicians of Egypt went out from the presence of their King in shame and confusion. And the King commanded in his wrath that all these men should be put to death.

When the chief butler heard this he sought the presence of the King, and in deep obeisance before him spoke as follows :

"O King, live for ever ! May thy greatness, O King, increase for ever through the land. Lo, thou wast wroth with thy servant, and thou didst place him in confinement. For a year was I imprisoned, I and the chief baker. And with us in our dungeon was a Hebrew servant who belonged to the captain of the guard. His name was Joseph, and his master growing wroth with him, had placed him in prison, where he served the captain of the guard, and he served us also.

"And it came to pass when we had been in the prison for a year we dreamed, each, a dream, and the Hebrew slave interpreted for each of us his dream. And lo, as he interpreted our dreams so was the reality. As he spoke so did it come to pass.

"Therefore, my lord King, I pray thee, do not kill the wise men of Egypt for naught. Behold, this slave is still in the prison. If it be pleasing in the eyes of the King let him be sent for. Let him listen to the dreams which trouble the mind of the King, and he will be able to solve them correctly."

The King listened to the words of the chief butler, and he ordered that Joseph should be brought before him. But he commanded his officers to be careful not to frighten the lad, lest through fear he should be unable to interpret correctly.

And the servants of the King brought Joseph forth from his dungeon, and shaved him and clothed him in new garments, and carried him before the King. The King was seated upon his throne, and the glare and glitter of the jewels which ornamented the throne dazzled and astonished the eyes of Joseph.

Now the throne of the King was reached by seven steps, and it was the custom of Egypt for a prince or noble who held audience with the King, to ascend to the sixth step; but when an inferior or a private citizen of the land was called into his presence, the King descended to the third step and from there spoke with him. So when Joseph came into the presence of the King he bowed to the ground at the foot of the throne, and the King descended to the third step and spoke to him.

And he said:

"Behold, I have dreamed a dream, and among all the wise men and magicians of the land there is not one able to read for me its meaning. I have heard that thou art far-sighted and blest with the gift of divination, and I have sent for thee to solve my dream."

And Joseph answered:

"O King, the power is not with me; but God will answer and give Pharaoh peace."

And Joseph found favour in the eyes of the King, and he told to him his dream. And the spirit of God was upon Joseph, and the King inclined his ears and heart to the words of Joseph.

And Joseph said to Pharaoh:

"Let not the King think that his dreams are two and distinct; they have but a single portent, and what the Lord intends doing upon the earth He has shown to Pharaoh in a vision. Let me advise thee, O King, how thou mayest preserve thy life and the lives of all the inhabitants of thy land from the grievous evils of the famine which is soon to drain and dry up its fruitfulness and its plenty. Let the King appoint a man wise and discreet, a man well versed in the laws of the country, and let him appoint other officers under him to go out through all the length and breadth of the land to gather food during the years of plenty and store it carefully away for future use, that the land may not die in the years of famine which will follow. And let the King command the people of the land, that they shall each and every one gather and store up in the years of plenty of the produce of the fields, to provide for their wants when the ground shall be barren and the fields unproductive."

And the King answered, "How knowest thou that thou hast read the dream aright?"

And Joseph said, "Lo, this shall be a sign that my words are true. A son shall be born to the King, and upon the day of his birth, thy first-born son, who is now two years old, shall die."

And when Joseph finished speaking these words, he bowed low before the King and departed from his presence.

The occurrence which Joseph predicted came to pass. The queen bore a son, and upon the day when it was told to the King he rejoiced greatly. But as the messenger of glad tidings retired, the servants of the King found his first-born son dead, and there was a great crying and wailing in the palace of the King.

And when Pharaoh inquired as to the cause of this great cry he was informed of his loss, and remembering the words of Joseph he acknowledged them as true.

After these things the King sent and gathered together all his princes, officers, and men of rank, and when they came before him, he said: "You have seen and heard all the words of this Hebrew, and you know that as he spoke so has the thing occurred; therefore must we believe that his solution of my dream was the correct one, and that his words of advice were of good weight and consideration. We must take measures of protection against the famine which is surely to come upon us. Therefore search, I pray you, over all Egypt for a man with wisdom and knowledge in his heart, that we may appoint him over the land."

And they answered the King: "The advice of this Hebrew was very good; behold, the country is in the hands of the King to do with it what is pleasing in his eyes; but the Hebrew has proved himself wise and skilful, why should our lord the King not select and appoint him as governor over the land?"

"Yea, surely," said the King, "if God has made these things known to the Hebrew, then there is none among us as wise and discreet as he is. What you have suggested is in accordance with my own thoughts; we will appoint the Hebrew our governor, and through his wisdom shall our country be saved the pangs of want."

And Pharaoh sent for Joseph and said to him: "Thou didst advise me to appoint a wise and discreet man to deliver the land from the anguish of famine. Surely, there can be none more discreet than thyself to whom God has made known all these things. Thy name shall no more be Joseph, but 'Zaphenath-Päaneah' (Revealer of hidden things) shalt thou hereafter be called among men.

"Thou shalt be second to me only, and according to thy words shall the land of Egypt be ruled; only upon the throne shall I be greater than thyself."

Then the King removed his ring from his finger and placed it upon the hand of Joseph. And he dressed Joseph in royal apparel, and placed a crown upon his head and a chain of gold about his neck. And Pharaoh commanded that Joseph should ride in his second chariot throughout the land of Egypt. And the people followed him with music, and a large concourse accompanied him upon his journey.

Five thousand soldiers with drawn swords in their hands, swords glittering in the sunlight, preceded him, and twenty thousand soldiers followed. And the people of the land, men, women, and children, gazed upon the pageant from windows and from house-tops, and the beauty of Joseph pleased all eyes.

And flowers were strewn in his path when he walked, and the air was made sweet with perfume, and the savoury odour of balms and spices. And proclamations were placed in prominent places declaring the authority of Joseph, and threatening death to those who failed to pay him homage; for he was considered as dishonouring his King who failed to honour the man made second in the kingdom. The people bowed down and shouted, "Long live the King and his Viceroy!" And Joseph, seated in his chariot, lifted his eyes to heaven, and exclaimed in the fulness of his heart, "He raiseth the poor from the dust; from the dunghill He lifteth up the needy. O Lord of Hosts, happy is the man who trusteth in thee!"

And it came to pass after this, that Joseph saw Osnath, the daughter of Potipharah, a pearl among the beauties of the land, and he loved her and she became his wife. And Joseph was but thirty years old when he was elevated to his honourable and trustworthy position. He built for himself a palace, elegant and complete in its details and surroundings, so elaborate that three years' time was required for its completion. And the Lord was with Joseph, and increased his wisdom and understanding, and blessed him with manners so affable and deserving that he quickly won the love and favour of all the inhabitants of the country.

And during seven years, as Joseph had foretold, the Lord increased the produce of Egypt sevenfold. And Joseph appointed officers to gather up the plenty. They built huge storehouses* and heaped up corn during the seven years of plenty, till the amount stored grew so great that no man could number it. And Joseph and his officers were watchful and diligent that their stores of grain should not suffer from moth or mould. The people of the land, too, stored up their surplus crop, but they were not as careful and watchful as was Joseph and his assistants.

And the wife of Joseph bore him two sons, Manassah and Ephraim, and their father taught them diligently the way of truth; they listened to his

---

* The Pyramids.—J. V. G.

words and departed not from the paths of pleasantness either to the right hand or to the left.

They grew up bright and intelligent lads, and were honoured among the people as were the children of the King.

But the seven years of plenty drew to an end, and the fields became barren and the trees gave forth no fruit, and the famine which Joseph had predicted threw its gloomy shadow and threatening presence over the once fruitful land.

And when the people opened their storehouses, they found to their sorrow that moth and mould had taken advantage of their neglect. And they cried aloud to Pharaoh, " Give us food; let us not die of hunger before thee, we and our children; give to us, we pray thee, from the plenty of thy storehouses."*

And Pharaoh answered, " Why cry ye unto me, O careless people? did Joseph not tell ye of the famine which has come upon us? Why did ye not hearken to his voice, and obey his commands to be frugal and painstaking?"

" By thy life, our lord," replied the people, "as Joseph spoke, so did we, and gathered in our corn during the years of plenty, but lo, when the pangs of hunger and the barrenness of the land bid us open our granaries, the moth had destroyed the provisions which we had garnered."

The King became alarmed lest all their precaution should prove unavailing against the famine's blight, and he bade the people to go to Joseph. " Obey his commands and rebel not against his words."

* The Pyramids.—J. V. G.

And the people repeated to Joseph the cry for food they had addressed to Pharaoh.

When Joseph heard the words of the people and learned the result of their want of care, he opened the storehouses of the King and sold food unto the hungry people.

And the famine grew sore in the land of Egypt and spread through Canaan and the land of the Philistines, and to the other side of the Jordan. And when the inhabitants of these countries heard that corn could be obtained in Egypt, they came all of them into that country to buy, so that Joseph was obliged to appoint many officers to sell corn to the large multitude of people.

And Joseph's thoughts reverted to his father's home, and he knew that his brothers would be obliged to come to Egypt to purchase food, for the famine was very grievous in their neighbourhood. Therefore he gave orders that no man desiring corn should send his servant to purchase it, but the head of each family should personally appear as a purchaser; either the father of a family or his sons. He proclaimed also, as the order of the King and his viceroy, that no man should be allowed to purchase corn in Egypt to sell it again in other countries, but only such as he required for the support of his immediate family; neither should any purchaser be allowed to buy more corn than one animal could carry.

And he put guards at all the gates of Egypt, and every man who passed through the gates was obliged to record his name and the name of his father in a book, which was brought by the guards every night for Joseph's inspection.

Thus did Joseph design to ascertain when his brothers came to buy food; and all the commands which he had given were faithfully executed.

Now, when the patriarch Jacob learned that food could be purchased in Egypt, he bade his sons proceed thither and obtain a stock of provisions, for the famine was growing very severe, and he feared that his family would suffer from its pangs. Jacob instructed his sons to enter the city by different gates, so that no objection should be made to the amount of their purchases; and as he commanded, so they did.

Thus did the sons of Jacob go down to Egypt, and while upon the way they thought of their brother Joseph, and their hearts chid them for their cruelty towards him, and they said one to the other:

"Behold, we know that Joseph was carried down to Egypt; now, when we come to the city let us seek for him, perchance we may discover his whereabouts, and then we will redeem him from his master."

And so did Jacob's ten sons travel to Egypt. Benjamin was not with them, for his father feared that mischief might befall him as it did the other son of Rachel, and he kept him at home by his side.

By ten different gates did the ten sons of the patriarch enter into the land of Egypt, and the guards at the gates took down their names, which were sent with the other names to Joseph at the close of the day. When Joseph read the names he commanded that all the storehouses* save one should be closed, and he ordered further, that every purchaser at this storehouse should be required to give his name; and mentioning the names of his brethren,

* The Pyramids.—J. V. G.

he said, "If these men come before ye, see that ye seize them, every one."

When the sons of Jacob had entered the city they met together, and before buying their corn they resolved to make a thorough search for their brother. They visited all places of public resort, and the houses of divination, but though they continued their search for three days, it proved unavailing.

Now when three days had passed, and his brothers had not put in an appearance at the storehouse, Joseph wondered at their delay, and he sent sixteen of his servants to search for them quietly through the city. They were found among the Egyptian players, and brought straightway before the viceroy.

Joseph was seated upon his throne dressed in his royal apparel, with his officers around him, when his brothers bowed to the ground before him. They wondered exceedingly at the magnificence, the handsome appearance and the majestic presence of the powerful man before them, but they did not recognise in him their brother.

And Joseph spoke to them, saying, "Whence came ye?" "From the land of Canaan," they answered, "and to buy food, for lo! the famine is sore in the land; and thy servants learning that corn might be purchased in Egypt, have journeyed hither to provide for their support and the support of their families."

But Joseph said, "Nay, ye are spies, else why did ye enter the city by ten different gates?"

They answered, "We are true men; thy servants have never been spies. Thy servants are brothers, the sons of one father, and by his command did we enter the city separately, for coming together he feared our appearance might attract unfavourable attention."

But Joseph repeated, "Ye are spies; to spy out the nakedness of our land have ye come. Behold, every man who comes to buy corn, makes his purchase and departs; but ye, lo, three days have ye been in the city, in public places and among the players; it is as I have spoken, ye are spies."

"God forbid!" they exclaimed; "our lord misjudges us. We are altogether twelve brothers, the sons of Jacob, in the land of Canaan; Jacob, the son of Isaac, and grandson of Abraham the Hebrew. Behold, our youngest brother is with his father, we ten are here, and the other brother, alas, he is not with us, we know not where he is. We thought perchance he might be in your land, therefore have we searched all public places these three days."

"And what should the son of Jacob be doing in the public places?" asked Joseph.

"We heard," they answered, "that the Ishmaelites had sold him in Egypt, and being of very handsome appearance, we thought he might have been sold in one of the play-houses, therefore we went there hoping to find and to redeem him."

"Suppose you had found him," said Joseph, "and his master had asked for him an enormous amount of money; were you prepared to comply with extraordinary demands?"

The brothers answered in the affirmative, and Joseph continued:

"Suppose again that you should find him and his master should refuse to sell or deliver him to you under any circumstances, what would you do in such a case?"

"In such a case," they answered, "if neither prayers nor money should prove of avail, we would rescue our brother by violence: aye, even the death of his master, and flee with him to our father's house."

"It is as I have said," retorted Joseph; "ye are spies; lo, with evil designs upon the inhabitants of our city ye have come. We have heard and know indeed how ye killed all the males of Shechem in the land of Canaan on your sister's account, and now ye would treat the men of Egypt in the same way for the sake of a brother. But yet we will give ye an opportunity to prove yourselves true men. Send one of your number to your father's house to bring hither the youngest brother of whom you have spoken. If ye will do this, I shall know that you have spoken truly. Take three days to consider."

And in obedience to Joseph's commands his brothers were held in ward for three days.

After this time the brothers concluded to leave one of their number as a hostage, while the others returned to Canaan to bring Benjamin down to Egypt. So Menasseh, the son of Joseph, chose Simeon as the hostage, and he was kept in ward.

Ere his brothers departed, Joseph spoke to them once more. "Take heed," said he, "that ye forget not my commands. If ye bring this brother to me, I shall consider ye true men, and ye shall be free to traffic in the land; neither will I do harm to your brother; he shall be at liberty to return with ye to your father's house in peace."

They bowed down to the ground and departed from Egypt. As they proceeded upon their homeward journey, they stopped at an inn to feed their asses, and Levi opened his sack to provide the corn for the meal. And lo, when he opened the sack, his money which he had paid for the corn was lying on the top. And he was exceedingly afraid, and he told the thing to his brethren, and they, too, were filled with alarm. And when every man found his money returned they cried aloud :

"What is this that God has done to us ? Has the Lord withdrawn from us the mercy which He showed to our ancestors, to Abraham, to Isaac, and to Jacob, that He has given us into the hands of Egypt's prince to mock us and make merry with us ?"

But Judah said, "It is just ! Are we not guilty and sinful before the Lord ? We sold our brother, our flesh. Why should we now complain that the favour God has lavished on our ancestors is denied to us ?"

"Did I not warn ye, 'sin not against the child ?'" said Reuben, "and ye would not hearken to my words. His blood is upon us. Why do ye say, therefore, 'Where is the kindness which the Lord promised unto our fathers ?' Verily we have forfeited His protection."

When Jacob's sons approached their home, and the patriarch came forth to meet them, he quickly missed the face of Simeon, and he asked, "Where is Simeon, your brother ?"

Then the brothers told their father all that had happened to them in Egypt, and Jacob said to them :

"What is this that ye have done to me? Your brother Joseph I sent to ye to inquire of your welfare, and his face I looked upon no more,—his bloody garments ye brought me, saying, 'Lo, the wild beasts of the forest have destroyed thy son.' Simeon I sent with ye to purchase food, and ye tell me that he is imprisoned in a cruel land; and now Benjamin ye wish to take also,—for Joseph and for Benjamin ye would bring my grey hairs in sorrow to the grave. No, my son shall not go with ye."

And Reuben said, "The lives of my two sons I place in your hands; if we do not bring back Benjamin safely to thee, their lives shall prove the forfeit."

But Jacob said, "Neither shall ye return again to Egypt; stay here, for my son shall not go with ye, to die as did his brother."

And Judah said to his brothers, "Urge him no more at present. Let us wait until these provisions have been consumed, and when cruel want and hunger press us he will consent to what we ask."

And it came to pass when the provisions were gone, that the sons of his children gathered around Jacob and cried to him, "Oh, give us bread."

And the heart of Jacob was torn with anguish at the cry, and summoning his sons, he said to them, "Hear ye not the voices of your children crying for food? 'Give us bread,' they cried to me, and I— I have none to give them. Get ye down to Egypt, I pray ye, and buy us a little food."

Then Judah answered, and said to his father, "If thou wilt send Benjamin with us, we will go,—otherwise we cannot. The King of Egypt is a mighty potentate; we dare not trifle with him. Should we return to Egypt, and our youngest brother be not with us, lo, he would destroy us all. Our father, we cannot disobey this King; greater even is he than Abimelech, the Philistine. Thou hast not seen, as we have, his throne, his palace, his myriads of officers; thou hast not witnessed, as have we, his wisdom, knowledge, and understanding. God has blessed him with unequalled gifts; greater is he than all on earth beside. Our names he told us; what had happened to us in our youth; he inquired of thee, saying, 'Is your father yet alive? Are all things well with him?' Thou hast not heard, as we have, of his power; over his people he is supreme; upon his word they go out, and upon his word they come in; his word governs, and the voice of his master, Pharaoh, is not required. Oh, my father, send the lad,—we cannot go without him; if thou refusest, we must see our children die with hunger."

And Jacob said, in his sorrow: "Why did ye tell the man ye had a brother? Oh, evil, evil is this thing which ye have done!" "Give the boy into my hands," said Judah, "and let us go down to Egypt and buy the corn. If I do not return him safely to thee, a sinner against my father shall I be considered all my days. Our children weep before thee, and we have naught to stay their cries; have mercy on them, send our brother with us. Hast thou not often told us of the mercy which our God has promised to thee? Lo, He will protect thy son and return him to thee safely. Pray unto the Lord for our sakes, entreat Him to give us grace and favour in the eyes of Egypt's prince. Lo, had we not tarried thus long, we should have now been back with food; yea, back twice to thee, and with thy son in safety."

And Jacob answered : "The Lord God give you grace in the eyes of the King and officers of Egypt. In Him will I put my trust. Arise, go unto the man, take with ye gifts, the best the land affords ; the Lord will be with ye, and ye shall bring back to me your brothers, Benjamin and Simeon."

Then the sons of Jacob went down again to Egypt. And they took Benjamin with them, and they took, also, presents and twofold money.

"Take heed of the lad," were Jacob's parting words ; "separate not from him either in Egypt or upon the road"; and when they had gone, he sought the presence of the Almighty in prayer.

And the wives of Jacob's sons, and his grandchildren, they, too, lifted their eyes and hearts to Heaven.

Jacob also addressed the following letter, to be delivered by his sons into the hands of Joseph :

"From thy servant, Jacob, the son of Isaac, the son of Abraham the Hebrew.

"The prince of God unto the mighty and wise King Zaphenath-Päaneah, the King of Egypt, peace.

"My lord, the King, knows well that the famine is sore in the land of Canaan; therefore I sent my sons to thee to buy food for our sustenance. I charged them not to enter the city by the same gate, lest coming together they might attract the attention of the inhabitants. And, lo, their obedience to my orders has caused them to be accused by thee as spies. Oh, my lord, could not an intelligent man, such as thou art, read truth upon the faces of my sons? Much have I heard of thy wisdom and the understanding which thou didst display in the interpretation of Pharaoh's dreams, in foretelling this grievous famine,—how, then, was it possible that thou shouldst suspect my sons?

"Behold, I am surrounded with children; I am very old, and my eyes wax dim; tearful have they been for twenty years in lamenting the loss of my son Joseph, and now I have sent to thee his brother Benjamin as thou didst command; I pray thee, O my lord, to be good to him, and return him to me with his brothers. The strength of God has ever been with us; He has listened to our prayers, and He has never forsaken us; protect thou my son who is coming unto thee, and God will look favourably upon thee and upon thy kingdom. Send him home again with his brothers, and Simeon also send with them in peace."

This letter was entrusted into Judah's hands.

Thus the sons of Jacob went down again to Egypt with Benjamin and with the presents, and they stood before Joseph. And Joseph released Simeon from prison, and restored him to his brethren. And Simeon told them of the kind treatment which he had received since their departure.

Then Judah took Benjamin and brought him before Joseph, and they prostrated themselves to the ground. And the brothers gave Joseph the presents which their father had sent to him. And Joseph asked them whether all went well with their children and with their old father, and they answered, "It is well with all of us."

Then Judah delivered his father's letter to Joseph, and the latter recognised his father's hand, and his feelings grew too strong for him; the recollections of his youth overpowered him, and retiring into a side apartment he wept bitterly.

Returning to the presence of his brothers, Joseph's eyes rested upon Benjamin, his mother's son, and he asked, " Is this your youngest brother of whom ye told me ? " And when Benjamin drew near, Joseph laid his hand upon his brother's head, and said, " God be gracious unto thee, my son."

Then restraining his feelings, he ordered his officers to prepare the dining-tables.

Then when the meal was ready Joseph took into his hand a cup,—a cup of solid silver, set with precious stones, and holding it in his hand in the presence of his brothers, Joseph said, "I know by this cup that Reuben is the first-born of your father, therefore shall he sit first, and Simeon, Levi, Judah, Issachar, and Zebulun shall follow him in this order, according to their ages; the rest shall follow these according to their ages."

And he said further, " I know that your youngest brother has no mother, neither have I a mother, therefore will we two sit together."

And the men marvelled much at the words of Joseph, as they ate and drank with Joseph upon that day.

In the morning Joseph dismissed his brethren, and bade them return to their father in peace. But when they had departed he called his servants, and ordered them to pursue after, overtake them, and bring them back.

And when the servants of Joseph overtook them, and said to them, "Why have ye done this thing to steal our master's cup?" the brothers of Joseph were indignant, and they answered, "If ye find the cup in the possession of any one of us, lo, he shall die, and we, his brethren, shall be your master's slaves"; but when the cup was found where Joseph had ordered it to be put, in Benjamin's sack, they returned, grieving and crestfallen, to the presence of Joseph.

The viceroy was seated upon his throne, and his officers of state were gathered about him when his brethren entered, and speaking roughly to them, he said: "What evil deed is this which you have wrought? Why did ye take my silver cup? Is it because you could not find that brother you spoke of in the country that you stole the cup instead? Answer and tell me why have ye done this thing?"

And Judah spoke, saying, "What shall we say unto my lord? What shall we speak, for how shall we justify ourselves? God hath found out the iniquity of thy servants, and sent this calamity upon us."

Then Joseph arose, and grasping hold of Benjamin he led him to another room, and pushing him therein closed the door upon him. He then told the others to return to their homes in peace, saying, "I will keep the one in whose possession the cup was found; return ye in peace."

Then Judah answered: "Know that I became a surety with our father for the lad's safe return. 'If he comes not back with us,' I said, 'lo, I shall be considered as sinning before thee all my days.' Oh, my lord, let me find grace in thy eyes; let me but take the lad home to his father, and I will return to take his place as thy servant. See, I am stronger and older than he is, let me be thy servant instead of Benjamin."

"Upon one condition," replied Joseph, "the lad may go with you. Bring before me his brother, his mother's son of whom you have spoken, and I will take him in place of Benjamin. You did become a surety for him to your father, therefore let me have him, and the brother for whom you did become a surety shall return home with you."

Then Simeon drew near and answered: "Did we not tell my lord, when first we came before him, that this lost brother we could not find? Wherefore will my lord speak such idle words? We know not, alas! whether this brother be alive or dead."

"Suppose, then," said Joseph, "that I should call him before me, will ye then give him to me in place of Benjamin?" And, raising his voice, he called aloud, "Joseph! Joseph! appear Joseph, and sit before thy brethren."

The sons of Jacob wondered much at these words, and their blood grew chill as they looked around in fear and amazement to see from whence their brother was to appear.

And Joseph said to them: "Why do ye look around? Your brother is before you. I am Joseph whom ye sold to Egypt. But nay, be not alarmed, ye were but instruments, and to save life did God send me hither."

And the men were much frightened, and Judah especially was terrified at the startling words. Benjamin, who was in the inner court, heard them, and hurrying before Joseph, he threw himself upon the latter's breast, and kissing him, they wept together. The other brothers too were much affected, and the people about wondered, and the report of the occurrence reached Pharaoh's palace.

Pharaoh was pleased with the news, and sent a deputation of his officers to welcome Joseph's brethren, and to bid them, in his name, to bring their families and their household goods and make their homes in Egypt.

And Joseph clad his brethren in new and elegant garments, and made them many generous presents, and gave to each of them three hundred pieces of silver; and then he took them before Pharaoh and introduced them to the King.

And when Pharaoh saw what goodly men the sons of Jacob were he was much pleased and very gracious towards them.

And when it became time for them to return to Canaan, Joseph procured eleven of Pharaoh's chariots and added to them his own, for their accommodation. And he sent rich presents to his father, and garments and presents to the children of his brothers and sister, and to his brothers' wives. And he accompanied his brethren upon their journey to the boundaries of Egypt, and parting with them, he said: "Do not, my brethren, quarrel on the way. This thing was wrought through God's wisdom; ye were but the instruments to save from famine and hunger a vast multitude." He also commanded them to be careful in imparting the great news they carried to their father, lest speaking suddenly, it might have a bad effect upon so old a man. And the sons of

Jacob returned unto the land of Canaan in gladness with happy hearts.

And it came to pass when they drew near to Canaan that they said one to the other, "How shall we break this news unto our father? We cannot tell him suddenly that Joseph is still alive."

But it chanced when they reached Beer-Shebah that Serach, the daughter of Asher, came to meet her father and her uncles. And Serach was a sweet singer, and she played upon the harp. So they said unto her, "Take thy harp, and go and sit before our father and play to him, and as thou playest, sing; sing of his son Joseph, and let him know in this manner that Joseph lives."

And the maiden did as she was bid, and sitting before her grandfather, she sang to him a song, wherein she repeated seven times these words:

> "Lo, Joseph is not dead; he lives,
> My uncle rules o'er Egypt's land."

And Jacob was pleased with her singing and playing; happiness seemed to find birth in his heart at her sweet voice, and he smiled upon the maiden and blessed her. And while he was talking to her his sons arrived with their horses and chariots, and Jacob arose and met them at the door, and they said to him, "We have joyful tidings for our father. Joseph, our brother, is still alive, and he is ruler over all the land of Egypt."

But Jacob remained cool and unaffected, for he did not believe their words, until he saw the presents which Joseph had sent, and all the signs of his greatness; then his eyes brightened and gladness sparkled in their depths, and he said: "Enough, my son lives; I will go and see him before I die."

And the inhabitants of Beer-Shebah and the surrounding countries heard the news, and came and congratulated Jacob, and he made a great feast for them. And he said, "I will go down to Egypt and see my son, and then will I return to Canaan, as the Lord has spoken to Abraham, giving this land unto his seed."

And the word of the Lord came to Jacob, saying, "Go down to Egypt; be not afraid, for I am with thee, and will make of thee a great nation."

And Jacob commanded his sons and their families to prepare to go down with him to Egypt, as the Lord had spoken, and they arose and started upon the way. And Jacob sent Judah in advance, to announce his coming and to select a place for his residence.

And when Joseph learned that his father was upon the way he gathered together his friends and officers, and soldiers of the realm, and they attired themselves in rich garments and gold and silver ornaments, and the troops were armed with all the implements of war, and they gathered together and formed a great company to meet Jacob upon the way and escort him to Egypt. Music and gladness filled the land, and all the people, the women and the children, assembled upon the house-tops to view the magnificent display.

Joseph was dressed in royal robes, with the crown of state upon his head; and when he came within fifty cubits of his father's company, he descended from his chariot and walked to meet his father. And when the nobles and princes saw this, they too descended from their steeds and chariots and walked with him.

And when Jacob saw all this great procession he wondered exceedingly, and he was much pleased thereat, and turning to Judah he asked, "Who is the man who marcheth at the head of this great array in royal robes?" and Judah answered, "That is thy son." And when Joseph drew nigh to his father he bowed down before him, and his officers also bowed low to Jacob.

And Jacob ran towards his son and fell upon his neck and kissed him, and they wept. And Joseph greeted his brethren with affection.

And Jacob said to Joseph, "Now let me die. I have seen thy face; my eyes have beheld thee living and in great honour."

And the great company escorted Jacob and his family to Egypt, and there Joseph gave to his relatives the best of the land, even Goshen.

And Joseph lived in the land and governed it wisely. And the two sons of Joseph were great favourites with their grandfather, and were ever in his house.* And Jacob taught them the ways of the Lord, and pointed out to them the path of happiness and peace in His service.

And Jacob and his family lived in Goshen, and had possession of the land and multiplied therein exceedingly.†

* The Palace, known as the Labyrinth.—J. V. G.
† These Hebrews are mentioned in Egyptian history as Shepherd Kings or Hycsos.—J. V. G.

APPENDIX II.

An Account of the Translation of the Jewish Laws from the Hebrew into Greek, as contained in the Works of Flavius Josephus.*

WHEN Alexander had reigned twelve years, and after him Ptolemy Soter forty years, Philadelphus then took the kingdom of Egypt, and held it forty years within one. He procured the law to be interpreted, and set free those that were come from Jerusalem into Egypt, and were in slavery there, who were a hundred and twenty thousand. The occasion was this :—Demetrius Phalerius, who was library-keeper to the King, was now endeavouring, if it were possible, to gather together all the books that were in the habitable earth, and buying whatsoever was anywhere valuable, or agreeable to the King's inclination (who was very earnestly set upon collecting of books) ; to which inclination of his, Demetrius was zealously subservient.

And when once Ptolemy asked how many ten

* *The Antiquities of the Jews,* bk. xii. ch. 2.

thousands of books he had collected, he replied that he had already about twenty times ten thousand; but that, in a little time, he should have fifty times ten thousand.

But he said he had been informed that there were many books of laws among the Jews worthy of inquiring after, and worthy of the King's library, but which, being written in characters and in a dialect of their own, will cause no small pains in getting them translated into the Greek tongue : that the character in which they are written seems to be like to that which is the proper character of the Syrians, and that its sound, when pronounced, is like to theirs also ; and that this sound appears to be peculiar to themselves. Wherefore, he said, that nothing hindered why they might not get those books to be translated also; for while nothing is wanting that is necessary for that purpose, we may have their books also in this library.

So the King thought that Demetrius was very zealous to procure him abundance of books, and that he suggested what was exceeding proper for him to do; and therefore he wrote to the Jewish high priest that he should act accordingly.

Now there was one Aristeus, who was amongst the King's most intimate friends, and, on account of his modesty, very acceptable to him. This Aristeus resolved frequently, and that before now, to petition the King that he would set all the captive Jews in his kingdom free; and he though this to be a convenient opportunity for the making that petition. So he discoursed, in the first place, with the captains of the King's guards, Sosibius of Tarentum and Andreas, and persuaded them to assist him in what he was going to intercede with the King for.

Accordingly, Aristeus embraced the same opinion with those that have been before mentioned, and went to the King and made the following speech to him: "It is not fit for us, O King, to overlook things hastily, or to deceive ourselves, but to lay the truth open : for since we have determined not only to get the laws of the Jews transcribed, but interpreted also, for thy satisfaction, by what means can we do this, while so many of the Jews are now slaves in thy kingdom?

"Do thou, then, what will be agreeable to thy magnanimity, and to thy good-nature: free them from the miserable condition they are in, because that God, who supporteth thy kingdom, was the author of their laws, as I have learned by particular inquiry; for both these people and we also worship the same God, the framer of all things. We call him, and that truly, by the name of Ζηνα (or life, or Jupiter), because He breathes life into all men. Wherefore, do thou restore these men to their own country; and this do to the honour of God, because these men pay a peculiarly excellent worship to Him.

"And know this further, that though I be not of kin to them by birth, nor one of the same country with them, yet do I desire these favours to be done them, since all men are the workmanship of God; and I am sensible that He is well pleased with those that do good. I do therefore put up this petition to thee, to do good to them."

When Aristeus was saying thus, the King looked upon him with a cheerful and joyful countenance, and said, "How many ten thousands dost thou suppose there are of such as want to be made free?" To which Andreas replied, as he stood by, and said, "A few more than ten times ten thousand." The King made answer, "And is this a small gift that thou askest, Aristeus?" But Sosibius, and the rest that stood by, said that he ought to offer such a thank-offering as was worthy of his greatness of soul, to that God who had given him his kingdom.

With this answer he was much pleased; and gave order that when they paid the soldiers their wages, they should lay down twenty drachmæ for every one of the slaves. And he promised to publish a magnificent decree about what they requested, which should confirm what Aristeus had proposed, and especially what God willed should be done; whereby, he said, he would not only set those free who had been led away captive by his father and his army, but those who were in his kingdom before, and those also, if any such there were, who had been brought away since. And when they said that their redemption-money would amount to above four hundred talents, he granted it. A copy of which decree I have determined to preserve, that the magnanimity of this king may be made known. Its contents were as follows:—

"Let all those who were soldiers under our father, and who, when they overran Syria and Phœnicia, and laid waste Judea, took the Jews captives, and made them slaves, and brought them into our cities, and into this country, and then sold them; as also all those that were in my kingdom before them, and if there be any that have lately been brought thither, be made free by those that possess them ; and let them accept of twenty drachmæ for every slave.

"And let the soldiers receive this redemption-money with their pay, but the rest out of the King's treasury : for I suppose that they were made captives without our father's consent, and against equity ; and that their country was harassed by the insolence of the soldiers, and that, by removing them into Egypt, the soldiers have made a great profit by them.

"Out of regard, therefore, to justice, and out of pity to those that have been tyrannized over contrary to equity, I enjoin those that have such Jews in their service to set them at liberty, upon the receipt of the before-mentioned sum: and that no one use any deceit about them, but obey what is here commanded.

"And I will that they give in their names within three days after the publication of this edict, to such as are appointed to execute the same, and to produce the slaves before them also, for I think it will be for the advantage of my affairs : and let everyone that will, inform against those that do not obey this decree; and I will that their estates be confiscated into the King's treasury."

When this decree was read to the King, it at first omitted those Jews that had formerly been brought, and those brought afterwards, which had not been distinctly mentioned; so he added these clauses out of his humanity, and with great generosity. He also gave order that the payment, which was likely to be done in a hurry, should be divided among the King's ministers, and among the officers of his treasury.

When this was over, what the King had decreed was quickly brought to a conclusion: and this in no more than seven days' time; the number of the talents paid for the captives being above four hundred and sixty, and this, because their masters required the twenty drachmæ for the children also, the King having, in effect, commanded that these should be paid for, when he said, in his decree, that they should receive the fore-mentioned sum for every slave.

Now when this had been done after so magnificent a manner, according to the King's inclinations, he gave order to Demetrius to give him in writing his sentiments concerning the transcribing of the Jewish books; for no part of the administration is done rashly by these kings, but all things are managed with great circumspection. On which account I have subjoined a copy of these epistles, and set down the multitude of the vessels sent as gifts (to Jerusalem), and the construction of every one, that the exactness of the artificers' workmanship, as it appeared to those that saw them, and which workmen made every vessel, may be made manifest, and this on account of the excellency of the vessels themselves. Now the copy of the epistle was to this purpose:—

"Demetrius to the great King. When thou, O King, gavest me a charge concerning the collection of books that were wanting to fill your library, and concerning the care that ought to be taken about such as are imperfect, I have used the utmost diligence about those matters. And I let you know, that we want the books of the Jewish legislation, with some others; for they are written in the Hebrew characters, and, being in the language of that nation, are to us unknown.

"It hath also happened to them, that they have been transcribed more carelessly than they should have been, because they have not had hitherto royal care taken about them. Now it is necessary that thou shouldst have accurate copies of them. And indeed this legislation is full of hidden wisdom, and entirely blameless, as being the legislation of God: for which cause it is, as Hecateus of Abdera says, that the poets and historians make no mention of it, nor of those men who lead their lives according to it,* since it is a holy law, and ought not to be published by profane mouths.

"If then it please thee, O King, thou mayst write to the high priest of the Jews, to send six of the elders out of every tribe, and those such as are most skilful of the laws, that by their means we may learn the clear and agreeing sense of those books, and may obtain an accurate intepretation of their contents, and so may have such a collection of these as may be suitable to thy desire."

When this epistle was sent to the King, he commanded that an epistle should be drawn up for Eleazar, the Jewish high priest, concerning these matters; and that they should inform him of the release of the Jews that had been in slavery among them. He also sent fifty talents of gold, for the making of large basins, and vials, and cups, and an immense quantity of precious stones. He also gave order to those who had the custody of the chests that

---

* That accounts for the ignorance of Tacitus as to who the Jews were.—J. V. G.

contained those stones, to give the artificers leave to choose out what sorts of them they pleased. He withal appointed that a hundred talents in money should be sent to the temple for sacrifices, and for other uses.

Now I will give a description of these vessels, and the manner of their construction, but not till after I have set down a copy of the epistle which was written to Eleazar the high priest, who had obtained that dignity on the occasion following:—

When Onias the high priest was dead, his son Simon became his successor. He was called Simon the Just, because of both his piety towards God, and his kind disposition to those of his own nation. When he was dead, and had left a young son, who was called Onias, Simon's brother Eleazar, of whom we are speaking, took the high priesthood; and he it was to whom Ptolemy wrote, and that in the manner following:—

"King Ptolemy to Eleazar the high priest, sendeth greeting. There are many Jews who now dwell in my kingdom, whom the Persians, when they were in power, carried captives. These were honoured by my father; some of whom he placed in the army, and gave them greater pay than ordinary; to others of them, when they came with him into Egypt, he committed his garrisons, and the guarding of them, that they might be a terror to the Egyptians; and when I had taken the government, I treated all men with humanity, and especially those that are thy fellow-citizens, of whom I have set free above a hundred thousand that were slaves, and paid the price of their redemption to their masters out of my own revenues; and those that are of a fit age, I have admitted into the number of my soldiers; and for such as are capable of being faithful to me, and proper for my court, I have put them in such a post, as thinking this (kindness done to them) to be a very great and acceptable gift, which I devote to God for His providence over me; and as I am desirous to do do what will be grateful to these, and to all the other Jews in the habitable earth, I have determined to procure an interpretation of your law, and to have it translated out of Hebrew into Greek, and to be deposited in my library.*

"Thou wilt therefore do well to choose out and send to me men of a good character, who are now elders in age, and six in number out of every tribe. These, by their age, must be skilful in the laws, and of abilities to make an accurate interpretation of them; and when this shall be finished, I shall think that I have done a work glorious to myself.

"And I have sent to thee Andreas, the captain of my guard, and Aristeus, men whom I have in very great esteem; by whom I have sent those first-fruits which I have dedicated to the temple, and to the sacrifices, and to other uses, to the value of a hundred talents; and if thou wilt send to us, to let us know what thou wouldst have further, thou wilt do a thing acceptable to me."

When this epistle of the King was brought to Eleazar, he wrote an answer to it with all the respect possible:—

"Eleazar the high priest to King Ptolemy, sendeth greeting. If thou and thy queen Arsinoe, and thy

* At Alexandria.—J. V. G.

children, be well, we are entirely satisfied. When we received thy epistle, we greatly rejoiced at thy intentions; and when the multitude were gathered together, we read it to them, and thereby made them sensible of the piety thou hast towards God. We also showed them the twenty vials of gold, and thirty of silver, and the five large basins, and the table for the shew-bread; as also the hundred talents for the sacrifices, and for the making what shall be needful, at the temple: which things Andreas and Aristeus, those most honoured friends of thine, have brought us; and truly they are persons of an excellent character, and of great learning, and worthy of thy virtue.

"Know then that we will gratify thee in what is for thy advantage, though we do what we used not to do before; for we ought to make a return for the numerous acts of kindness which thou hast done to our countrymen. We immediately, therefore, offered sacrifices for thee and thy sister, with thy children and friends; and the multitude made prayers, that thy affairs may be to thy mind; and that thy kingdom may be preserved in peace, and that the translation of our law may come to the conclusion thou desirest, and be for thy advantage.

"We have also chosen six elders out of every tribe, whom we have sent, and the law with them. It will be thy part, out of thy piety and justice, to send back the law when it hath been translated; and to return those to us that bring it in safety. Farewell!"

This was the reply which the high priest made; but it does not seem to me to be necessary to set down the names of the seventy elders who were sent by

Eleazar, and carried the law, which yet were subjoined at the end of the Epistle.

However, I thought it not improper to give an account of those very valuable and artificially contrived vessels which the King sent to God, that all may see how great a regard the King had for God, for the King allowed a vast deal of expenses for these vessels, and came often to the workmen, and viewed their work, and suffered nothing of carelessness or negligence to be any damage to their operations; and I will relate how rich they were as well as I am able, although, perhaps, the nature of this history may not require such a description; but I imagine I shall thereby recommend the elegant taste and magnanimity of this King to those that read this history.

And, first, I will describe what belongs to the table. It was, indeed, in the King's mind to make this table vastly large in its dimensions; but then he gave orders that they should learn what was the magnitude of the table which was already at Jerusalem, and how large it was, and whether there were a possibility of making one larger than it; and when he was informed how large that was which was already there, and that nothing hindered but a larger might be made, he said that he was willing to have one made that should be five times as large as the present table; but his fear was, that it might be then useless in their sacred ministrations by its too great largeness; for he desired that the gifts he presented them should not only be there for show, but should be useful also in their sacred ministrations.

According to which reasoning, that the former

table was made of so moderate a size for use, and not for want of gold, he resolved that he would not exceed the former table in largeness, but would make it exceed it in the variety and elegancy of its materials; and as he was sagacious in observing the nature of all things, and in having a just notion of what was new and surprising, and where there were no sculptures, he would invent such as were proper by his own skill, and would show them to the workmen, he commanded that such sculptures should now be made; and that those which were delineated should he most accurately formed, by a constant regard to their delineation.

When therefore the workmen had undertaken to make the table, they framed it in length two cubits, in breadth one cubit, and in height one cubit and a half; and the entire structure of the work was of gold. They withal made a crown of a hand-breadth round it, with wave-work wreathed about it, and with an engraving which imitated a cord, and was admirably turned on its three parts; for as they were of a triangular figure, every angle had the same disposition of its sculptures, that when you turned them about, the very same form of them was turned about without any variation.

Now that part of the crown-work that was enclosed under the table had its sculptures very beautiful; but that part which went round on the outside was more elaborately adorned with most beautiful ornaments, because it was exposed to sight, and to the view of the spectators; for which reason it was that both those sides which were extant above the rest were acute, and none of the angles, which we before told you were three, appeared less than another when the table was turned about.

Now into the cord-work thus turned were precious stones inserted, in rows parallel one to the other, enclosed in golden buttons, which had ouches in them; but the parts which were on the side of the crown, and were exposed to the sight, were adorned with a row of oval figures obliquely placed, of the most excellent sort of precious stones, which imitated rods laid close, and encompassed the table round about; but under these oval figures thus engraven, the workmen had put a crown all round it, where the nature of all sorts of fruit was represented, insomuch that the bunches of grapes hung up ; and when they had made the stones to represent all the kinds of fruit before mentioned, and that each in its proper colour, they made them fast with gold round the whole table.

The like disposition of the oval figures, and of the engraved rods, was framed under the crown, that the table might on each side show the same appearance of variety and elegancy of its ornaments, so that neither the position of the wave-work nor of the crown might be different, although the table were turned on the other side, but that the prospect of the same artificial contrivances might be extended as far as the feet; for there was made a plate of gold four fingers broad, through the entire breadth of the table, into which they inserted the feet, and then fastened them to the table by buttons and buttonholes, at the place where the crown was situate, that so on what side soever of the table one should stand, it might exhibit the very same view of the exquisite workmanship, and of the vast expenses bestowed upon it.

But upon the table itself they engraved a meander, inserting into it very valuable stones in the middle like stars, of various colours; the carbuncle and the emerald, each of which sent out agreeable rays of light to the spectators; with such stones of other sorts also as were most curious and best esteemed, as being most precious in their kind.

Hard by this meander a texture of network ran round it, the middle of which appeared like a rhombus, into which were inserted rock-crystal and amber, which, by the great resemblance of the appearance they made, gave wonderful delight to those that saw them.

The chapiters of the feet imitated the first budding of lilies, while their leaves were bent and laid under the table, but so that the chives were seen standing upright within them. Their bases were made of a carbuncle; and the place at the bottom, which rested on that carbuncle, was one palm deep, and eight fingers in breadth.

Now they had engraven upon it, with a very fine tool, and with a great deal of pains, a branch of ivy, and tendrils of the vine, sending forth clusters of grapes, that you would guess they were nowise different from real tendrils; for they were so very thin, and so very far extended at their extremities, that they were moved with the wind, and made one believe that they were the product of nature, and not the representation of art.

They also made the entire workmanship of the table appear to be three-fold, while the joints of the several parts were so united together as to be invisible, and the places where they joined could not be distinguished. Now the thickness of the table was not less than half a cubit.

So that this gift by the King's great generosity, by the great value of the materials, and the variety of its exquisite structure, and the artificer's skill in imitating nature with graving tools, was at length brought to perfection, while the King was very desirous, that though in largeness it were not to be different from that which was already dedicated to God, yet that in exquisite workmanship, and the novelty of the contrivances, and in the splendour of its construction, it should far exceed it, and be more illustrious than that was.

Now of the cisterns of gold there were two, whose sculpture was of scale-work, from its basis to its belt-like circle, with various sorts of stones enchased in the spiral circles. Next to which there was upon it a meander of a cubit in height: it was composed of stones of all sorts of colours; and next to this was the rod-work engraven; and next to that was a rhombus in a texture of net-work, drawn out to the brim of the basin, while small shields, made of stones, beautiful in their kind, and of four fingers' depth, filled up the middle parts.

About the top of the basin were wreathed the leaves of lilies, and of the convolvulus, and the tendrils of vines in a circular manner; and this was the construction of the two cisterns of gold, each containing two firkins;—but those which were of silver were much more bright and splendid than looking-glasses; and you might in them see images that fell upon them more plainly than in the other.

The King also ordered thirty vials; those of which the parts that were of gold, and filled up with precious stones, were shadowed over with the leaves of ivy and vines, artificially engraven; and these were the vessels that were, after an extraordinary manner, brought to this perfection, partly by the skill of the workmen, who were admirable in such fine work, but much more by the diligence and generosity of the King, who not only supplied the artificers abundantly, and with great generosity, with what they wanted, but he forbade public audiences for the time, and came and stood by the workmen, and saw the whole operation; and this was the cause why the workmen were so accurate in their performance, because they had regard to the King, and to his great concern about the vessels, and so the more indefatigably kept close to the work.

And these were what gifts were sent by Ptolemy to Jerusalem, and dedicated to God there. But when Eleazar the high priest had devoted them to God, and had paid due respect to those that brought them, and had given them presents to be carried to the King, he dismissed them.

And when they were come to Alexandria, and Ptolemy heard that they were come, and that the seventy elders were come also, he presently sent for Andreas and Aristeus, his ambassadors, who came to him, and delivered him the epistle which they brought him from the high priest, and made answer to all the questions he put to them by word of mouth. He then made haste to meet the elders that came from

Jerusalem for the interpretation of the laws; and he gave command, that everybody who came on other occasions should be sent away, which was a thing surprising, and what he did not use to do; for those that were drawn thither upon such occasions used to come to him on the fifth day, but ambassadors at the month's end.

But when he had sent those away, he waited for these that were sent by Eleazar; but as the old men came in with the presents, which the high priest had given them to bring to the King, and with the membranes, upon which they had their laws written in golden letters, he put questions to them concerning those books; and when they had taken off the covers wherein they were wrapt up, they showed him the membranes.

So the King stood admiring the thinness of those membranes, and the exactness of the junctures, which could not be perceived (so exactly were they connected one with another); and this he did for a considerable time. He then said that he returned them thanks for coming to him, and still greater thanks to him that sent them; and, above all, to that God whose laws they appeared to be.

Then did the elders, and those that were present with them, cry out with one voice, and wished all happiness to the King. Upon which he fell into tears by the violence of the pleasure he had, it being natural to men to afford the same indications in great joy that they do under sorrow.

And when he had bidden them deliver the books to those that were appointed to receive them, he saluted the men, and said that it was but just to discourse, in the first place, of the errand they were sent about, and then to address himself to themselves. He promised, however, that he would make this day on which they came to him remarkable and eminent every year through the whole course of his life; for their coming to him, and the victory which he gained over Antigonus by sea, proved to be on the very same day. He also gave orders that they should sup with him; and gave it in charge that they should have excellent lodgings provided for them in the upper part of the city.

Now he that was appointed to take care of the reception of strangers, Nicanor by name, called for Dorotheus, whose duty it was to make provision for them, and bade him prepare for every one of them what should be requisite for their diet and way of living; which thing was ordered by the King after this manner: he took care that those that belonged to every city, which did not use the same way of living, that all things should be prepared for them according to the custom of those that came to him, that being feasted according to the usual method of their own way of living, they might be the better pleased, and might not be uneasy at anything done to them from which they were naturally averse.

And this was now done in the case of these men by Dorotheus, who was put into this office because of his great skill in such matters belonging to common life: for he took care of all such matters as concerned the reception of strangers, and appointed them double seats for them to sit on, according as the King had commanded him to do; for he had commanded that half of their seats should be set at his right hand,

and the other half behind his table, and took care that no respect should be omitted that could be shown them.

And when they were thus set down, he bid Dorotheus to minister to all those that were come to him from Judea, after the manner they used to be ministered to; for which cause he sent away their sacred heralds, and those that slew the sacrifices, and the rest that used to say grace: but called to one of those that were come to him, whose name was Eleazar, who was a priest, and desired him to say grace: who then stood in the midst of them, and prayed that all prosperity might attend the King and those that were his subjects. Upon which an acclamation was made by the whole company, with joy and a great noise; and when that was over, they fell to eating their supper, and to the enjoyment of what was set before them.

And at a little interval afterward, when the King thought a sufficient time had been interposed, he began to talk philosophically to them, and he asked every one of them a philosophical question, and such a one as might give light in those inquiries; and when they had explained all the problems that had been proposed by the King about every point, he was well pleased with their answers. This took up the twelve days in which they were treated; and he that pleases may learn the particular questions in that book of Aristeus, which he wrote on this very occasion.

And while not the King only, but the philosopher Menedus also, admired them, and said, that all things were governed by Providence, and that it was probable that thence it was that such force or beauty was discovered in these men's words,—they then left off asking any more questions. But the King said that he had gained very great advantages by their coming, for that he had received this profit from them, that he had learned how he ought to rule his subjects. And he gave order that they should have every one three talents given them; and that those that were to conduct them to their lodgings should do it.

Accordingly, when three days were over, Demetrius took them, and went over the causeway seven furlongs long : it was a bank in the sea to an island. And when they had gone over the bridge, he proceeded to the northern parts, and showed them where they should meet, which was in a house which was built near the shore, and was a quiet place, and fit for their discoursing together about their work.

When he had brought them thither, he entreated them (now they had all things about them which they wanted for the interpretation of their law), that they would suffer nothing to interrupt them in their work. Accordingly, they made an accurate interpretation, with great zeal and great pains; and this they continued to do till the ninth hour of the day; after which time they relaxed and took care of their body, while their food was provided for them in great plenty : besides, Dorotheus, at the King's command, brought them a great deal of what was provided for the King himself. But in the morning they came to the court, and saluted Ptolemy, and then went away to their former place, where, when they had washed their hands and purified themselves, they betook themselves to the interpretation of the laws.

Now when the law was transcribed, and the labour of interpretation was over, which came to its conclusion in seventy-two days, Demetrius gathered all the Jews together to the place where the laws were translated, and where the interpreters were, and read them over. The multitude did also approve of those elders that were the interpreters of the law. They withal commended Demetrius for his proposal, as the inventor of what was greatly for their happiness; and they desired that he would give leave to their rulers also to read the law.

Moreover they all, both the priests and the ancientest of the elders, and the principal men of their commonwealth, made it their request, that since the interpretation was happily finished, it might continue in the state it now was, and might not be altered. And when they all commended that determination of theirs, they enjoined, that if any one observed either anything superfluous, or anything omitted, that he would take a view of it again, and have it laid before them, and corrected; which was a wise action of theirs, that when the thing was judged to have been well done, it might continue for ever.

So the King rejoiced when he saw that his design of this nature was brought to perfection, to so great advantage: and he was chiefly delighted with hearing the laws read to him; and was astonished at the deep meaning and wisdom of the legislator. And he began to discourse with Demetrius, "How it came to pass that, when this legislation was so wonderful, no one, either of the poets or of the historians, had made mention of it." Demetrius made answer, "that no one durst be so bold as to touch upon the description of these laws, because they were Divine and venerable, and because some that had attempted it were afflicted by God."

He also told him that "Theopompus was desirous of writing somewhat about them, but was thereupon disturbed in his mind for above thirty days' time; and upon some intermission of his distemper he appeased God (by prayer), as suspecting that his madness proceeded from that cause." Nay, indeed, he further saw in a dream that his distemper befell him while he indulged too great a curiosity about Divine matters, and was desirous of publishing them among common men; but when he left off that attempt, he recovered his understanding again.

Moreover he informed him of Theodectes, the tragic poet, concerning whom it was reported that, when in a certain dramatic representation, he was desirous to make mention of things that were contained in the sacred books, he was afflicted with a darkness in his eyes; and that upon his being conscious of the occasion of his distemper, and appeasing God (by prayer), he was freed from that affliction.

And when the King had received these books from Demetrius, as we have said already, he adored them; and gave order, that great care should be taken of them, that they might remain uncorrupted. He also desired that the interpreters would come often to him out of Judea, and that both on account of the respect which he would pay them, and on account of the presents he would make them; for he said, it was now but just to send them away, although if, of their own accord, they would come to him hereafter, they should obtain all that their own wisdom might justly require, and what his generosity was able to give them.

So he sent them away, and gave to every one of them three garments of the best sort, and two talents of gold, and a cup of the value of one talent, and the furniture of the room wherein they were feasted. And these were the things he presented to them. But by them he sent to Eleazar the high priest ten beds, with feet of silver, and the furniture to them belonging, and a cup of the value of thirty talents, and besides these, ten garments, and purple, and a very beautiful crown, and a hundred pieces of the finest woven linen; as also vials and dishes, and vessels for pouring, and two golden cisterns, to be dedicated to God.

He also desired him, by an epistle, that he would give these interpreters leave, if any of them were desirous of coming to him; because he highly valued a conversation with men of such learning, and should be very willing to lay out his wealth upon such men. And this was what came to the Jews, and was much to their glory and honour, from Ptolemy Philadelphus.*

* This took place about 284 B.C.—J. V. G.

APPENDIX III.

An Extract from the Works of Herodotus* concerning the Pyramids of Egypt.

THE Egyptians say that this Cheops† reigned fifty years; and when he died, his brother Chephren succeeded to the kingdom; and he followed the same practices as the other, both in other respects, and in building a pyramid; which does not come up to the dimensions of his brother's, for I myself measured them; nor has it subterraneous chambers; nor does a channel from the Nile flow to it, as to the other; but

---

* *Euterpe*, 2.
† Joseph the Hebrew, son of Jacob.—In the thirty-second year after the children of Israel went down into Egypt, the Pharaoh the friend of Joseph died. Joseph was then seventy-one years of age. Before his death, Pharaoh commanded his son who succeeded him to obey Joseph in all things, and the same instructions he left in writing. Thus, while this Pharaoh reigned over Egypt the country was governed by Joseph's advice and counsel. Joseph lived in Egypt ninety-three years, as a prince of the country eighty years of that time. Chephren the brother was no other than Benjamin, who was Joseph's brother. Joseph's age when he died was one hundred and ten years; and his body was embalmed and afterwards laid in the ground near the banks of the river Nile, in the subterranean island near the Great Pyramid. During Joseph's lifetime the temples were closed, and the God of Abraham, Isaac, and Jacob was worshipped.

this flows through an artificial aqueduct round an island within, in which they say the body of Cheops is laid.

Having laid the first course of variegated Ethiopian stones, less in height than the other by forty feet, he built it near the large Pyramid. They both stand on the same hill,* which is about a hundred feet high. Chephren, they said, reigned fifty-six years.

Thus one hundred and six years are reckoned during which the Egyptians suffered all kind of calamities,† and for this length of time the temples were closed and never opened. From the hatred they bear them, the Egyptians are not very willing to mention their names; but call the Pyramids after Philition,‡ a shepherd, who at that time kept his cattle in those parts.

* The Mokattam Hill.
† The memorable famine recorded in the Holy Bible, and its dire consequences.
‡ Corrupted from Psothom Phaneeh (the revealer of secrets), the name given to Joseph the son of Israel the Hebrew, by Pharaoh the King of Egypt. He was a shepherd by profession, as all his ancestors were. It was, therefore, Joseph who built all the Pyramids to store corn in, against the famine that he declared would take place in Egypt.—J. V. G.

APPENDIX IV.

On the Hebrew and Grecian Feast of First-Fruits.

These extracts are given as showing the real nationality of the first colonists of ancient Greece; their mysterious intercourse with the Hyperboreans, who were the followers of Moses in the Far East; their observance of the law given by Moses to the Hebrews, and commemorative representation of the marvellous escape from Egypt into Arabia; and include a description of the Islands of Delos and Rhenea.

" Then sang Moses and the children of Israel this song unto the Lord, and spake, saying, I will sing unto the Lord, for he hath triumphed gloriously : the horse and his rider hath he thrown into the sea.

" The Lord is a man of war : the Lord is his name. Pharaoh's chariots and his host hath he cast into the sea : his chosen captains also are drowned in the Red Sea. The depths have covered them : they sank into the bottom as a stone.

" The enemy said, I will pursue, I will overtake, I will divide the spoil; my lust shall be satisfied upon them; I will draw my sword, my hand shall destroy them.

"Thou didst blow with thy wind, the sea covered them : they sank as lead in the mighty waters."*

"Thou shalt keep the feast of unleavened bread : (thou shalt eat unleavened bread seven days, as I commanded thee, in the time appointed of the month Abib ; for in it thou camest out of Egypt : and none shall appear before me empty:)

"And the feast of harvest, the first-fruits of thy labours, which thou hast sown in the field : and the feast of ingathering, which is in the end of the year, when thou hast gathered in thy labours out of the field."†

The following narrative describes the manner in which the Greeks practised the above law, and represented the crossing of the Red Sea.

"This‡ charming season (spring) brought with it festivals still more charming : I mean those which are celebrated every four years in Delos, in honour of Diana and Apollo. The worship of these two divinities has subsisted in that island for a long succession of ages. But as it latterly began to decline, the Athenians instituted, during the Peloponnesian war, games which drew thither a great concourse of people from various nations.

"The youth of Athens were eager to distinguish themselves in these, and the whole city was in motion. Preparations were likewise made for the

* Exodus xv. † Exodus xxiii. 15, 16.
‡ Abbé Barthelemi, *Travels of Anacharsis the Younger in Greece*, ch. 76, pp. 309, &c.

solemn deputation which is annually sent to the temple of Delos, to present a tribute of gratitude for the victory which Theseus gained over the Minotaur. The voyage is made in the same ship which carried that hero to Crete; and already the priest of Apollo had crowned its stern with his sacred hands. The sea was covered with small vessels which were getting under sail for Delos.

"On the next day we coasted Scyros, and, leaving Tenos on the left, entered into the channel which separates Delos from the island of Rhenea. We immediately came in sight of the temple of Apollo, which we saluted with new transports of joy; and the city of Delos was almost entirely displayed to our view.

"With an eager eye we ran over the superb edifices, elegant porticoes, and forests of columns by which it is embellished; and this prospect, momentarily varying, suspended in us the desire to arrive at the land.

"When we had reached the shore, we ran to the temple, which is distant from it only about a hundred paces. It is more than a thousand years since Erisichthon, son of Cecrops,* laid the first foundation of this edifice, to which the different states of Greece continually add new embellishments. It was covered with festoons and garlands, which, by the contrast of their colours, gave a new lustre to the Parian marble of which it is built.

"Within we saw the statue of Apollo, less celebrated for the delicacy of the workmanship than its

* Cecrops left Egypt the same year that Moses fled from the Court of Pharaoh.—J. V. G.

antiquity. The god is represented holding his bow in one hand ; and to signify that music owes to him its origin and charms, with his left he supports the three Graces, who are represented, the first with a lyre, the second with flutes, and the third with a pipe.

"Near the statue is that altar which is esteemed one of the wonders of the world. It is not gold or marble which is admired in it; horns of animals, forcibly bent, and artfully interwoven, form a whole equally solid and regular. Some priests, whose employment it is to adorn it with flowers and boughs, made us observe the ingenious contexture of its parts.

"'It was the god himself,' exclaimed a young priest, 'who in his childhood interwove them as you see. Those menacing horns, which you behold suspended on the wall, and those of which the altar is composed, are the spoils of the wild goats which fed on Mount Cynthus, and which fell beneath the shafts of Diana. Here the eye meets nothing but prodigies. This palm-tree, which displays its branches over our heads, is the sacred tree that supported Latona when she brought forth the divinities we adore.

"'The form of this altar has become celebrated by a problem in geometry, of which an exact solution will perhaps never be given. The plague laid waste our island, and Greece was ravaged by war. The oracle, being consulted by our ancestors, declared that these calamities would cease if they could make this altar double the size it is of at present. They imagined it would be sufficient to make it twice as large every way ; but they found, with surprise, that they were constructing an enormous mass that would contain the altar in question eight times. After other attempts, equally fruitless, they sent to consult Plato, then just returned from Egypt; who told their messengers, that the god, by this oracle, sported with the ignorance of the Greeks, and exhorted them to cultivate the accurate sciences, rather than to be continually occupied in dissensions and wars. At the same time he proposed a simple and mechanical method of resolving the problem; but the plague had ceased when his answer arrived.'

" These words, though pronouned in a low voice, engaged the attention of a citizen of Delos, who approached us, and showing us an altar less embellished than the former : ' This,' said he, ' is never drenched with the blood of victims ; on this the devouring flame is never kindled. Hither Pythagoras came, to offer, after the example of the people, cakes, barley, and wheat; and beyond all doubt the god was better pleased with the enlightened worship of that great man than with all those streams of blood with which our altars are perpetually inundated.'

" The Island of Delos is only seven or eight miles in circuit, and its breadth is but about one third of its length. Mount Cynthus, which extends from north to south, terminates in a plain that on the west side reaches to the sea. The city stands in this plain. The rest of the island presents only an uneven and sterile soil, if we except some pleasant valleys, which are formed by several hills, on the south side. The source of the Inopus is the only spring with which it is favoured by nature; but we find, in different places, cisterns and lakes, which preserve the rain-water during several months.

"Delos was originally governed by kings, who united the priesthood to the regal authority. It afterwards fell under the power of the Athenians, who purified it, during the Peloponnesian war. The tombs of its ancient inhabitants were removed to the Isle of Rhenea; and there their successors have seen for the first time the light of day, and there are they to behold it for the last. But if they are deprived of the advantage of being born and dying in their own country, they enjoy there a profound tranquillity during their lives.

"The fury of barbarians, the enmity of nations, and the animosities of individuals, all subside at the view of this sacred land; nor ever have the coursers of Mars trodden it with their ensanguined feet. Everything that can present the image of war is rigorously banished; and even the animal most faithful to man is not suffered to remain in it, because he would destroy the weaker and more timid creatures.

"At length the day arrived which had been expected with so much impatience. The morning faintly indicated in the horizon the course of the sun, when we arrived at the foot of Cynthus.

"This mountain is but of a moderate height. It is a block of granite, of different colours, and containing pieces of a blackish and shining talc. From its top a surprising number of islands of various sizes are discoverable. They are dispersed in the midst of the ocean, in the same beautiful disorder as the stars are scattered in the heavens. Here the bosom of the waves is become the habitation of mortals. We behold a city scattered over the surface of the sea; and view the picture of Egypt when the Nile has inundated the plains, and appears to bear on its waters the hills which afford a retreat to the inhabitants. The greater part of these islands are named Cyclades, because they form a kind of circle round Delos. Sesostris, King of Egypt, subjected a part of them by his arms ; and Minos, King of Crete, governed some of them by his laws. The Phœnicians, the Carians, the Persians, the Greeks, and all the nations which have possessed the empire of the sea, have successively conquered or colonized them: but the colonies of the latter have effaced all traces of those of other nations; and powerful interests have for ever attached the destiny of the Cyclades to that of Greece.

"Their inhabitants are separated by the sea, but united by pleasure. They have festivals which are common to them, and which assemble them together sometimes in one place and sometimes in another; but these cease the moment our solemnities commence. Thus, according to Homer, the gods suspend their profound deliberations, and arise from their thrones, when Apollo appears in the midst of them. The neighbouring temples are about to be deserted ; the divinities there adored permit the incense destined to them to be conveyed to Delos. Solemn deputations, known by the name of Theoriæ, are charged with this illustrious commission. They bring with them choruses of boys and maidens, who are the triumph of beauty, and the principal ornament of our festivals. They repair hither from the coasts of Asia, the islands of the Ægean sea, the continent of Greece, and the most distant countries. They arrive to the sound of musical instruments, to the voice of pleasure, and with all the pomp that taste and magnificence can furnish. The vessels which bring them are covered with flowers; chaplets of flowers are worn by the mariners and pilots; and their joy is the more expressive as they consider it as a religious duty to forget every care by which it may be destroyed or abated. The small fleets which bring the offerings to Delos had already left the ports of Mycone and Rhenea, and other fleets appeared at a distance. An infinite number of vessels of every kind flew over the surface of the sea, resplendent with a thousand different colours. They were seen to issue from the channels which separate the islands, cross, pursue, and join each other. A fresh gale played in their purple sails; and the waves beneath their oars were covered with a foam, which reflected the rays of the rising sun.

"At the foot of the mountain an immense multitude overspread the plain. The crowds of people advanced, and fell back, with a motion resembling that of a field of corn when agitated by the wind; and the transports of joy by which they were animated produced a vague and confused sound that seemed to float over that vast body.

"In the meantime, the Theoria of the Athenians was perceived at a distance. A number of light vessels seemed to sport round the sacred galley. At sight of them, some old men, who had with difficulty come down to the beach, regretted their youthful days, when Nicias, the general of the Athenians, was appointed to conduct the Theoria. He did not proceed with it, said they to us, immediately to Delos; but brought it secretly to the Isle of Rhenea, which you see before you. *The whole night was employed in erecting over the channel between the two islands a bridge, the materials of which, prepared long before, and richly gilt and painted, only required to be joined together.* It was nearly four *stadia* (about 3 furlongs and 145 yards) in length, covered with superb carpets, and ornamented with garlands; *and on the day following*, at early dawn, the Theoria crossed the sea, not, like the army of Xerxes, to ravage and lay waste nations, but bringing to them pleasures in its train; and, that they might taste the first-fruits of these, it remained long suspended over the waves, chanting sacred songs, and delighting all eyes with a glorious spectacle which the sun will never again behold.

"The number of those foreign merchants whom the situation of the island, the privileges it enjoys, the vigilant attention of the Athenians, and the celebrity of the festivals, bring in crowds to Delos; whither they come to exchange their respective riches for the corn, wine, and commodities of the neighbouring islands; for the scarlet linen tunics, which are made in the isle of Amorgos, the rich purple stuffs of *Cos*, the highly-esteemed alum of Melos, and the valuable copper that from time immemorial has been extracted from the mines of Delos, and of which are made elegant vases. The island was become as it were the storehouse of the treasures of nations; and near the place where they were collected, the inhabitants of Delos, obliged by an express law to furnish water to the whole multitude of strangers, set out, on long tables, cakes, and eatables prepared in haste.*

"A sudden shout announced the arrival of the Theoria of the Tenians, who, besides their own offerings, brought also those of the Hyperboreans.

"The latter people dwell towards the north of Greece: they especially pay adoration to Apollo; and there is still to be seen at Delos the tomb of two of his priestesses, who came thither to add new rites to the worship of that god. They also preserve there, in an edifice dedicated to Diana, the ashes of the last Theori, whom the Hyperboreans sent to their island. They unfortunately perished; and, since that event, that nation has sent the first-fruits of their harvests through a foreign channel.

"A neighbouring tribe of the Scythians receive them from their hands, and transmit them to other nations, who convey them to the shores of the Adriatic sea, from whence they are carried to Epirus, cross Greece, arrive at Eubœa, and are brought to Tenos.

"The fleets of the Theoriæ presented their prows to the shore, and these prows art had decorated with the symbols peculiar to each nation. Those of the Phthiotes were distinguished by the figures of Nereides. On the Athenian galley, Pallas was represented guiding a resplendent car; and the ships of the Bœotians were ornamented with an image of Cadmus holding a serpent."

* See Deut. xvi. 1-3.

APPENDIX V.

Predictions regarding the land of Egypt, recorded in the Holy Bible.

"In that day shall there be an altar to the Lord in the midst of the land of Egypt, and a pillar at the border thereof to the Lord. And it shall be for a sign and for a witness unto the Lord of hosts in the land of Egypt: for they shall cry unto the Lord because of the oppressors, and he shall send them a saviour, and a great one, and he shall deliver them. And the Lord shall be known to Egypt, and the Egyptians shall know the Lord in that day, and shall do sacrifice and oblation; yea, they shall vow a vow unto the Lord, and perform it.

"And the Lord shall smite Egypt: he shall smite and heal it: and they shall return even to the Lord, and he shall be intreated of them, and shall heal them.

"In that day shall there be a highway out of Egypt to Assyria, and the Assyrian shall come into Egypt, and the Egyptian into Assyria, and the Egyptians shall serve with the Assyrians.

"In that day shall Israel be the third with Egypt and with Assyria, even a blessing in the midst of the land: whom the Lord of hosts shall bless, saying, Blessed be Egypt my people, and Assyria the work of my hands, and Israel mine inheritance."—Isa. xix. 19–25.

MARCH 1885.

BOOKS, &c.,

ISSUED BY

MESSRS. W. H. ALLEN & Co.,

Publishers & Literary Agents to the India Office

COMPRISING

MISCELLANEOUS PUBLICATIONS IN GENERAL LITERATURE.

MILITARY WORKS, INCLUDING THOSE ISSUED BY THE GOVERNMENT.

INDIAN AND MILITARY LAW.

MAPS OF INDIA, &c.

LONDON:
W. H. ALLEN & CO., 13 WATERLOO PLACE, PALL MALL, S.W.

Works issued from the India Office, and sold by W. H. ALLEN & Co.

Illustrations of Ancient Buildings in Kashmir.
Prepared at the Indian Museum under the authority of the Secretary of State for India in Council. From Photographs, Plans, and Drawings taken by Order of the Government of India. By Henry Hardy Cole, Lieut. R.E., Superintendent Archæological Survey of India, North-West Provinces. In 1 vol.; half-bound, Quarto. 58 Plates. £3 10s.

The Illustrations in this work have been produced in Carbon from the original negatives, and are therefore permanent.

Pharmacopœia of India.
Prepared under the Authority of the Secretary of State for India. By Edward John Waring. M.D. Assisted by a Committee appointed for the Purpose. 8vo. 6s.

The Stupa of Bharhut. A Buddhist Monument.
Ornamented with numerous Sculptures illustrative of Buddhist Legend and History in the Third Century B.C. By Alexander Cunningham, C.S.I., C.I.E., Major-General, Royal Engineers (Bengal Retired); Director-General Archæological Survey of India. 4to. 57 Plates. Cloth gilt. £3 3s.

Archæological Survey of Western India.
Report of the First Season's Operations in the Belgâm and Kaladgi Districts. January to May 1874. Prepared at the India Museum and Published under the Authority of the Secretary of State for India in Council. By James Burgess, Author of the "Rock Temples of Elephanta," &c. &c., and Editor of "The Indian Antiquary." Half-bound. Quarto. 58 Plates and Woodcuts. £2 2s.

Archæological Survey of Western India. Vol. II.
Report on the Antiquities of Káthiâwâd and Kachh, being the result of the Second Season's Operations of the Archæological Survey of Western India. 1874-1875. By James Burgess, F.R.G.S., M.R.A.S., &c., Archæological Surveyor and Reporter to Government, Western India. 1876. Half-bound. Quarto. 74 Plates and Woodcuts. £3 3s.

Archæological Survey of Western India. Vol. III.
Report on the Antiquities in the Bidar and Aurungabad Districts in the Territory of H.H. the Nizam of Haidarabad, being the result of the Third Season's Operations of the Archæological Survey of Western India. 1875-1876. By James Burgess, F.R.G.S., M.R.A.S., Membre de la Societé Asiatique, &c., Archæological Surveyor and Reporter to Government, Western India. Half-bound. Quarto. 66 Plates and Woodcuts. £2 2s.

Illustrations of Buildings near Muttra and Agra.
Showing the Mixed Hindu-Mahomedan Style of Upper India. Prepared at the India Museum under the Authority of the Secretary of State for India in Council, from Photographs, Plans, and Drawings taken by Order o the Government of India. By Henry Hardy Cole, Lieut. R.E., late Superintendent Archæological Survey of India, North-West Provinces. 4to. With Photographs and Plates. £3 10s.

The Cave Temples of India.
By James Ferguson, D.C.L., F.R.A.S., V.P.R.A.S., and James Burgess, F.R.G.S., M.R.A.S., &c. Printed and Published by Order of Her Majesty's Secretary of State, &c. Roy. 8vo. With Photographs and Woodcuts. £2 2s.

MESSRS. W. H. ALLEN & CO.'S CATALOGUE OF BOOKS, &c.

[All bound in cloth unless otherwise stated.]

ABERIGH-MACKAY, GEORGE.
    Twenty-one Days in India. Being the Tour of Sir Ali Baba, K.C.B. Post 8vo. 4s. An Illustrated Edition. Demy 8vo. 10s. 6d.

ABBOTT, Capt. JAMES.
    Narrative of a Journey from Herat to Khiva, Moscow, and St. Petersburg, during the late Russian Invasion of Khiva. With some Account of the Court of Khiva and the Kingdom of Khaurism. 2 vols. 8vo. With Map and Portrait. 24s.

Academy Sketches, including Various Exhibitions. Edited by Henry Blackburn, Editor of "Academy" and "Grosvenor" Notes. First year, 1883, nearly 200 Illustrations, 2s. Second year, 1884, 200 Illustrations. Demy 8vo. 2s.

Æsop, the Fables of, and other Eminent Mythologists. With Morals and Reflections. By Sir Roger L'Estrange, kt. A facsimile reprint of the Edition of 1669. Fcap. Folio, antique, sheep. 21s.

Aids to Prayer. Thirteenth Thousand. 24mo., cloth antique. 1s. 6d.

Akbar: An Eastern Romance. By Dr. P. A. S. Van Limburg Brouwer. Translated from the Dutch by M. M. With Notes and Introductory Life of the Emperor Akbar, by Clements R. Markham, C.B., F.R.S. Cr. 8vo. 10s. 6d.

ALBERG, ALBERT.
    Snowdrops: Idylls for Children. From the Swedish of Zach Topelius. Cr. 8vo. 3s. 6d.
    Whisperings in the Wood: Finland Idylls for Children. From the Swedish of Zach Topelius. Cr. 8vo. 3s. 6d.
    Queer People. A Selection of Short Stories from the Swedish of "Leah." 2 vols. Illus. Cr. 8vo. 12s.

Alexander II., Emperor of all the Russias, Life of. By the Author of "Science, Art, and Literature in Russia," "Life and Times of Alexander I.," &c. Cr. 8vo. 10s. 6d.

ALFORD, HENRY, D.D., the late Dean of Canterbury.
    The New Testament. After the Authorised Version. Newly compared with the original Greek, and Revised. Long Primer, Cr. 8vo., cloth, red edges, 6s.; Brevier, Fcap. 8vo., cloth, 3s. 6d.; Nonpareil, small 8vo., 1s. 6d., or in calf extra, red edges, 4s. 6d.
    How to Study the New Testament. Vol. I. The Gospels and the Acts. Vol. II. The Epistles, Part 1. Vol. III. The Epistles, Part 2, and The Revelation. Three vols. Small 8vo. 3s. 6d. each.

AMEER ALI, SYED, MOULVI, M.A., LL.B., Barrister-at-Law.
The Personal Law of the Mahommedans (according to all the Schools). Together with a Comparative Sketch of the Law of Inheritance among the Sunnis and Shiahs. Demy 8vo. 15s.

ANDERSON, EDWARD L.
How to Ride and School a Horse. With a System of Horse Gymnastics. Cr 8vo 2s. 6d.
A System of School Training for Horses. Cr. 8vo. 2s. 6d.

ANDERSON, P.
The English in Western India. Demy 8vo. 14s.

ANDERSON, THOMAS, Parliamentary Reporter, &c.
History of Shorthand. With an analysis and review of its present condition and prospects in Europe and America. With Portraits. Cr. 8vo. 12s. 6d.
Catechism of Shorthand; being a Critical Examination of the various Styles, with special reference to the question, Which is the best English System of Shorthand? Fcap. 8vo. 1s.

ANDREW, Sir WILLIAM PATRICK, C.I.E., M.R.A.S., F.R.G.S., F.S.A.
India and Her Neighbours. With Two Maps. Demy 8vo. 15s.
Our Scientific Frontier. With Sketch-Map and Appendix. Demy 8vo. 6s.
Euphrates Valley Route, in connection with the Central Asian and Egyptian Questions. Lecture delivered at the National Club, 16th June 1882. Roy. 8vo., with 2 Maps. 5s.
Through Booking of Goods between the Interior of India and the United Kingdom. Demy 8vo. 2s.
Indian Railways as Connected with the British Empire in the East. Fourth Edition. With Map and Appendix. Demy 8vo. 10s. 6d.

ANGELL, H. C., M.D.
The Sight, and How to Preserve it. With Numerous Illustrations. Fifth Thousand. Fcap. 8vo. 1s. 6d.

ANSTED, Professor DAVID THOMAS, M.A., F.R.S., &c.
Physical Geography. Fifth Edition. With Illustrative Maps. Post 8vo. 7s.
Elements of Physiography. For the Use of Science Schools. Fcap. 8vo. 1s. 4d.
The World We Live In. Or, First Lessons in Physical Geography. For the use of Schools and Students. Twenty-fi th Thousand, with Illustrations. Fcap. 8vo. 2s.
The Earth's History. Or, First Lessons in Geology. For the use of Schools and Students. Third Thousand. Fcap. 8vo. 2s.
Two Thousand Examination Questions in Physical Geography. pp. 180. Fcap. 8vo. 2s.
Water, and Water Supply. Chiefly with reference to the British Islands. Part I.—Surface Waters. With Maps. Demy 8vo. 18s.
The Applications of Geology to the Arts and Manufactures. Illustrated. Fcap. 8vo., cloth. 4s.

ANSTED, Professor, and LATHAM, ROBERT GORDON, M.A., M.D., F.R.S., &c.
Channel Islands. Jersey, Guernsey, Alderney, Sark, &c. New and Cheaper Edition in one handsome 8vo. Volume, with 72 Illustrations on Wood by Vizetelly, Loudon, Nicholls, and 'Iart. With Map Demy 8vo. 16s.

Antiquity and Genuineness of the Gospels. With some Prefatory Remarks on the Remoter Sources of Unbelief. Cr. 8vo. 2s.

AQUARIUS.
Books on Games at Cards. Piquet and Cribbage—Games at Cards for Three Players—Tarocco—Familiar Round Games at Cards—Norseman—New Games with Cards and Dice—Écarté. Cr. 16mo. 1s. each.

ARCHER, Capt. J. H. LAWRENCE, Bengal H. P.
Commentaries on the Punjaub Campaign—1848-49, including some additions to the History of the Second Sikh War, from original sources. Cr. 8vo. 8s.

ARMSTRONG, ANNIE E.
Ethel's Journey to Strange Lands in Search of Her Doll. With Illustrations by Chas. Whymper. Cr. 8vo. 2s. 6d.

Army and Navy Calendar for the Financial Year 1884-85. Being a Compendium of General Information relating to the Army, Navy, Militia, and Volunteers, and containing Maps, Plans, Tabulated Statements, Abstracts, &c. Compiled from authentic sources. Published Annually. Demy 8vo. 2s. 6d.

Army and Navy Magazine. Vols. I. to VII. are issued. Demy 8vo. 7s. 6d. each. Monthly, 1s.

AYNSLEY, Mrs. J. C. MURRAY.
Our Visit to Hindustan, Kashmir, and Ladakh. 8vo. 14s.

BAILDON, SAMUEL, Author of "Tea in Assam."
The Tea Industry in India. A Review of Finance and Labour, and a Guide for Capitalists and Assistants. Demy 8vo. 10s. 6d.

BARNARD, H.
Oral Training Lessons in Natural Science and General Knowledge: Embracing the subjects of Astronomy, Anatomy, Physiology, Chemistry, Mathematics and Geography. Cr. 8vo. 2s. 6d.

BAYLISS, WYKE.
The Higher Life in Art; with a Chapter on Hobgoblins, by the Great Masters. Cr. 8vo., cloth, Illustrated. 6s.

Belgium of the East, The. By the Author of "Egypt under Ismail Pasha," "Egypt for the Egyptians," &c. Cr. 8vo. 6s.

BELLEW, Captain.
Memoirs of a Griffin; or, A Cadet's First Year in India. Illustrated from Designs by the Author. A New Edition. Cr. 8vo. 10s. 6d

BENTON, SAMUEL, L.R.C.P., &c.
Home Nursing, and How to Help in Cases of Accident. Illustrated with 19 Woodcuts. Cr. 8vo., cloth. 2s. 6d.

BERDMORE, SEPTIMUS (NIMSHIVICH).
A Scratch Team of Essays never before put together. Reprinted from the "Quarterly" and "Westminster" Reviews. The Kitchen and the Cellar — Thackeray — Russia — Carriages, Roads, and Coaches. Cr. 8vo. 7s. 6d.

BLACK, Rev. CHARLES INGRAM, M.A., Vicar of Burley in Wharfedale, near Leeds.
The Proselytes of Ishmael. Being a short Historical Survey of the Turanian Tribes in their Western Migrations. With Notes and Appendices. Second Edition. Cr. 8vo. 6s.

BLANCHARD, SIDNEY LAMAN.
Yesterday and To-day in India. Post 8vo. 6s.

BLENKINSOPP, Rev. E. L., M.A., Rector of Springthorpe.
Doctrine of Development in the Bible and in the Church. Second Edition. Cr. 8o. 6s.

BOILEAU, Major-General J. T.
A New and Complete Set of Traverse Tables, showing the Differences of Latitude and the Departures to every Minute of the Quadrant and to Five Places of Decimals. Together with a Table of the Lengths of each Degree of Latitude and corresponding Degree of Longitude from the Equator to the Poles; with other Tables useful to the Surveyor and Engineer. Fourth Edition, thoroughly revised and corrected by the Author. Roy. 8vo. 12s. London, 1876.

BOULGER, DEMETRIUS CHARLES, M.R.A.S.
History of China. Demy 8vo. Vol. I., with Portrait, 18s. Vol. II., 18s. Vol. III., with Portraits and Map, 28s.

England and Russia in Central Asia. With Appendices and Two Maps, one being the latest Russian Official Map of Central Asia. 2 vols. Demy 8vo. 36s.

Central Asian Portraits; or, The Celebrities of the Khanates and the Neighbouring States. Cr. 8vo. 7s. 6d.

The Life of Yakoob Beg, Athalik Ghazi and Badaulet, Ameer of Kashgar. With Map and Appendix. Demy 8vo. 16s.

BOWLES, THOMAS GIBSON, Master Mariner.
Flotsam and Jetsam. A Yachtsman's Experiences at Sea and Ashore. Cr. 8vo. 7s. 6d.

BOYD, R. NELSON, F.R.G.S., F.G.S., &c.
Chili and the Chilians, during the War 1879-80. Cloth, Illustrated. Cr. 8vo. 10s. 6d.

Coal Mines Inspection: Its History and Results. Demy 8vo. 14s.

BRADSHAW, JOHN, LL.D., Inspector of Schools, Madras.
The Poetical Works of John Milton, with Notes, explanatory and philological. 2 vols., Post 8vo. 12s. 6d.

BRAITHWAITE, R., M.D., F.L.S., &c.
The Sphagnaceæ, or Peat Mosses of Europe and North America. Illustrated with 29 Plates, coloured by hand. Imp. 8vo., cloth. 25s.

BRANDE, Professor, D.C.L., F.R.S., &c., and Professor, A. S. TAYLOR, M.D., F.R.S., &c.
Chemistry, a Manual of. Fcap. 8vo. 900 pages. 12s. 6d.

BRANDIS, Dr., Inspector-General of Forests to the Government of India.
The Forest Flora of North-Western and Central India. Text Demy 8vo. and Plates Roy. 4to. £2 18s.

BRERETON, WILLIAM H., late of Hong Kong, Solicitor.
The Truth about Opium. Being the Substance of Three Lectures delivered at St. James's Hall. Demy 8vo. 7s. 6d. Cheap edition, sewed, Cr. 8vo., 1s.

BRIGHT, W., late Colour-Sergeant 19th Middlesex R.V.
Red Book for Sergeants. Fifth and Revised Edition, 1880. Fcap. 8vo., interleaved. 1s.

BRISTOWE, J.S., M.D., F.R.C.P., *Senior Physician and Joint Lecturer on Medicine, St. Thomas's Hospital.*
    The Physiological and Pathological Relations of the Voice and Speech. Illustrated. Demy 8vo. 7s. 6d.

British Painters of the 18th and 19th Centuries. With 80 Examples of their Work, engraved on Wood. Handsomely bound in cloth, gilt. Demy 4to. 21s.

BUCKLAND, C.T., F.Z.S.
    Whist for Beginners. Second Edition. Cr. 16mo. 1s.
    Sketches of Social Life in India. Cr. 8vo. 5s.

BUCKLE, *the late Captain E., Assistant Adjutant-General, Bengal Artillery.*
    Bengal Artillery. A Memoir of the Services of the Bengal Artillery from the formation of the Corps. Edited by Sir J. W. Kaye. Demy 8vo. 10s.

BUCKLEY, ROBERT B., A.M.I.C.E., *Executive Engineer to the Public Works Department of India.*
    The Irrigation Works of India, and their Financial Results. Being a brief History and Description of the Irrigation Works of India, and of the Profits and Losses they have caused to the State. With Map and Appendix. Demy 8vo. 9s.

BURBIDGE, F. W.
    Cool Orchids, and How to Grow Them. With Descriptive List of all the best Species in Cultivation. Illustrated with numerous Woodcuts and Coloured Figures of 13 varieties. Cr. 8vo. 6s.

BURGESS, *Captain F., Bengal Staff Corps.*
    Sporting Fire-arms for Bush and Jungle; or, Hints to Intending Griffs and Colonists on the Purchase, Care, and Use of Fire-arms, with Useful Notes on Sporting Rifles, &c. Illustrated by the Author. Cr. 8vo. 5s.

BURGOYNE, *Lieutenant-Colonel Sir JOHN M., Bart.*
    Regimental Records of the Bedfordshire Militia. Cr. 8vo. 5s.

BURKE, PETER, *Serjeant-at-Law.*
    Celebrated Naval and Military Trials. Post 8vo. 10s. 6d.

BURROWS, MONTAGU, *Captain R.N., Retired List, Chichele Professor of Modern History in the University of Oxford.*
    Life of Edward Lord Hawke, Admiral of the Fleet, Vice-Admiral of Great Britain, and First Lord of the Admiralty from 1766 to 1771. Demy 8vo. 21s.

Byron Birthday Book, The. Compiled and edited by James Burrows. New Edition. 16mo. 2s. 6d.

By the Tiber. By the Author of "Signor Monaldini's Niece." 2 vols. Cr. 8vo. 21s.

CANNING, *The Hon. ALBERT S. G.*
    Thoughts on Shakespeare's Historical Plays. Demy 8vo. 12s.

CARLYLE, THOMAS.
    Memoirs of the Life and Writings of, With Personal Reminiscences and Selections from his Private Letters to numerous Correspondents. Edited by Richard Herne Shepherd, Assisted by Charles N. Williamson. 2 vols. With Portrait and Illustrations. Cr. 8vo. 21s.

CARRINGTON, B., M.D., F.R.S.
 British Hepaticæ. Containing Descriptions and Figures of the Native Species of Jungermannia, Marchantia, and Anthoceros. Imp. 8vo., sewed, Parts 1 to 4, each 2s. 6d. plain; 3s. 6d. coloured. To be completed in about 12 Parts.

CAVENAGH, Gen. Sir ORFEUR, K.C.S.I.
 Reminiscences of an Indian Official. Cr. 8vo. 10s. 6d.

CHAFFERS, WILLIAM, Author of "Hall Marks on Plate."
 Gilda Aurifabrorum: A History of London Goldsmiths and Plate-workers, with their Marks stamped on Plate, copied in fac-simile from celebrated Examples and the Earliest Records preserved at Goldsmiths' Hall, London, with their Names, Addresses, and Dates of Entry. 2,500 Illustrations. Roy. 8vo. 18s.

 Challenge of Barletta, The. By Massimo D'Azeglio. Rendered into English by Lady Louisa Magenis. 2 vols., Cr. 8vo. 21s.

CHAMISSO, ADALBERT VON.
 Peter Schlemihl. Translated by Sir John Bowring, LL.D., &c. trations on India paper by George Cruikshank. Large paper, Cr. 4to., half-Roxburghe, 10s. 6d.

CLARKE, Mrs. CHARLES, Lady Superintendent of the National Training School for Cookery, S. Kensington, S.W.
 Plain Cookery Recipes as Taught in the School. Paper cover. Cr. 8vo. 1s.

 Clever Things said by Children. Edited by Howard Paul. Roy. 16mo. 2s. 6d.

 Collection Catalogue for Naturalists. A Ruled Book for keeping a Permanent Record of Objects in any branch of Natural History, with Appendix for recording interesting particulars, and lettered pages for general Index. Strongly bound, 200 pages, 7s. 6d.; 300 pages, 10s.; and 2s. 6d. extra for every additional 100 pages. Working Catalogues, 1s. 6d. each.

COLLETTE, CHARLES HASTINGS.
 The Roman Breviary. A Critical and Historical Review, with Copious Classified Extracts. Second Edition. Revised and enlarged. Demy 8vo. 5s.

 Henry VIII. An Historical Sketch as affecting the Reformation in England. Post 8vo. 6s.

 St. Augustine (Aurelius Augustinus Episcopus Hipponiensis), a Sketch of his Life and Writings as affecting the Controversy with Rome. Cr. 8vo. 5s.

COLLINS, MABEL.
 The Story of Helena Modjeska (Madame Chlapowska). Cr. 8vo. 7s. 6d.

COLOMB, Colonel.
 Bluestockings. A Comedy in Five Acts. Adapted from the French of Molière. Cr. 8vo. 3s. 6d.

COLQUHOUN, Major J. A. S., R.A.
 With the Kurrum Force in the Caubul Campaign of 1878-79. With Illustrations from the Author's Drawings, and two Maps. Demy 8vo. 16s.

Companion to the Writing-Desk. How to Address Titled People, &c. Roy. 32mo. 1s.

COOKE, M. C., M.A., LL.D.
The British Fungi: A Plain and Easy Account of. With Coloured Plates of 40 Species. Third Edition, Revised. Cr. 8vo., cloth, 6s.

Rust, Smut, Mildew, and Mould. An Introduction to the Study of Microscopic Fungi. Illustrated with 269 Coloured Figures by J. E. Sowerby. Fourth Edition, with Appendix of New Species. Cr. 8vo. 6s.

A Manual of Structural Botany. Revised Edition, with New Chemical Notation. Illustrated with 200 Woodcuts. Twenty-fifth Thousand. 32mo. 1s.

A Manual of Botanic Terms. New Edition, greatly Enlarged. Illustrated with over 300 Woodcuts. Fcap. 8vo. 2s. 6d.

COOKE, M. C., M.A., A.L.S., et L. QUELET, M.D., O.A., Inst. et Sorb. laur.
Clavis Synoptica Hymenomycetum Europæorum. Fcap. 8vo. 7s. 6d.

COOLIDGE, SUSAN.
Crosspatch, and other Stories. New Edition. Illustrated. Cr. 8vo. 3s. 6d.

Cooper's Hill Royal Indian Engineering College, Calendar of. Published (by Authority) in January each year. Demy 8vo. 5s.

CORBET, Mrs. M. E.
A Pleasure Trip to India, during the Visit of H.R.H. the Prince of Wales, and afterwards to Ceylon. Illustrated with Photos. Cr. 8vo. 7s. 6d.

CRESSWELL, C. N., of the Inner Temple.
Woman, and her Work in the World. Cr. 8vo. 3s. 6d.

CROLL, JAMES, LL.D., F.R.S.
Climate and Time in their Geological Relations. Illustrated with 8 Coloured Plates and 11 Woodcuts. 577 pp. Demy 8vo. 24s.

CROSLAND, Mrs. NEWTON.
Stories of the City of London: Retold for Youthful Readers. With 10 Illustrations. Cr. 8vo. 6s.

Crown of Life, The. By M. Y. W. With elegantly illuminated borders from designs by Arthur Robertson, Fcap. 4to. 6s.

Cruise of H.M.S. "Galatea," Captain H.R.H. the Duke of Edinburgh, K.G., in 1867-1868. By the Rev. John Milner, B.A., Chaplain; and Oswald W. Brierly. Illustrated by a Photograph of H.R.H. the Duke of Edinburgh; and by Chromo-lithographs and Graphotypes from Sketches taken on the spot by O. W. Brierly. Demy 8vo. 16s.

CUNNINGHAM, H. S., M.A., one of the Judges of the High Court of Calcutta, and late Member of the Famine Commission.
British India, and its Rulers. Demy 8vo. 10s. 6d.

CUVIER, BARON.
The Animal Kingdom. With considerable Additions by W. B. Carpenter, M.D., F.R.S., and J. O. Westwood, F.L.S. New Edition, Illustrated with 500 Engravings on Wood and 36 Coloured Plates. Imp. 8vo. 21s.

DAUMAS, E., *General of the Division Commanding at Bordeaux, Senator, &c. &c.*
Horses of the Sahara, and the Manners of the Desert. With Commentaries by the Emir Abd-el-Kadir (Authorized Edition). Demy 8vo. 6s.

DAVIES, THOMAS.
The Preparation and Mounting of Microscopic Objects. New Edition, greatly Enlarged and brought up to the Present Time by John Matthews, M.D., F.R.M.S., Vice-President of the Quekett Microscopical Club. Fcap. 8vo. 2s. 6d.

DAVIS, GEORGE E., F.R.M.S., F.C.S., F.I.C., &c.
Practical Microscopy. Illustrated with 257 Woodcuts and a Coloured Frontispiece. Demy 8vo. 7s. 6d.

DEIGHTON, K., *Principal of Agra College.*
Shakespeare's King Henry the Fifth. With Notes and an Introduction. Cr. 8vo. 5s.

Destruction of Life by Snakes, Hydrophobia, &c., in Western India. By an Ex-Commissioner. Fcap. 2s. 6d.

DICKENS, CHARLES.
Plays and Poems, with a few Miscellanies in Prose. Now first collected. Edited, Prefaced, and Annotated by Richard Herne Shepherd. 2 vols. 8vo. 21s.
Edition de Luxe. 2 vols. Imp. 8vo. (Only 150 copies printed.)

DICKINS, FREDERICK V., *Sc.B. of the Middle Temple, Barrister-at-law* (translator).
Chiushingura: or the Loyal League. A Japanese Romance. With Notes and an Appendix containing a Metrical Version of the Ballad of Takasako, and a specimen of the Original Text in Japanese character. Illustrated by numerous Engravings on Wood, drawn and executed by Japanese artists and printed on Japanese paper. Roy. 8vo. 10s. 6d.

Diplomatic Study on the Crimean War, 1852 to 1856. (Russian Official Publication.) 2 vols. Demy 8vo. 28s.

DORAN, Dr. J., F.S.A.
"Their Majesties' Servants": Annals of the English Stage. Actors Authors, and Audiences, from Thomas Betterton to Edmund Kean. Post 8vo. 6s.

DOUGLAS, Mrs. MINNIE.
Countess Violet; or, What Grandmamma saw in the Fire. A Book for Girls. Illustrated. Cr. 8vo 3s. 6d.
Grandmother's Diamond Ring. A Tale for Girls. Cr. 8vo., 2s. 6d.

DRURY, Col. HEBER.
The Useful Plants of India, with Notices of their chief value in Commerce, Medicine, and the Arts. Second Edition, with Additions and Corrections. Roy. 8vo. 16s.

DUKE, JOSHUA, F.R.A.S., *Bengal Medical Service.*
Recollections of the Kabul Campaign 1879-1880. Illustrations and Map. Demy 8vo. 15s.

DUMERGUE, EDWARD, M.R.A.S., *Member of the Leyden Society of Orientalists.*
The Chotts of Tunis; or, the Great Inland Sea of North Africa in Ancient Times. With Map. Cr. 8vo., 2s. 6d.

DURAND, HENRY MARION, C.S.I., *Bengal Civil Service, Barrister-at-law.*
The Life of Major-General Sir Henry Marion Durand, K.C.S.I., C.B., of the Royal Engineers. With Portrait. 2 vols. Demy 8vo. 42s.

DUTTON, *Major the Hon. CHARLES.*
 Life in India. Cr. 8vo. 2s. 6d.

DWIGHT, HENRY O.
 Turkish Life in War Time. Cr. 8vo. 12s.

DYER, *The Rev. T. F. THISTLETON, M.A.*
 English Folk-lore. Second Edition. Cr. 8vo. 3s. 6d.

EDWARDS, G. SUTHERLAND.
 A Female Nihilist. By Ernest Lavigne. Translated from the French by G. Sutherland Edwards. Cr. 8vo. 9s.

EDWARDS, H. SUTHERLAND.
 The Lyrical Drama: Essays on Subjects, Composers, and Executants of Modern Opera. 2 vols. Cr. 8vo. 21s.
 The Russians at Home and the Russians Abroad. Sketches, Unpolitical and Political, of Russian Life under Alexander II. 2 vols. Cr. 8vo. 21s.

EMINENT WOMEN SERIES. Edited by JOHN H. INGRAM. Cr. 8vo. 3s. 6d.
  BLIND, MATHILDE.
    George Eliot.
  ROBINSON, A. MARY F.
    Emily Bronte.
  THOMAS, BERTHA.
    George Sand.
  GILCHRIST, ANNE.
    Mary Lamb.
  HOWE, JULIA WARD.
    Margaret Fuller.
  ZIMMERN, HELEN.
    Maria Edgeworth.
  PITMAN, *Mrs. E. R.*
    Elizabeth Fry.
  LEE, VERNON.
    Countess of Albany.
  MILLER, *Mrs. FENWICK.*
    Harriet Martineau.

ENSOR, F. SYDNEY, C.E.
 Incidents of a Journey through Nubia to Darfoor. 10s. 6d.

 The Queen's Speeches in Parliament, from Her Accession to the present time. A Compendium of the History of Her Majesty's Reign told from the Throne. Cr. 8vo. 7s. 6d.

EYRE, *Major-General Sir V., K.C.S.I., C.B.*
 The Kabul Insurrection of 1841–42. Revised and corrected from Lieut. Eyre's Original Manuscript. Edited by Colonel G. B. Malleson, C.S.I. With Map and Illustrations. Cr. 8vo. 9s.

FARRAR, *The Rev. FREDERIC W., D.D., F.R.S., Canon of Westminster, &c.*
 Words of Truth and Wisdom. Cr. 8vo. 5s.

FEARON, ALEC.
 Kenneth Trelawny. 2 vols. Cr. 8vo. 21s.

FORBES, *Capt. C. J. F. S., of the British Burma Commission.*
    Comparative Grammar of the Languages of Further India.
    A Fragment; and other Essays, being the Literary Remains of the Author. Demy 8vo. 6s.

    Foreign Office, Diplomatic and Consular Sketches. Reprinted from "Vanity Fair." Cr. 8vo. 6s.

FORTESCUE-HARRISON, *Miss NELLIE.*
    For One Man's Pleasure. 2 vols., Cr. 8vo. 21s.

FOURNIER, ALFRED, *Professeur à la Faculté de Médecine de Paris, Médecin de l'Hôpital Saint Louis, Membre de l'Académie de Médecine.*
    Syphilis and Marriage: Lectures delivered at the Hospital of St. Louis. Translated by Alfred Lingard. Cr. 8vo. 10s. 6d.

FRASER, *Lieut.-Col. G. T., formerly of 1st Bombay Fusiliers, and recently attached to the Staff of H.M. Indian Army.*
    Records of Sport and Military Life in Western India. With an Introduction by Colonel G. B. Malleson, C.S.I. Cr. 8vo. 7s. 6d.

FRY, HERBERT.
    London in 1884. Its Suburbs and Environs. Illustrated with 18 Bird's-eye Views of the Principal Streets, and a Map. Fourth year of publication. Revised and Enlarged. Cr. 8vo. 2s.

Gazetteer of Southern India. With the Tenasserim Provinces and Singapore. Compiled from original and authentic sources. Accompanied by an Atlas, including plans of all the principal towns and cantonments. With 4to. Atlas. Roy. 8vo. £3 3s.

Gazetteers of India.
    THORNTON, 4 vols. Demy 8vo. £2 16s.
        „   Demy 8vo. 21s.
        „   (N.W.P., &c.) 2 vols. Demy 8vo. 25s.

Geography of India. Comprising an account of British India, and the various states enclosed and adjoining. pp. 250. Fcap. 8vo. 2s.

Geological Papers on Western India. Including Cutch, Scinde, and the south-east coast of Arabia. To which is added a Summary of the Geology of India generally. Edited for the Government by Henry J. Carter, Assistant Surgeon, Bombay Army. With folio Atlas of Maps and Plates; half-bound. Roy. 8vo. £2 2s.

GIBNEY, *Major R. D., late Adj. 1st Wilts R.V.*
    Earnest Madement; a Tale of Wiltshire. Dedicated by permission to Lieut.-Gen. Sir Garnet Wolseley, G.C.B. Cr. 8vo. 6s.

GILLMORE, PARKER (UBIQUE).
    Encounters with Wild Beasts. With 10 full-page Illustrations. Cr. 8vo. 7s. 6d.

    Prairie and Forest. A description of the Game of North America, with Personal Adventures in its Pursuit. With 37 Illustrations. Cr. 8vo. 7s. 6d.

    The Amphibion's Voyage.

GOLDSTÜCKER, *Prof. THEODORE, The late.*
    The Literary Remains of. With a Memoir. 2 vols. Demy 8vo. 21s.

GRAHAM, ALEXANDER.
    Genealogical and Chronological Tables, illustrative of Indian History. Demy 4to. 5s.

GRANT, JAMES.
    Derval Hampton ; A Story of the Sea. 2 vols. Cr. 8vo. 21s.

GRANVILLE, J. MORTIMER, M.D.
    The Care and Cure of the Insane. 2 vols. Demy 8vo., cloth. 36s.
    Change as a Mental Restorative. Demy 8vo. 1s.
    Nerves and Nerve Troubles. Fcap. 8vo, cloth. 1s.
    Common Mind Troubles. Fcap. 8vo., cloth. 1s.
    How to make the Best of Life. Fcap. 8vo., cloth. 1s.
    Youth : Its Care and Culture. Post. 8vo., cloth. 2s. 6d.
    The Secret of a Clear Head. Fcap. 8vo., cloth. 1s.
    The Secret of a Good Memory. Fcap. 8vo., cloth. 1s.
    Sleep and Sleeplessness. Fcap. 8vo., cloth. 1s.

GREENE, F. V., Lieut. U.S. Army, and lately Military Attaché to the U. S. Legation at St. Petersburg.
    The Russian Army and its Campaigns in Turkey in 1877-1878. Second Edition. Roy. 8vo. 32s.
    Sketches of Army Life in Russia. Cr. 8vo. 9s.

GRIESINGER, THEODOR.
    The Jesuits ; a Complete History of their Open and Secret Proceedings from the Foundation of the Order to the Present Time. Translated by A. J. Scott, M.D. 2 vols. Illustrated. Demy 8vo. 24s.
    Mysteries of the Vatican, or Crimes of the Papacy. 2 vols., post 8vo. 21s.

GRIFFIS, WILLIAM ELLIOT, late of the Imperial University of Tokio, Japan.
    Corea, the Hermit Nation. Roy. 8vo. 18s.

GRIFFITH, RALPH T. H.
    Birth of the War God. A Poem. By Kalidasa. Translated from the Sanskrit into English Verse. Cr. 8vo. 5s.

Grove's System of Medical Book-keeping. The Complete Set, 4to., £4 14s. 6d.

HAINES, C. B.
    A Vindication of England's Policy with regard to the Opium Trade. Cr. 8vo., cloth. 2s. 6d.

HALL, Mrs. CECIL.
    A Lady's Life on a Farm in Manitoba. Fcap. 8vo. 2s. 6d.

HALL, E. HEPPLE, F.S.S.
    Lands of Plenty for Health, Sport, and Profit. British North America. A Book for all Travellers and Settlers. With Maps. Cr. 8vo. 6s.

HALL, The Rev. T. G., M.A., Prof. of Mathematics in King's College, London.
    The Elements of Plane and Spherical Trigonometry. With an Appendix, containing the solution of the Problems in Nautical Astronomy. For the use of Schools. 12mo. 2s.

HAMILTON, LEONIDAS LE CENCI, M.A.
    Ishtar and Izdubar. The Epic of Babylon, or the Babylonian goddess of love, and the hero and warrior king. Illustrated. Demy 8vo. 8s. 6d.

HANCOCK, E. CAMPBELL.
Copies for China Painters. With Fourteen Chromo-Lithographs and other Illustrations. Demy 8vo. 10s.
Handbook of Reference to the Maps of India. Giving the Lat. and Long. of places of note. Demy 18mo. 3s. 6d.
** This will be found a valuable Companion to Messrs. Allen & Co.'s Maps of India.

HARCOURT, Maj. A. F. P., Bengal Staff Corps.
Down by the Drawle. 2 vols. in one, Cr. 8vo. 6s.

Hardwicke's Elementary Books: Chemistry, 6d.; Mechanics, 4d.; Hydrostatics, 2d.; Hydraulics, 2d.; Optics, 4d.; Pneumatics, 2d.

HARDWICKE, HERBERT JUNIUS, M.D., &c.
Health Resorts and Spas; or, Climatic and Hygienic Treatment of Disease. Fcap. 8vo. 2s. 6d.

HARTING, JAMES EDMUND.
Sketches of Bird Life. With numerous Illustrations. Demy 8vo. 10s. 6d.

HAWEIS, Rev. H. R.
Music and Morals. Twelfth Edition. Cr. 8vo. 7s. 6d.
My Musical Life. With Portraits. Cr. 8vo. 15s.

HAWEIS, Mrs.
Chaucer's Beads: A Birthday Book, Diary, and Concordance of Chaucer's Proverbs or Sooth-saws. Cr. 8vo., vellum. 5s.; paper boards, 4s. 6d.

Health Primers. 1. Premature Death. 2. Alcohol. 3. Exercise and Training. 4. The House. 5. Personal Appearances. 6. Baths and Bathing. 7. The Skin. 8. The Heart. 9. The Nervous System. 10. Health in Schools. Demy 16mo. 1s. each.

HEAPHY, THOMAS.
The Likeness of Christ. Being an Enquiry into the verisimilitude of the received Likeness of our Blessed Lord. Edited by Wyke Bayliss, F.S.A. Illustrated with Twelve Portraits Coloured as Facsimiles, and Fifty Engravings on Wood. Handsomely bound in cloth gilt, atlas 4to., price £5 5s.

HEATLEY, GEORGE S., M.R.C.V.S.
Sheep Farming. With Illustrations. Cr. 8vo. 7s. 6d.

HEINE, HEINRICH.
The Book of Songs. Translated from the German by Stratheir. Cr. 8vo. 7s. 6d.

HELMS, LUDWIG VERNER.
Pioneering in the Far East, and Journeys to California in 1849, and to the White Sea in 1878. With Illustrations from original Sketches and Photographs, and Maps. Demy 8vo. 18s.

HENNEBERT, Lieutenant-Colonel.
The English in Egypt; England and the Mahdi—Arabi and the Suez Canal. Translated from the French (by permission) by Bernard Pauncefote. 3 Maps. Cr. 8vo. 2s. 6d.

HENSMAN, HOWARD, *Special Correspondent of the "Pioneer" (Allahabad), and the "Daily News" (London).*
 The Afghan War, 1879-80. Being a complete Narrative of the Capture of Cabul, the Siege of Sherpur, the Battle of Ahmed Khel, the brilliant March to Candahar, and the Defeat of Ayub Khan, with the Operations on the Helmund, and the Settlement with Abdur Rahman Khan. With Maps. Demy 8vo. 21s.

HERRICK, SOPHIE BLEDSOE.
 The Wonders of Plant Life under the Microscope. With numerous Illustrations. Small 4to. 6s.

HERSCHEL, Sir JOHN F. W., Bt., K.H., &c., *Member of the Institute of France, &c.*
 Popular Lectures on Scientific Subjects. Cr. 8vo. 6s.

HOLDEN, EDWARD S., *United States Naval Observatory.*
 Sir William Herschel: His Life and Works. Cr. 8vo. 6s.

Holland. Translated from the Italian of Edmondo Amicis, by Caroline Tilton. Cr. 8vo. 10s. 6d.

HOLMES, T. R. E.
 A History of the Indian Mutiny, and of the Disturbances which accompanied it among the Civil Population. With Maps and Plans. Demy 8vo. 21s.

HOOKER, Sir W. J., F.R.S., *and* J. G. BAKER, F.L.S.
 Synopsis Filicum; or, a Synopsis of all Known Ferns, including the Osmundaceæ, Schizæaceæ, Marratiaceæ, and Ophioglossaceæ (chiefly derived from the Kew Herbarium), accompanied by Figures representing the essential Characters of each Genus. Second Edition, brought up to the present time. Coloured Plates. Demy 8vo. £1 8s.

HOSSAIN, SYED M.
 Our Difficulties and Wants in the Path of the Progress of India. Cr. 8vo. 3s. 6d.

HOWDEN, PETER, V.S.
 Horse Warranty: a Plain and Comprehensive Guide to the various Points to be noted, showing which are essential and which are unimportant. With Forms of Warranty. Fcap. 8vo. 3s. 6d.

HOUGH, *Lieutenant-Colonel* W.
 Precedents in Military Law. Demy 8vo. 25s.

HUGHES, Rev. T. P.
 Notes on Muhammadanism. Second Edition, revised and enlarged. Fcap. 8vo. 6s.

HUNT, *Major* S. LEIGH, *Madras Army, and* ALEX. S. KENNY, M.R.C.S.E., A.K.C., *Senior Demonstrator of Anatomy at King's College, London.*
 On Duty under a Tropical Sun. Being some Practical Suggestions for the Maintenance of Health and Bodily Comfort, and the Treatment of Simple Diseases; with Remarks on Clothing and Equipment for the Guidance of Travellers in Tropical Countries. Second Edition. Cr. 8vo. 4s.
 Tropical Trials. A Handbook for Women in the Tropics. Cr. 8vo. 7s. 6d.

HUNTER, J., *late Hon. Sec. of the British Bee-Keepers' Association.*
 A Manual of Bee-Keeping. Containing Practical Information for Rational and Profitable Methods of Bee Management. Full Instructions on Stimulative Feeding, Ligurianizing and Queen-raising, with descriptions of the American Comb Foundation, Sectional Supers, and the best Hives and Apiarian Appliances on all systems. With Illustrations. Fourth Edition. Cr. 8vo. 3s. 6d.

HUTTON, JAMES.
    The Thugs and Dacoits of India. A Popular Account of the Thugs and Dacoits, the Hereditary Garotters and Gang Robbers of India. Post 8vo. 5s.

India Directory, The. For the Guidance of Commanders of Steamers and Sailing Vessels. Founded upon the Work of the late Captain James Horsburgh, F.R.S.
    Part I.—The East Indies, and Interjacent Ports of Africa and South America. Revised, Extended, and Illustrated with Charts of Winds, Currents, Passages, Variation, and Tides. By Commander Alfred Dundas Taylor, F.R.G.S., Superintendent of Marine Surveys to the Government of India. Sup. roy. 8vo. £1 18s.
    Part II.—The China Sea, with the Ports of Java, Australia, and Japan, and the Indian Archipelago Harbours, as well as those of New Zealand. Illustrated with Charts of the Winds, Currents, Passages, &c. By the same. (*In preparation.*)

INGRAM, JOHN H.
    The Haunted Homes and Family Traditions of Great Britain. First Series. Cr. 8vo., 7s. 6d.
    Second Series. Cr. 8vo., 7s. 6d.

In the Company's Service. A Reminiscence. Demy 8vo. 10s. 6d.

IRWIN, H. C., B.A., *Oxon, Bengal Civil Service.*
    The Garden of India; or, Chapters on Oudh History and Affairs. Demy 8vo. 12s.

JACKSON, LOWIS D'A., A.M.I.C.E., *Author of " Hydraulic Manual and Statistics," &c.*
    Canal and Culvert Tables. With Explanatory Text and Examples. New and corrected edition, with 40 pp. of additional Tables. Roy. 8vo. 28s.
    Pocket Logarithms and Other Tables for Ordinary Calculations of Quantity, Cost, Interest, Annuities, Assurance, and Angular Functions, obtaining Results correct in the Fourth Figure. 16mo. Cloth, 2s. 6d.; leather, 3s. 6d.
    Accented Four-Figure Logarithms, and other Tables. For purposes both of Ordinary and of Trigonometrical Calculation, and for the Correction of Altitudes and Lunar Distances. Cr. 8vo. 9s.
    Accented Five-Figure Logarithms of Numbers from 1 to 99999, without Differences. Roy. 8vo. 16s.
    Units of Measurement for Scientific and Professional Men. Cr. 4to. 2s.

JAMES, Mrs. A. G. F. ELIOT.
    Indian Industries. Cr. 8vo. 9s.

JENKINSON, Rev. THOMAS B., B.A,, *Canon of Maritzburg.*
    Amazulu. The Zulu People: their Manners, Customs, and History, with Letters from Zululand descriptive of the Present Crisis. Cr. 8vo. 6s.

JERROLD, BLANCHARD.
    At Home in Paris. Series I., 2 vols., Cr. 8vo., 16s. Series II., 2 vols., Cr. 8vo., 21s.

JEWITT, LLEWELLYN, F.S.A.
    Half - Hours among English Antiquities. Contents: Arms, Armour, Pottery, Brasses, Coins, Church Bells, Glass. Tapestry, Ornaments, Flint Implements, &c. With 304 Illustrations. Second Edition. Cr. 8vo. 5s.

JOHNSON, R. LOCKE, L.R.C.P., L.R.C.I., L.S.A., &c.
 Food Chart. Giving the Names, Classification, Composition, Elementary Value, Rates of Digestibility, Adulterations, Tests, &c., of the Alimentary Substances in General Use. In wrapper, 4to., 2s. 6d.; or on roller, varnished, 6s.

JOYNER, Mrs. A. BATSON.
 Cyprus: Historical and Descriptive. Adapted from the German of Herr Franz von Löher. With much additional matter. With 2 Maps. Cr. 8vo. 10s. 6d.

KAYE, Sir J. W.
 History of the War in Afghanistan. New Edition. 3 vols. Cr. 8vo. £1 6s.
 Lives of Indian Officers. 3 vols. Cr. 8vo. 6s. each.
 The Sepoy War in India. A History of the Sepoy War in India, 1857-1858. By Sir John William Kaye. Demy 8vo. Vol. I., 18s. Vol. II., £1. Vol. III., £1.
 (For continuation, *see* **History of the Indian Mutiny**, by Colonel G. B. Malleson, Vol. I. of which is contemporary with Vol. III. of Kaye's work.)

KEATINGE, Mrs.
 English Homes in India. 2 vols. Post 8vo. 16s.

KEENE, HENRY GEORGE, C.I.E., B.C.S., M.R.A.S., &c.
 The Fall of the Moghul Empire. From the Death of Aurungzeb to the overthrow of the Mahratta Power. Second Edition. With Map. Demy 8vo. 10s. 6d.
 This Work fills up a blank between the ending of Elphinstone's and the commencement of Thornton's Histories.
 Administration in India. Post 8vo. 5s.
 Peepul Leaves. Poems written in India. Post 8vo. 5s.
 Fifty-Seven. Some account of the Administration of Indian Districts during the Revolt of the Bengal Army. Demy 8vo. 6s.
 The Turks in India. Historical Chapters on the Administration of Hindostan by the Chugtai Tartar, Babar, and his Descendants. Demy 8vo. 12s. 6d.

KEMPSON, M., M.A.
 The Repentance of Nussooh. Translated from the original Hindustani tale by Sir William Muir, K.C.S.I. Cr. 8vo. 3s. 6d.

KENNY, ALEXANDER S., M.R.C.S. Edin., &c.
 The Tissues, and their Structure. Fcap. 8vo. 6s.

KENT, W. SAVILLE, F.L.S., F.Z.S., F.R.M.S., formerly Assistant in the Nat. Hist. Department of the British Museum.
 A Manual of the Infusoria. Including a Description of the Flagellate, Ciliate, and Tentaculiferous Protozoa, British and Foreign, and an account of the Organization and Affinities of the Sponges. With numerous Illustrations. Super-roy. 8vo., cloth. £4 4s.

KINAHAN, G. H.
 A Handy Book of Rock Names. Fcap. 8vo., cloth. 4s.

Knots, the Book of. Illustrated by 172 Examples, showing the manner of making every Knot, Tie, and Splice. By "Tom Bowling." Third Edition. Cr. 8vo., 2s. 6d

KING, DAVID BENNETT, Professor in Lafayette College, U.S.A.
The Irish Question. Cr. 8vo. 9s.

LANE-POOLE, STANLEY, Laureat de l'Institut de France.
Studies in a Mosque. Demy 8vo. 12s.

LANKESTER, Mrs.
Talks about Health: A Book for Boys and Girls. Being an Explanation of all the Processes by which Life is sustained. Illustrated. Small 8vo. 1s.
British Ferns: Their Classification, Arrangement of Genera, Structures, and Functions, Directions for Out-door and Indoor Cultivation, &c. Illustrated with Coloured Figures of all the Species. New and Enlarged Edition. Cr. 8vo. 3s. 6d.
Wild Flowers Worth Notice: A Selection of some of our Native Plants which are most attractive for their Beauty, Uses, or Associations. With 108 Coloured Figures by J. E. Sowerby. New Edition. Cr. 8vo. 5s.

LANKESTER, E., M.D., F.R.S., F.L.S.
Our Food. Illustrated. New Edition. Cr. 8vo. 4s.
Half-hours with the Microscope. With 250 Illustrations. Seventeenth Thousand, enlarged. Fcap. 8vo., plain, 2s. 6d.; coloured, 4s.
Practical Physiology: A School Manual of Health. Numerous Woodcuts. Sixth Edition. Fcap. 8vo. 2s. 6d.
The Uses of Animals in Relation to the Industry of Man. Illustrated. New Edition. Cr. 8vo. 4s.
Sanitary Instructions: A Series of Handbills for General Distribution. Each, 1d.; doz. 6d.; 100, 4s.; 1,000, 30s.

LATHAM, Dr. R. G.
Russian and Turk, from a Geographical, Ethnological, and Historical Point of View. Demy 8vo. 18s.

LAURIE, Col. W. F. B.
Burma, the Foremost Country: A Timely Discourse. To which is added, How the Frenchman sought to win an Empire in the East. With Notes on the probable effects of French success in Tonquin on British interests in Burma. Cr. 8vo. 2s.
Our Burmese Wars and Relations with Burma. With a Summary of Events from 1826 to 1879, including a Sketch of King Theebau's Progress. With Local, Statistical, and Commercial Information. With Plans and Map. Demy 8vo. 16s.
Ashe Pyee, the Superior Country; or the great attractions of Burma to British Enterprise and Commerce. Cr. 8vo. 5s.

LAW AND PROCEDURE, INDIAN CIVIL.
Mahommedan Law of Inheritance, &c. A Manual of the Mahommedan Law of Inheritance and Contract; comprising the Doctrine of Soonee and Sheea Schools, and based upon the text of Sir H. W. Macnaghten's Principles and Precedents, together with the Decisions of the Privy Council and High Courts of the Presidencies in India. For the use of Schools and Students. By Standish Grove Grady, Barrister-at-Law, Reader of Hindoo, Mahommedan, and Indian Law to the Inns of Court. Demy 8vo. 14s.
Hedaya, or Guide, a Commentary on the Mussulman Laws, translated by order of the Governor-General and Council of Bengal. By Charles Hamilton. Second Edition, with Preface and Index by Standish Grove Grady. Demy 8vo. £1 15s.

Law and Procedure, Indian Civil—*cont.*

Institutes of Menu in English. The Institutes of Hindu Law or the Ordinances of Menu, according to Gloss of Collucca. Comprising the Indian System of Duties, Religious and Civil, verbally translated from the Original, with a Preface by Sir William Jones, and collated with the Sanscrit Text by Graves Chamney Haughton, M.A., F.R.S., Professor of Hindu Literature in the East India College. New Edition, with Preface and Index by Standish G. Grady, Barrister-at-Law, and Reader of Hindu, Mahommedan, and Indian Law to the Inns of Court. Demy 8vo. 12s.

Indian Code of Civil Procedure. Being Act X. of 1877. Demy 8vo. 6s.

Indian Code of Civil Procedure. In the form of Questions and Answers, with Explanatory and Illustrative Notes. By Angelo J. Lewis, Barrister-at-Law. Imp. 12mo. 12s. 6d.

Hindu Law. Defence of the Daya Bhaga. Notice of the Case on Prosoono Coomar Tajore's Will. Judgment of the Judicial Committee of the Privy Council. Examination of such Judgment. By John Cochrane, Barrister-at-Law. Roy. 8vo. 20s.

Law and Customs of Hindu Castes, within the Dekhan Provinces subject to the Presidency of Bombay, chiefly affecting Civil Suits. By Arthur Steele. Roy. 8vo. £1 1s.

Moohummudan Law of Inheritance, and Rights and Relations affecting it (Sunni Doctrine). By Almaric Rumsey. Demy 8vo. 12s.

A Chart of Hindu Family Inheritance. By Almaric Rumsey Second Edition, much enlarged. Demy 8vo. 6s. 6d.

INDIAN CRIMINAL.

Including the Procedure in the High Courts, as well as that not in the Courts not established by Royal Charter; with Forms of Charges and Notes on Evidence, illustrated by a large number of English Cases, and Cases decided in the High Courts of India; and an Appendix of selected Acts passed by the Legislative Council relating to Criminal matters. By M. H. Starling, Esq., LL.B., and F. B. Constable, M.A. Third Edition. Medium 8vo. £2 2s.

Indian Code of Criminal Procedure. Being Act X. of 1872, Passed by the Governor-General of India in Council on the 25th of April 1872. Demy 8vo. 12s.

Indian Penal Code. In the form of Questions and Answers. With Explanatory and Illustrative Notes. By Angelo J. Lewis, Barrister-at-Law. Imp. 12mo. 7s. 6d.

Indian Code of Criminal Procedure, Act of 1882. Roy. 8vo. cloth. 6s.

MILITARY.

Manual of Military Law. For all ranks of the Army, Militia, and Volunteer Services. By Colonel J. K. Pipon, Assistant Adjutant-General at Head-quarters, and J. F. Collier, Esq., of the Inner Temple, Barrister-at-Law. Third and Revised Edition. Pocket size. 5s.

Precedents in Military Law; including the Practice of Courts-Martial; the Mode of Conducting Trials; the Duties of Officers at Military Courts of Inquests, Courts of Inquiry, Courts of Requests, &c. &c. By Lieut.-Col. W. Hough, late Deputy Judge-Advocate-General, Bengal Army, and Author of several Works on Courts-Martial. One thick Demy 8vo. vol. 25s.

Military—*cont.*
    The Practice of Courts-Martial. By Hough and Long. Thick Demy 8vo. London, 1825. 26s.
LEE, *The Rev. F. G., D.D.*
    The Church under Queen Elizabeth. An Historical Sketch. 2 vols. Cr. 8vo. 21s.
    Reginald Barentyne; or, Liberty without Limit. A Tale of the Times. With Portrait of the Author. Second Edition. Cr. 8vo. 5s.
    The Words from the Cross: Seven Sermons for Lent, Passion-Tide, and Holy Week. Third Edition revised. Fcap. 8vo. 3s. 6d.
    Order Out of Chaos. Two Sermons. Fcap. 8vo. 2s. 6d.
LEES, *Col. WILLIAM NASSAU, LLD.*
    The Drain of Silver to the East. Post 8vo. 8s.
LE MESSURIER, *Maj. A., R.E., Brigade Major with the Quetta Column.*
    Kandahar in 1879. Cr. 8vo. 8s.
LETHBRIDGE, *ROPER, C.I.E., M.A.*
    High Education in India. A Plea for the State Colleges. Cr. 8vo. 5s.
LEWIN, *Capt. T. H., Dep. Comm. of Hill Tracts.*
    Wild Races of the South-Eastern Frontier of India. Including an Account of the Loshai Country. Post 8vo. 10s. 6d.
LIANCOURT, *COUNT C. A. DE GODDES, and FREDERIC PINCOTT, M.R.A.S., &c.*
    The Primitive and Universal Laws of the Formation and Development of Language; a Rational and Inductive System founded on the Natural Basis of Onomatops. Demy 8vo. 12s. 6d.
LLOYD, *Mrs. JESSIE SALE.*
    Shadows of the Past. Second Edition. Cr. 8vo. 6s.
    Honesty Seeds and How they Grew; or, Tony Wigston's Firm Bank. Illustrated. Cr. 8vo. 2s. 6d.
LOCKWOOD, *EDWARD, B.S.C.*
    Natural History, Sport and Travel. With numerous Illustrations. Cr. 8vo. 9s.
LOVELL, *The late Vice-Adm. WM. STANHOPE, R.N., K.H.*
    Personal Narrative of Events from 1799 to 1815. With Anecdotes. Second Edition. Fcap. 8vo. 4s.
LOW, *CHARLES RATHBONE.*
    Major-General Sir Frederick S. Roberts, Bart., V.C., G.C.B., C.I.E., R.A.: a Memoir. With Portrait. Demy 8vo. 18s.
    Pollock, Field-Marshal Sir George, The Life and Correspondence of. With Portrait. Demy 8vo. 18s.
LUPTON, *JAMES IRVINE, F.R.C.V.S.*
    The Horse, as he Was, as he Is, and as he Ought to Be. Illustrated. Cr. 8vo. 3s. 6d.
MACDONALD, *The late DUNCAN GEO. FORBES, LL.D., C.E., J.P., F.R.G.S.*
    Grouse Disease; its Causes and Remedies. Illustrated. Third Edition. Demy 8vo. 10s. 6d.
MACGREGOR, *Col. C.M., C.S.I., C.I.E., Beng. Staff Corps.*
    Narrative of a Journey through the Province of Khorassan and on the N.W. Frontier of Afghanistan in 1875. With Map and Numerous illustrations. 2 vols. 8vo. 30s.
    Wanderings in Balochistan. With Illustrations and Map. Demy 8vo. 18s.

MACKAY, CHARLES, LL.D.
Luck; and what came of it. A Tale of our Times. 3 vols. Cr. 8vo. 31s. 6d.

MACKENZIE, Capt. C. F. (El Musannif).
The Romantic Land of Hind. Cr. 8vo. 6s

MACKENZIE,
Tables, &c.

MALABARI, BEHRAMJI, M.
Gujerat and the Gujeratis. Pictures of Men and Manners taken from Life. Cr. 8vo. 6s.

MALLESON, Col. G. B., C.S.I.
Final French Struggles in India and on the Indian Seas. Including an Account of the Capture of the Isles of France and Bourbon, and Sketches of the most eminent Foreign Adventurers in India up to the Period of that Capture. With an Appendix containing an Account of the Expedition from India to Egypt in 1801. New Edition. Cr. 8vo. 6s.
History of the Indian Mutiny, 1857-1858, commencing from the close of the Second Volume of Sir John Kaye's History of the Sepoy War. Vol. I. With Map. Demy 8vo. 20s.—Vol. II. With 4 plans. Demy 8vo. 20s.—Vol. III. With plans. Demy 8vo. 20s.
History of Afghanistan, from the Earliest Period to the Outbreak of the War of 1878. Second Edition. With Map. Demy 8vo. 18s.
The Decisive Battles of India, from 1746-1849. With a Portrait of the Author, a Map, and Three Plans. Demy 8vo. 18s.
Herat: The Garden and Granary of Central Asia. With Map and Index. Demy 8vo. 8s.
Founders of the Indian Empire. Clive, Warren Hastings, and Wellesley. Vol. I.—LORD CLIVE. With Portraits and 4 Plans. Demy 8vo. 20s.
Captain Musafir's Rambles in Alpine Lands. Illustrated by G. Strangman Handcock. Cr. 4to. 10s. 6d.
Battle-fields of Germany. With Maps and Plan. Demy 8vo. 16s.

MALLOCK, W. H.
A Chart showing the Proportion borne by the Rental of the Landlords to the Gross Income of the People. Cr. 1s.

MANGNALL, Mrs.
Historical and Miscellaneous Questions (generally known as "Mangnall's Questions"). New and Improved Edition. 18mo. 1s.

MANNING, Mrs.
Ancient and Mediæval India. Being the History, Religion, Laws, Caste, Manners and Customs, Language, Literature, Poetry, Philosophy, Astronomy, Algebra, Medicine, Architecture, Manufactures, Commerce, &c. of the Hindus, taken from their Writings. With Illustrations. 2 vols. Demy 8vo. 30s.

MARVIN, CHARLES.
The Eye-Witnesses' Account of the Disastrous Russian Campaign against the Akhal Tekke Turcomans: Describing the March across the Burning Desert, the Storming of Dengeel Tepe, and the Disastrous Retreat to the Caspian. With numerous Maps and Plans. Demy 8vo. 18s

Marvin, Charles—*cont.*
The Russians at Merv and Herat, and their Power of invading India. With 24 Illustrations and 3 Maps. Demy 8vo. 24s.
Merv, the Queen of the World; and the Scourge of the Man-stealing Turcomans. With Portraits and Maps. Demy 8vo. 18s.
Colonel Grodekoff's Ride from Samarcand to Herat, through Balkh and the Uzbek States of Afghan Turkestan. With his own March-route from the Oxus to Herat. With Portrait. Cr. 8vo. 8s.
The Region of the Eternal Fire. An Account of a Journey to the Caspian Region in 1883. 21 Maps and Illustrations. Demy 8vo. 21s.

MATEER, The Rev. SAMUEL, of the London Miss. Soc.
Native Life in Travancore. With Numerous Illustrations and Map. Demy 8vo. 18s.

MATSON, NELLIE.
Hilda Desmond, or Riches and Poverty. Cr. 8vo. 10s. 6d.

MAYHEW, EDWARD, M.R.C.V.S.
Illustrated Horse Doctor. Being an Accurate and Detailed Account, accompanied by more than 400 Pictorial Representations, characteristic of the various Diseases to which the Equine Race are subjected; together with the latest Mode of Treatment, and all the requisite Pre-scriptions written in Plain English. New and Cheaper Edition. Half-bound. Demy 8vo. 10s. 6d.
Illustrated Horse Management. Containing descriptive remarks upon Anatomy, Medicine, Shoeing, Teeth, Food, Vices, Stables; likewise a plain account of the situation, nature, and value of the various points; together with comments on grooms, dealers, breeders, breakers, and trainers; Embellished with more than 400 engravings from Original designs made expressly for this work. A new Edition, revised and im-proved by J. I. Lupton, M.R,C.V,S, New and Cheaper Edition. Half-bound. Demy 8vo. 7s. 6d.

MAYHEW, HENRY.
German Life and Manners. As seen in Saxony. With an account of Town Life—Village Life—Fashionable Life—Married Life—School and University Life, &c. Illustrated with Songs and Pictures of the Student Customs at the University of Jena. With numerous Illustra-tions. 2 vols. Demy 8vo. 18s. A Popular Edition of the above. With Illustrations. Cr. 8vo. 7s.

MAYO, Earl of.
De Rebus Africanus. The Claims of Portugal to the Congo and Adjacent Littoral. With Remarks on the French Annexation. With Map. Demy 8vo. 3s. 6d.

McCARTHY, T. A.
An Easy System of Calisthenics and Drilling, including Light Dumb-Bell and Indian Club Exercises. Fcap. 8vo. 1s. 6d.

McCOSH, JOHN, M.D.
Advice to Officers in India. Post 8vo. 8s.

MENZIES, SUTHERLAND.
Turkey Old and New: Historical, Geographical, and Statistical. With Map and numerous Illustrations. Third Edition. Demy 8vo. 21s.

MICHOD, C. J.
Good Condition: A Guide to Athletic Training for Amateurs and Pro-fessionals. Small 8vo. 1s.

Microscope, How to Choose a. By a Demonstrator. With 80 Illustrations. Demy 8vo. 1s.

MILITARY WORKS.

A Treatise on Scales. By Major F. Hart-Dyke. 2s.

Red Book for Sergeants. By William Bright, Colour-Sergeant, 19th Middlesex R.V. Fcap. 8vo. 1s.

Volunteer Artillery Drill-Book. By Captain W. Brooke Hoggan, R.A., Adjutant 1st Shropshire and Staffordshire V.A. Square 16mo. 2s

Principles of Gunnery. By John T. Hyde, M.A., late Professor of Fortification and Artillery, Royal Indian Military College, Addiscombe. Second Edition, revised and enlarged. With many Plates and Cuts, and Photograph of Armstrong Gun. Roy. 8vo. 14s.

Treatise on Fortification and Artillery. By Major Hector Straith. Revised and re-arranged by Thomas Cook, R.N., by John T. Hyde, M.A. Seventh Edition. Illustrated and 400 Plans, Cuts, &c. Roy. 8vo. £2 2s.

Elementary Principles of Fortification. A Text-Book for Military Examinations. By J. T. Hyde, M.A. With numerous Plans and Illustrations. Roy. 8vo. 10s. 6d.

Military Surveying and Field Sketching. The Various Methods of Contouring, Levelling, Sketching without Instruments, Scale of Shade, Examples in Military Drawing, &c. &c. &c. As at present taught in the Military Colleges. By Major W. H. Richards, 55th Regiment, Chief Garrison Instructor in India, Late Instructor in Military Surveying, Royal Military College, Sandhurst. Second Edition, Revised and Corrected. Roy. 12s.

Celebrated Naval and Military Trials. By Peter Burke. Post 8vo. 10s. 6d.

Military Sketches. By Sir Lascelles Wraxall. Post 8vo. 6s.

Military Life of the Duke of Wellington. By Jackson and Scott. 2 vols. Maps, Plans, &c. Demy 8vo. 12s.

Single Stick Exercise of the Aldershot Gymnasium. Paper cover. Fcap. 8vo. 6d.

An Essay on the Principles and Construction of Military Bridges. By Sir Howard Douglas. Demy 8vo. 15s.

Hand-book Dictionary for the Militia and Volunteer Services, containing a variety of useful information, Alphabetically arranged. Pocket size, 3s. 6d.; by post, 3s. 8d.

Lectures on Tactics for Officers of the Army, Militia, and Volunteers. By Major F. H. Dyke, Garrison Instructor, E.D. Fcap. 4to. 3s. 6d

Precedents in Military Law. By Lieut.-Col. W. Hough. Demy 8vo. 25s.

The Practice of Courts-Martial. By Hough and Long. Demy 8vo. 26s.

Reserve Force; Guide to Examinations, for the use of Captains and Subalterns of Infantry, Militia, and Rifle Volunteers, and for Sergeants of Volunteers. By Capt. G. H. Greaves. Second Edition. Demy 8vo. 2s.

Military Works—*cont.*
The Military Encyclopædia; referring exclusively to the Military Sciences, Memoirs of distinguished Soldiers, and the Narratives of Remarkable Battles. By J. H. Stocqueler. Demy 8vo. 12s.
Cavalry Remounts. By Capt. Nolan. With Illustrations. Demy 8vo. 10s. 6d.

Messrs. W. H. ALLEN and CO. are Agents for the Sale of Government Naval and Military Publications.

MILL, JAMES.
History of British India, With Notes and Continuation by H. H. Wilson. 9 vols. Cr. 8vo. £2 10s.

Misterton, or, Through Shadow to Sunlight. By Unus. Cr. 8vo. 5s.

MITCHINSON, ALEXANDER WILLIAM.
The Expiring Continent; A Narrative of Travel in Senegambia, with Observations on Native Character; Present Condition and Future Prospects of Africa and Colonisation. With 16 full-page Illustrations and Map. 8vo. 18s.

MITFORD, EDWARD L.
A Land March from England to Ceylon Forty Years Ago. With Map and numerous Illustrations. 2 vols. Demy 8vo. 24s.

MITFORD, Major R. C. W., 14th Bengal Lancers.
To Caubul with the Cavalry Brigade. A Narrative of Personal Experiences with the Force under General Sir F. S. Roberts, G.C.B. With Map and Illustrations from Sketches by the Author. Second Edition. Demy 8vo. 9s.

Modern Parallels to the Ancient Evidences of Christianity. Being an attempt to Illustrate the Force of those Evidences by the Light of Parallels supplied by Modern Affairs. Demy 8vo. 10s. 6d.

MULLER, MAX.
Rig-Veda-Sanhita. The Sacred Hymns of the Brahmins; together with the Commentary of Sayanacharya. Published under the Patronage of the Right Honourable the Secretary of State for India in Council. Demy 4to. 6 vols. £2 10s. per volume.

NAVE, JOHANN.
The Collector's Handy-Book of Algæ, Diatoms, Desmids, Fungi, Lichens, Mosses, &c. Translated and Edited by the Rev. W. W. Spicer, M.A. Illustrated with 114 Woodcuts. Fcap. 8vo. 2s. 6d.

NEVILLE, RALPH.
The Squire's Heir. 2 vols. Cr. 8vo. 21s.

NEWMAN, The Late EDWARD, F.Z.S.
British Butterflies and Moths. With over 800 Illustrations. Super-roy. 8vo., cloth gilt. 25s.
The above Work may also be had in Two Volumes, sold separately. Vol. I., Butterflies, 7s. 6d.; Vol. II., Moths, 20s.

NEWMAN, The Rev. JOHN HENRY (now Cardinal).
Miscellanies from the Oxford Sermons of John Henry Newman, D.D. Cr. 8vo. 6s.

NICHOLSON, Capt. H. WHALLEY
From Sword to Share; or, a Fortune in Five Years at Hawaii. With Map and Photographs. Cr. 8vo. 12s. 6d.

Nirgis and Bismillah. NIRGIS; a Tale of the Indian Mutiny, from the Diary of a Slave Girl: and BISMILLAH; or, Happy Days in Cashmere. By Hafiz Allard. Post 8vo. 10s. 6d.

NORRIS-NEWMAN, CHARLES L., *Special Correspondent of the London "Standard."*
  In Zululand with the British, throughout the War of 1879. With Plans and Four Portraits. Demy 8vo. 16s.
  With the Boers in the Transvaal and Orange Free State in 1880-81. With Maps. Demy 8vo. 14s.

Notes on Collecting and Preserving Natural History Objects. Edited by J. E. Taylor, F.L.S., F.G.S., Editor of "Science Gossip." With numerous Illustrations. Cr. 8vo. 3s. 6d.

Notes on the North-Western Provinces of India. By a District Officer. Second Edition. Post 8vo. 5s.

O'DONOGHUE, Mrs. POWER.
  Ladies on Horseback. Learning, Park Riding, and Hunting. With Notes upon Costume, and numerous Anecdotes. With Portrait. Second Edition. Cr. 8vo. 5s.

OLDFIELD, The Late HENRY ARMSTRONG, M.D., H.M. Indian Army.
  Sketches from Nipal, Historical and Descriptive; with Anecdotes of the Court Life and Wild Sports of the Country in the time of Maharaja Jung Bahadur, G.C.B.; to which is added an Essay on Nipalese Buddhism, and Illustrations of Religious Monuments, Architecture, and Scenery, from the Author's own Drawings. 2 vols. Demy 8vo. 36s.

OLIVER, Capt. S. P.
  On and Off Duty. Being Leaves from an Officer's Note Book, in Turania, Lemuria, and Columbia. With 38 Illustrations. Cr. 4to. 14s.
  On Board a Union Steamer. A compilation; to which is added "A Sketch Abroad," by Miss Doveton. With Frontispiece. Demy 8vo. 8s.

OSBORNE, Mrs. WILLOUGHBY.
  A Pilgrimage to Mecca. By the Nawab Sikandar Begum of Bhopal. Translated from the original Urdu by Mrs. Willoughby Osborne. Followed by a Sketch of the History of Bhopal by Colonel Willoughby Osborne, C.B. With Photographs. Dedicated, by permission, to Her Majesty Queen Victoria. Post 8vo. £1 1s.

OSWALD, FELIX S.
  Zoological Sketches: a Contribution to the Out-door Study of Natural History. With 36 Illustrations by Hermann Faber. Cr. 8vo. 7s. 6d.

OWEN, SIDNEY, M.A.
  India on the Eve of the British Conquest. A Historical Sketch. Post 8vo. 8s.

OXENHAM, Rev. HENRY NUTCOMBE, M.A.
  Catholic Eschatology and Universalism. An Essay on the Doctrine of Future Retribution. Second Edition, revised and enlarged. Cr. 8vo. 7s. 6d.
  Catholic Doctrine of the Atonement. An Historical Inquiry into its Development in the Church, with an Introduction on the Principle of Theological Development. Third Edition and enlarged. 8vo. 14s.
  The First Age of Christianity and the Church. By John Ignatius Döllinger, D.D., Professor of Ecclesiastical History in the University of Munich, &c. &c. Translated from the German by H. N. Oxenham, M.A. Third Edition. 2 vols., Cr. 8vo. 18s.

OZANAM, A. F.
   History of Civilisation in the Fifth Century. Translated from the French by the Hon. A. C. Glyn. 2 vols., Post 8vo. 21s.

PANTON, J. E.
   Country Sketches in Black and White. Cr. 8vo. 6s.

PAYNE, JOHN.
   Lautrec. A Poem. New Edition. Paper cover. Fcap. 8vo. 2s. 6d.
   Intaglios. New Edition. Fcap. 8vo. 3s. 6d.
   Songs of Life and Death. New Edition. Cr. 8vo. 5s.
   Marque of Shadows. New Edition. Cr. 8vo. 5s.
   New Poems. New Edition. Cr. 8vo. 7s. 6d.

PEBODY, CHARLES.
   Authors at Work. Francis Jeffrey—Sir Walter Scott—Robert Burns—Charles Lamb—R. B. Sheridan—Sydney Smith—Macaulay—Byron—Wordsworth—Tom Moore—Sir James Mackintosh. Post 8vo. 10s. 6d.

PEILE, Rev. W. O., M.A.
   Tay. A Novel. Cr. 8vo. 10s. 6d.

PELLY, Colonel Sir LEWIS, K.C.B., K.C.S.I., &c.
   The Miracle Play of Hasan and Husain. Collected from Oral Tradition by Colonel Sir Lewis Pelly, K.C.B., K.C.S.I. Revised, with Explanatory Notes, by Arthur N. Wollaston, H.M. Indian (Home) Service, Translator of Anwar-i-Suhaili, &c. 2 vols., Roy. 8vo. 32s.

   Pen and Ink Sketches of Military Subjects. By "Ignotus." Reprinted, by permission, from the "Saturday Review." Cr. 8vo. 5s.

   Personal Piety: a Help to Christians to walk worthy of their Calling. 24mo. 1s. 6d.

PHILLIPS, Mrs. ALFRED.
   Man Proposes. A Novel. 3 vols., Cr. 8vo. 31s. 6d.

PINCOTT, FREDERIC, M.R.A.S.
   Analytical Index to Sir John Kaye's History of the Sepoy War, and Colonel G. B. Malleson's History of the Indian Mutiny. (Combined in one volume.) Demy 8vo. 10s. 6d.

PINKERTON, THOMAS A.
   Agnes Moran: A Story of Innocence and Experience. 3 vols., Cr. 8vo. 31s. 6d.

PITTENGER, Rev. W.
   Capturing a Locomotive. A History of Secret Service in the late American War. With 13 Illustrations. Cr. 8vo. 6s.

   Plutarch, Our Young Folks'. Edited by Rosalie Kaufmann. With Maps and Illustrations. Small 4to. 10s. 6d.

POPE, Rev. G. U., D.D., Fellow of Madras University.
   Text-Book of Indian History; with Geographical Notes, Genealogical Tables, Examination Questions, and Chronological, Biographical, Geographical, and General Indexes. For the use of Schools, Colleges, and Private Students. Third Edition, thoroughly revised. Fcap. 4to. 12s.

PRICHARD, I. I.
   The Chronicles of Budgepore, &c.; or, Sketches of Life in Upper India. 2 vols., Fcap. 8vo. 12s.

PRINSEP, H. T.
> **Historical Results.** Deducible from Recent Discoveries in Afghanistan. Demy 8vo. 15s.
> **Tibet, Tartary, and Mongolia.** Second Edition. Post 8vo. 5s.
> **Political and Military Transactions in India.** 2 vols., Demy 8vo. 18s.
> **Private Theatricals.** Being a Practical Guide to the Home Stage, both Before and Behind the Curtain. By an Old Stager. Illustrated with Suggestions for Scenes after designs by Shirley Hodson. Cr. 8vo. 3s. 6d.

PROCTOR, RICHARD A., B.A., F.R.A.S.
> **Half-Hours with the Stars.** Demy 4to. 3s. 6d.
> **Half-Hours with the Telescope.** Illustrated. Fcap. 8vo. 2s. 6d.

PROCTER, WILLIAM, Stud Groom.
> **The Management and Treatment of the Horse** in the Stable, Field, and on the Road. New and revised edition. Cr. 8vo. 6s.

RALFE, CHARLES H., M.A., M.D. Cantab.; F.R.C.P. Lond.; late Teacher of Physiological Chemistry, St. George's Hospital, &c.
> **Demonstrations in Physiological and Pathological Chemistry.** Arranged to meet the requirements for the Practical Examination in these subjects at the Royal College of Physicians and College of Surgeons. Fcap. 8vo. 5s.

RAMANN, Fraulein L.
> **Franz Liszt, Artist and Man.** Translated from the German by Miss E. Cowdery. 2 vols., Cr. 8vo. 21s.

RANSOME, A. H.
> **Sunday Thoughts for the Little Ones.** 24mo. 1s. 6d.

RICE, WILLIAM, Major-General (Retired) Indian Army.
> **Indian Game: from Quail to Tiger.** With 12 Coloured Plates. Imp. 8vo. 21s.

RIDLEY, MARIAN S.
> **A Pocket Guide to British Ferns.** Fcap. 8vo. 2s. 6d.

RIMMER, R., F.L.S.
> **The Land and Fresh Water Shells of the British Isles.** Illustrated with 8 Photographs and 3 Lithographs, containing figures of all the principal Species. Cr. 8vo. 10s. 6d.

ROWE, RICHARD.
> **Picked up in the Streets:** or, Struggles for Life among the London Poor. Illustrated. Cr. 8vo. 6s.

SACHAU, Dr. C. EDWARD, Professor Royal University of Berlin.
> **The Chronology of Ancient Nations.** An English Version of the Arabic Text of the Athar-ut-Bâkiya of Albirûnî, or "Vestiges of the Past." Collected and reduced to writing by the Author in A.H. 390-1, A.D. 1000. Translated and Edited, with Notes and Index. Roy. 8vo. 42s.

SANDERSON, G. P., Officer in Charge of the Government Elephant Keddahs at Mysore.
> **Thirteen Years among the Wild Beasts of India;** their Haunts and Habits, from Personal Observation. With an account of the Modes of Capturing and Taming Wild Elephants. With 21 full-page Illustrations and 3 Maps. Second Edition. Fcap. 4to. £1 5s.

SCHAIBLE, CHARLES H., M.D., Ph.D.
> **First Help in Accidents:** Being a Surgical Guide in the absence, or before the arrival, of medical assistance. Fully Illustrated. 32mo. 1s.

SCHLEIDEN, J. M., M.D.
The Principles of Scientific Botany. Translated by Dr. Lankester. Numerous Woodcuts and Six Steel Plates. Demy 8vo. 10s. 6d.

SCUDAMORE, FRANK IVES, C.B.
France in the East. A Contribution towards the consideration of the Eastern Question. Cr. 8vo. 6s.

SECCOMBE, Lieut.-Col. T. S.
Comic Sketches from English History. For Children of various Ages. With Descriptive Rhymes. With 12 full-page Illustrations and numerous Woodcuts. 6s.

SEWELL, ROBERT, Madras Civil Service.
Analytical History of India. From the earliest times to the Abolition of the East India Company in 1858. Post 8vo. 8s.

Shadow of a Life (The). A Girl's Story. By Beryl Hope. 3 vols. Cr. 8vo. 31s. 6d.

SHERER, J. W., C.S.I.
The Conjuror's Daughter. A Tale. With Illustrations by Alf. T. Elwes and J. Jellicoe. Cr. 8vo. 6s.
Who is Mary? A Cabinet Novel, in one volume. Cr. 8vo. 10s. 6d.
At Home and in India. A Volume of Miscellanies. With Frontispiece. Cr. 8vo. 5s.

SHERIFF, DANIEL.
An Improved Principle of Single Entry Book-keeping. Roy. 8vo. 3s. 6d.
The Whole Science of Double Entry Book-keeping. Third Edition. 8vo. 4s.

Signor Monaldini's Niece. A Novel of Italian Life. By the Author of "The Jewel in the Lotus." Cr. 8vo. 6s.

SIMPSON, HENRY TRAILL, M.A., late Rector of Adel.
Archæologia Adelensis; or, a History of the Parish of Adel, in the West Riding of Yorkshire. Being an attempt to delineate its Past and Present Associations, Archæological, Topographical, and Scriptural. With numerous etchings by W. Lloyd Ferguson. Roy. 8vo. 21s.

Skobeleff, Personal Reminiscences of General. By Nemirovitch-Dantchenko. Translated by E. A. Brayley Hodgetts. With 3 Portraits. Demy 8vo. 10s. 6d.

SMALL, Rev. G., Interpreter to the Strangers' Home for Asiatics.
A Dictionary of Naval Terms, English and Hindustani. For the use of Nautical Men trading to India, &c. Cr. 8vo. 2s. 6d.

SMITH, J., A.L.S.
Ferns: British and Foreign. Fourth Edition, revised and greatly enlarged, with New Figures, &c. Cr. 8vo. 7s. 6d.

SMITH, WORTHINGTON, F.L.S.
Mushrooms and Toadstools; How to Distinguish easily the Difference between Edible and Poisonous Fungi. Two large Sheets, containing Figures of 29 Edible and 31 Poisonous Species, drawn the natural size, and Coloured from Living Specimens. With descriptive letterpress, 6s.; on canvas, in cloth case for pocket, 10s. 6d.; on canvas, on rollers and varnished, 10s. 6d. The letterpress may be had separately, with key-plates of figures, 1s.

SOLYMOS, B. (B. E. Falkonberg, C.E.).
    Desert Life. Recollections of an Expedition in the Soudan. Demy 8vo. 15s.

    Soldiers' Stories and Sailors' Yarns: A Book of Mess-Table Drollery and Reminiscence picked up Ashore and Afloat by Officers, Naval, Military, and Medical. Cr. 8vo. 9s.

    Songs of a Lost World. By a New Hand. Cr. 8vo. 6s.

STANLEY, ARTHUR P., D.D., Dean of Westminster.
    Scripture Portraits, and other Miscellanies. Cr. 8vo. 6s.

STEINMETZ, A.
    The Smoker's Guide, Philosopher, and Friend: What to Smoke —What to Smoke with—and the whole "What's What" of Tobacco, Historical, Botanical, Manufactural, Anecdotal, Social, Medical, &c. Roy. 32mo. 1s.

STENT, GEORGE CARTER, M.R.A.S., Chinese Imperial Customs Service.
    Entombed Alive, and other Songs and Ballads. (From the Chinese.) With 4 Illustrations. Cr. 8vo. 9s.

    Scraps from my Sabretasche. Being Personal Adventures while in 14th (King's Light) Dragoons. Cr. 8vo. 6s.

    The Jade Chaplet, in Twenty-four Beads. A Collection of Songs, Ballads, &c. from the Chinese. Second Edition. Cr. 8vo. 5s.

STOTHARD, ROBERT T., F.S.A.
    The A B C of Art. Being a system of delineating forms and objects in nature necessary for the attainments of a draughtsman. Fcap. 8vo. 1s.

    Sunday Evening Book (The): Short Papers for Family Reading. By J. Hamilton, D.D., Dean Stanley, J. Eadie, D.D., Rev. W. M. Punshon, Rev. T. Binney, J. R. Macduff, D.D. Cloth antique. 24mo. 1s. 6d.

SYMONDS, Rev. W. S., Rector of Pendock.
    Old Bones; or, Notes for Young Naturalists. With References to the Typical Specimens in the British Museum. Second Edition, much improved and enlarged. Numerous Illustrations. Fcap. 8vo. 2s. 6d.

SWINNERTON, Rev. C. Chaplain in the Field with the First Division, Peshawur Valley Field Force.
    The Afghan War. Gough's Action at Futtehabad With Frontispiece and 2 Plans. Cr. 8vo. 5s.

SWINTON, A. H.
    An Almanack of the Christian Era, containing a legitimate prediction of the Weather, Disasters by Wind and Rain, Shipwrecks and River Floods, Prognostics of the Harvest, Havoc by Vermin and Infection, Famines and Panics, Electrical Disturbances, Calamities by Earthquakes and Volcanic Eruptions, with much that is Important or Curious. A Record of the Past and Glimpse into the Future, based on Solar Physics. 4to. 6s.

TAUNTON, ALFRED GEORGE.
    The Family Register. A Key to such Official Entries of Births, Marriages, and Deaths at the Registrar-General's Office as may refer to any particular family. Half-bound. Demy folio. 21s.

TAYLER, WILLIAM, Retired B.C.S., late Commissioner of Patna.
Thirty-eight Years in India, from Jugunath to the Himalaya Mountains. 200 Illustrations from Original Sketches. 2 vols. Demy 8vo. 25s. each.
The Patna Crisis; or, Three Months at Patna during the Insurrection of 1857. Third Edition. Fcap. 8vo. 2s.

TAYLOR, J. E., F.L.S., F.G.S., &c.
The Aquarium : Its Inhabitants, Structure, and Management. With 238 Woodcuts. Second Edition. Cr. 8vo. 3s. 6d.
Flowers: Their Origin, Shapes, Perfumes, and Colours. Illustrated with 32 Coloured Figures by Sowerby, and 161 Woodcuts. Second Edition. Cr. 8vo. 7s. 6d.
Geological Stories. Numerous Illustrations. Fourth Edition. Cr. 8vo. 2s. 6d.
Nature's Bye-paths : A Series of Recreative Papers in Natural History. Cr. 8vo. 3s. 6d.
Half-Hours at the Sea-side. Illustrated with 250 Woodcuts. Fourth Edition. Cr. 8vo. 2s. 6d.
Half-Hours in the Green Lanes. Illustrated with 300 Woodcuts. Fifth Edition. Cr. 8vo., cloth. 2s. 6d.

THOMS, JOHN ALEXANDER.
A Complete Concordance to the Revised Version of the New Testament, embracing the Marginal Readings of the English Revisers as well as those of the American Committee. Roy. 8vo. 6s.

THOMSON, DAVID.
Lunar and Horary Tables. For New and Concise Methods of Performing the Calculations necessary for ascertaining the Longitude by Lunar Observations, or Chronometers; with directions for acquiring a knowledge of the Principal Fixed Stars and finding the Latitude of them. Sixty-fifth Edition. Roy. 8vo. 10s.

THORNTON, EDWARD.
The History of the British Empire in India. Containing a Copious Glossary of Indian Terms, and a Complete Chronological Index of Events, to aid the Aspirant for Public Examinations. Third Edition. With Map. 1 vol. Demy 8vo. 12s.
*** The Library Edition of the above in 6 volumes, 8vo., may be had, price £2 8s.

Gazetteer of India. Compiled from the records at the India Office. With Map. 1 vol. Demy 8vo., pp. 1015. 21s.
*** The chief objects in view in compiling this Gazetteer are:—
1st. To fix the relative position of the various cities, towns, and villages with as much precision as possible, and to exhibit with the greatest practicable brevity all that is known respecting them ; and
2ndly. To note the various countries, provinces, or territorial divisions, and to describe the physical characteristics of each, together with their statistical, social, and political circumstances.
To these are added minute descriptions of the principal rivers and chains of mountains; thus presenting to the reader, within a brief compass, a mass of information which cannot otherwise be obtained, except from a multiplicity of volumes and manuscript records.
The Library Edition.
4 vols. Demy 8vo, Notes, Marginal References and Map. £2 16s.

Thornton, Edward—*cont.*
Gazetteer of the Punjaub, Affghanistan, &c. Gazeteer of the Countries adjacent to India, on the north-west, including Scinde, Affghanistan, Beloochistan, the Punjaub, and the neighbouring States. 2 vols. Demy 8vo. £1 5s.

THORNTON, PERCY M.
Foreign Secretaries of the Nineteenth Century. Lord Grenville, Lord Hawkesbury, Lord Harrowby, Lord Mulgrave, C. J. Fox, Lord Howick, George Canning, Lord Bathurst, Lord Wellesley (together with estimate of his Indian Rule by Col. G. B. Malleson, C.S.I.), Lord Castlereagh, Lord Dudley, Lord Aberdeen, and Lord Palmerston. Also, Extracts from Lord Bexley's Papers, including lithographed letters of Lords Castlereagh and Canning, bearing on important points of public policy; never before published. With Ten Portraits, and a View showing Interior of the old House of Lords. Second Edition. 2 vols. Demy 8vo. 32s. 6d.
Vol. III. Second Edition. With Portraits. Demy 8vo. 18s.

THORNTON, T.
East India Calculator. Demy 8vo. 10s.
History of the Punjaub, and Present Condition of the Sikhs. 2 vols. Cr. 8vo. 8s.

TILLEY, HENRY A.
Japan, the Amoor and the Pacific. With Notices of other Places, comprised in a Voyage of Circumnavigation in the Imperial Russian Corvette *Rynda*, in 1858-1860. Eight Illustrations. Demy 8vo. 10s.

Time's Footprints: A Birthday Book of Bitter-Sweet. 16mo. 2s. 6d.

TINCKER, MARY AGNES.
The Jewel in the Lotos. A Novel. By the Author of "Signor Monaldini's Niece," &c. 5 Illustrations. Cr. 8vo. 7s. 6d.

TORRENS, W. T. McCULLAGH, M.P.
Reform of Procedure in Parliament to Clear the Block of Public Business. Second Edition. Cr. 8vo. 5s.

Treasury of Choice Quotations: Selections from more than 300 Eminent Authors. With a complete Index. Cr. 8vo. 3s. 6d.

TRIMEN, H., M.B. (Lond.), F.L.S., and DYER, W. T., B.A.
The Flora of Middlesex: A Topographical and Historical Account of the Plants found in the County. With Sketches of its Physical Geography and Climate, and of the Progress of Middlesex Botany during the last Three Centuries. With a Map of Botanical Districts. Cr. 8vo. 12s. 6d.

TRIMEN, Capt. R., late 35th Regiment.
Regiments of the British Army, Chronologically arranged. Showing their History, Services, Uniform, &c. Demy 8vo. 10s. 6d.

TROTTER, Capt. LIONEL JAMES, late Beng. Fusiliers.
History of India. The History of the British Empire in India, from the Appointment of Lord Hardinge to the Death of Lord Canning (1844 to 1862). 2 vols. Demy 8vo. 16s. each.
Lord Lawrence. A Sketch of his Career. Fcap. 8vo. 1s. 6d.
Warren Hastings, a Biography. Cr. 8vo. 9s.

TROTTER, M.E.
A Method of Teaching Plain Needlework in Schools. Illustrated with Diagrams and Samplers. New Edition, revised and arranged according to Standards. Demy 8vo. 2s. 6d.

TUPPER, MARTIN F., Author of "Proverbial Philosophy," &c.
Three Five-Act Plays and Twelve Dramatic Scenes. Suitable for Private Theatricals or Drawing-room Recitation. Cr. 8vo. 5s.

TURGENEV, IVAN, D.C.L.
First Love, and **Punin and Baburin.** Translated from the Russian by permission of the Author, with Biographical Introduction, by Sidney Jerrold. With Portrait. Cr. 8vo. 6s.

Under Orders. By the Author of "Invasions of India from Central Asia." Third Edition. 3 vols., Cr. 8vo. 31s. 6d.

UNDERWOOD, ARTHUR S., M.R.C.S, L.D.S.E., Assistant-Surgeon to the Dental Hospital of London.
Surgery for Dental Students. Cr. 8vo. 5s.

VALBEZEN, E. DE, late Consul-General at Calcutta, Minister Plenipotentiary.
The English and India. New Sketches. Translated from the French (with the Author's permission) by a Diplomate. Demy 8vo. 18s.

VAMBERY, ARMENIUS.
Sketches of Central Asia. Additional Chapters on My Travels and Adventures, and of the Ethnology of Central Asia. Demy 8vo. 16s.

VIBART, Major H.M., Royal (late Madras) Engineers.
The Military History of the Madras Engineers and Pioneers. 2 vols. With numerous Maps and Plans. Demy 8vo. 32s. each.

Victoria Cross (The), An Official Chronicle of Deeds of Personal Valour achieved in the presence of the Enemy during the Crimean and Baltic Campaigns, and the Indian, Chinese, New Zealand, and African Wars, from the Institution of the Order in 1856 to 1880. Edited by Robert W. O'Byrne. With Plate. Cr. 8vo. 5s.

VYSE, GRIFFIN W., late on special duty in Egypt and Afghanistan for H.M.'s Government.
Egypt: Political, Financial, and Strategical. Together with an Account of its Engineering Capabilities and Agricultural Resources. With Maps. Cr. 8vo. 9s.

WALFORD, M.A., &c. &c.
Holidays in Home Counties. With numerous Illustrations. Cr. 8vo. 3s. 6d.
Pleasant Days in Pleasant Places. Illustrated with numerous Woodcuts. Second Edition. Cr. 8vo. 3s. 6d.

WALL, A. J., M.D., F.R.C.S., Med. Staff H.M.'s Indian Army.
Indian Snake Poisons, their Nature and Effects. Cr. 8vo. 6s.

WATSON, Dr. J. FORBES, and JOHN WILLIAM KAYE.
Races and Tribes of Hindostan, A series of Photographic Illustrations of; prepared under the Authority of the Government of India; containing about 450 Photographs on mounts, in Eight Volumes, super royal 4to. £2 5s. per volume.

WATSON, MARGARET.
Money. Translated from the French of Jules Tardieu. Cr. 8vo. 7s. 6d.

WEBB, Dr. ALLAN, B.M.S.
Pathologia Indica. Based upon Morbid Specimens from all parts of the Indian Empire. Second Edition. Demy 8vo. 14s.

Wellesley's Despatches. The Despatches, Minutes, and Correspondence of the Marquis Wellesley, K.G., during his Administration in India. 5 vols. With Portrait, Map, &c. Demy 8vo. £6 10s.

Wellington in India. Military History of the Duke of Wellington in India. Cr. 8vo. 1s.

WHINYATES, *Col. F. A., late R.H.A., formerly commanding the Battery.*
From Coruna to Sevastopol. The History of "C" Battery, "A" Brigade, late "C" Troop, Royal Horse Artillery. With succession of officers from its formation to the present time. With 3 maps. Demy 8vo. 14s.

WHITE, *Col. S. DEWÉ, late Beng. Staff Corps.*
Indian Reminiscences. With 10 Photographs. Demy 8vo. 14s.

WILBERFORCE, *SAMUEL, D.D., Bishop of Winchester.*
Heroes of Hebrew History. New Edition. Cr. 8vo. 5s.

WILBERFORCE, *E.*
Franz Schubert. A Musical Biography. Translated from the German of Dr. Heinrich Kreisle von Heilborn. Cr. 8vo. 6s.

WILKIN, *Mrs. (Māră).*
The Shackles of an Old Love. Cr. 8vo. 7s. 6d.

WILKINS, *WILLIAM NOY.*
Visual Art; or Nature through the Healthy Eye. With some remarks on Originality and Free Trade, Artistic Copyright, and Durability. Demy 8vo. 6s.

WILLIAMS, *FOLKESTONE.*
Lives of the English Cardinals, from Nicholas Breakspeare, (Pope Adrien IV,) to Thomas Wolsey, Cardinal Legate. With Historical Notices of the Papal Court. 2 vols. Demy 8vo. 14s.

Life, &c. of Bishop Atterbury. The Memoir and Correspondence of Francis Atterbury, Bishop of Rochester, with his distinguished contemporaries. Compiled chiefly from the Atterbury and Stuart Papers. 2 vols. Demy 8vo. 14s.

WILLIAMS, *S. WELLS, LL.D. Professor of the Chinese Language and Literature at Yale College.*
The Middle Kingdom. A Survey of the Geography, Government, Literature, Social Life, Arts, and History of the Chinese Empire and Its Inhabitants. Revised Edition, with 74 Illustrations and a New Map of the Empire. 2 vols. Demy 8vo. 42s.

WILSON, *H. H.*
Glossary of Judicial and Revenue Terms, and of useful Words occurring in Official Documents relating to the Administration of the Government of British India. From the Arabic, Persian, Hindustani, Sanskrit, Hindi, Bengali, Uriya, Marathi, Guzarathi, Telugu, Karnata, Tamil, Malayalam, and other Languages. Compiled and published under the authority of the Hon. the Court of Directors of the E. I. Company. Demy 4to. £1 10s.

WOOD, *Rev. J. G., M.A., F.L.S., &c.*
Man and Beast, Here and Hereafter. Illustrated by more than 300 original Anecdotes. Fourth Edition. Post 8vo. 6s. 6d.

13 WATERLOO PLACE, PALL MALL.   35

WOLLASTON, ARTHUR N.
  Anwari Suhaili, or Lights of Canopus. Commonly known as Kalilah and Damnah, being an adaptation of the Fables of Bidpai. Translated from the Persian. Royal 8vo., 42s.; also with illuminated borders, designed specially for the work, cloth, extra gilt. Roy. 4to. £3 13s. 6d.

WOOLRYCH, HUMPHREY W., Serjeant-at-Law.
  Lives of Eminent Serjeants-at-Law of the English Bar. 2 vols. Demy 8vo. 30s.

WORDSWORTH, W.
  Poems for the Young. With 50 Illustrations by John Macwhirter and John Pettie, and a Vignette by J. E. Millais, R.A. Demy 16mo. 1s. 6d.

WRAXALL, Sir LASCELLES, Bart.
  Caroline Matilda, Queen of Denmark, Sister of George 3rd; from Family and State Papers. 3 vols. Demy 8vo. 18s.

WYNTER, ANDREW, M.D., M.R.C.P.
  Subtle Brains and Lissom Fingers: Being some of the Chisel Marks of our Industrial and Scientific Progress. Third Edition, revised and corrected by Andrew Steinmetz. Fcap. 8vo. 3s. 6d.
  Our Social Bees: Pictures of Town and Country Life. New Edition. Cr. 8vo. 5s.
  Curiosities of Civilization. Being Essays reprinted from the *Quarterly* and *Edinburgh Reviews.* Cr. 8vo. 6s.

YOUNG, Prof. J. R.
  Course of Mathematics. A Course of Elementary Mathematics for the use of candidates for admission into either of the Military Colleges; of applicants for appointments in the Home or Indian Civil Services; and of mathematical students generally. In one closely-printed volume. pp. 648. Demy 8vo. 12s.

YOUNG, MINNIE, and TRENT, RACHEL.
  A Home Ruler. A Story for Girls. Illustrated by C. P. Colnaghi. Cr. 8vo. 3s. 6d.

ZERFFI, G. G., Ph.D., F.R.S.L.
  Manual of the Historical Development of Art—Prehistoric, Ancient, Hebrew, Classic, Early Christian. With special reference to Architecture, Sculpture, Painting, and Ornamentation. Cr. 8vo. 6s.

A Selection from Messrs. ALLEN'S Catalogue of Books in the Eastern Languages, &c.

HINDUSTANI, HINDI, &c.

Dr. Forbes's Works are used as Class Books in the Colleges and Schools in India.

ABDOOLAH, SYED.
Singhasan Battisi. Translated into Hindi from the Sanscrit. A New Edition. Revised, Corrected, and Accompanied with Copius Notes. Roy. 8vo. 12s. 6d.
Akhlaki Hindi, translated into Urdu, with an Introduction and Notes. Roy. 8vo. 12s. 6d.

BALLANTYNE, JAMES R.
Hindustani Selections, with a Vocabulary of the Words. Second Edition. 1845. 5s.
Principles of Persian Caligraphy. Illustrated by Lithographic Plates of the Ta"lik Character, the one usually employed in writing the Persian and the Hindustani. Prepared for the use of the Scottish Naval and Military Academy. Second Edition. 4to. 3s. 6d.

EASTWICK, EDWARD B.
The Bagh-o-Bahar—literally translated into English, with copious explanatory notes. 8vo. 10s. 6d.
Hindostani Grammar. Post 8vo. 5s.
Prem Sagar. Demy 4to. £2 2s.

FORBES, DUNCAN, LL.D.
Hindustani-English Dictionary, in the Persian Character, with the Hindi words in Nagari also; and an English-Hindustani Dictionary in the English Character; both in one volume. Roy. 8vo. 42s.
Hindustani-English and English-Hindustani Dictionary, in the English Character. Roy. 8vo. 36s.
Smaller Dictionary, Hindustani and English, in the English Character. 12s.
Hindustani Grammar, with Specimens of Writing in the Persian and Nagari Characters, Reading Lessons, and Vocabulary. 8vo. 10s. 6d.
Hindustani Manual, containing a Compendious Grammar, Exercises for Translation, Dialogues, and Vocabulary, in the Roman Character. New Edition, entirely revised. By J. T. Platts. 18mo. 3s. 6d.
Bagh o Bahar, in the Persian Character, with a complete Vocabulary. Roy. 8vo. 12s. 6d.
Bagh o Bahar, in English, with Explanatory Notes, illustrative of Eastern Character. 8vo. 8s.
Bagh o Bahar, with Vocabulary. English Character. 5s.

Forbes, Duncan, LL.D.—*cont.*
Tota Kahani; or, "Tales of a Parrot," in the Persian Character, with a complete Vocabulary. Roy. 8vo. 8s.
Baital Pachisi; or, Twenty-five Tales of a Demon," in the Nagari Character, with a complete Vocabulary. Roy. 8vo. 9s.
Ikhwanu-s-Safa; or, "Brothers of Purity," in the Persian Character. Roy. 8vo. 12s. 6d.
[*For the higher standard for military officers' examinations.*]
Oriental Penmanship; a Guide to Writing Hindustani in the Persian Character. 4to. 8s.

MULVIHILL, P.
A Vocabulary for the Lower Standard in Hindustani. Containing the meanings of every word and idiomatic expression in "Jarrett's Hindu Period," and in "Selections from the Bagh o Bahar." 2s. 6d.

PINCOTT, FREDERIC, M.R.A.S., &c. &c.
Sakuntala in Hindi. Translated from the Bengali recension of the Sanscrit. Critically edited, with grammatical, idiomatical, and exegetical notes. 4to. 12s. 6d.
Alif Laila, ba-Zuban-i-Urdu (The Arabian Nights in Hindustani). Roman Character. 10s. 6d.
Hindi Manual. 6s.

PLATTS, J. T.
Hindustani Dictionary. Dictionary of Urdû and Classical Hindî. Super Roy. 8vo. £3 3s.
Grammar of the Urdu or Hindustani Language. 8vo. 12s.
Baital Pachisi; translated into English. 8vo. 8s.
Ikhwanu S Safa; translated into English. 8vo. 10s. 6d.

SMALL, Rev. G.
Tota Kahani; or, "Tales of a Parrot." Translated into English. 8vo. 8s.
Dictionary of Naval Terms, English and Hindustani. For the use of Nautical Men Trading to India, &c. Fcap. 2s. 6d.

SANSCRIT.
COWELL, E. B.
Translation of the Vikramorvasi. 8vo. 3s. 6d.

GOUGH, A. E.
Key to the Exercises in Williams's Sanscrit Manual. 18mo. 4s.

HAUGHTON, —.
Sanscrit and Bengali Dictionary, in the Bengali Character, with Index, serving as a reversed dictionary. 4to. 30s.
Menu, with English Translation. 2 vols. 4to. 24s.
Hitopadesa, with Bengali and English Translations. 10s. 6d.

JOHNSON, Prof. F.
Hitopadesa, with Vocabulary. 15s.

PINCOTT, FREDERIC, M.R.A.S., Corresponding Member of the Anjuman-i-Panjab.
Hitopadesa. A new literal Translation from the Sanskrit Text of Prof. F. Johnson. For the use of Students. 6s.

THOMPSON, J. C.
Bhagavat Gita. Sanscrit Text. 5s.

WILLIAMS, —.
English-Sanscrit Dictionary. 4to., cloth. £3 3s.
Sanscrit-English Dictionary. 4to. £4 14s. 6d.

WILLIAMS, MONIER.
Sanscrit Grammar. 8vo. 15s.
Sanscrit Manual; to which is added, a Vocabulary, by A. E. Gough. 18mo. 7s. 6d.
Sakuntala, with Literal English Translation of all the Metrical Passages, Schemes of the Metres, and copious Critical and Explanatory Notes. Roy. 8vo. 21s.
Sakuntala. Translated into English Prose and Verse. Fourth Edition. 8s.
Vikramorvasi. The Text. 8vo. 5s.

WILKIN, Sir CHARLES.
Sanscrit Grammar. 4to. 15s.

WILSON —.
Megha Duta, with Translation into English Verse, Notes, Illustrations, and a Vocabulary. Roy. 8vo. 6s.

PERSIAN.

BARETTO, —.
Persian Dictionary. 2 vols. 4to. Also in 2 vols. 8vo.

CLARKE, Captain H. WILBERFORCE, R.E.
The Persian Manual. A Pocket Companion.
Part I.—A Concise Grammar of the Language, with Exercises on its more Prominent Peculiarities, together with a Selection of Useful Phrases, Dialogues, and Subjects for Translation into Persian.
Part II.—A Vocabulary of Useful Words, English, and Persian, showing at the same time the Difference of idiom between the two Languages. 18mo. 7s. 6d.
The Bustan. By Shaikh Muslihu-d-Dín Sa'di Shírází. Translated for the first time into Prose, with Explanatory Notes and Index. With Portrait. 8vo. 30s.
The Sikandar Nama,e Bara, or, Book of Alexander the Great. Written, A.D. 1200, by Abu Muhammad Bin Yusuf Bin Mu'ayyid-i-Nizámu-d-Dín. Translated for the first time out of the Persian into Prose, with Critical and Explanatory Remarks, and an Introductory Preface, and a Life of the Author, collected from various Persian sources. Roy. 8vo. 42s.

FORBES, DUNCAN, LL.D.
Persian Grammar, Reading Lessons, and Vocabulary. Roy. 8vo. 12s. 6d.

IBRAHEEM, —.
Persian Grammar, Dialogues, &c. Roy. 8vo. 12s. 6d.

KEENE, Rev. H. G.
First Book of The Anwari Soheili. Persian Text. 8vo. 5s.
Akhlaki Mushini. Translated into English. 8vo. 3s. 6d.

OUSELEY, Col.
Anwari Soheili. 4to. 42s.
Akhlaki Mushini. Persian Text. 8vo. 5s.

PLATTS, J. T.
Gulistan. Carefully collated with the original MS., with a full Vocabulary. Roy. 8vo. 12s. 6d.
Gulistan. Translated from a revised Text, with copious Notes. 8vo. 12s. 6d.

RICHARDSON —.
Persian, Arabic, and English Dictionary. Edition of 1852. By F. Johnson. 4to. £4.

TOLBORT, T. W. H., Bengal Civil Service.
A Translation of Robinson Crusoe into the Persian Language. Roman Character. Cr. 8vo. 7s.

WOLLASTON, ARTHUR N.
Translation of the Anvari Soheili. Roy. 8vo. £2 2s.
English-Persian Dictionary. Compiled from Original Sources. 8vo. 25s.

BENGALI.

BATRI, —.
Singhasan. Demy 8vo. 5s.

FORBES, DUNCAN, LL.D.
Bengali Grammar, with Phrases and Dialogues. Roy. 8vo. 12s. 6d.
Bengali Reader, with a Translation and Vocabulary. Roy. 8vo. 12s. 6d.

HAUGHTON, —.
Bengali, Sanscrit, and English Dictionary, adapted for Students in either language; to which is added an Index, serving as a reversed dictionary. 4to. 30s.

Nabo Nari. 12mo. 7s.
Tota Itahas. Demy 8vo. 5s.

ARABIC.

FORBES, DUNCAN, LL.D.
Arabic Grammar, intended more especially for the use of young men preparing for the East India Civil Service, and also for the use of self-instructing students in general. Royal 8vo., cloth. 18s.
Arabic Reading Lessons, consisting of Easy Extracts from the best Authors, with Vocabulary. Roy. 8vo., cloth. 15s.

KAYAT, ASSAAD YAKOOB.
The Eastern Traveller's Interpreter; or, Arabic Without a Teacher. Oblong. 2s. 6d.

PALMER, Prof. E. H., M.A., &c.
Arabic Grammar. 8vo. 18s.
The Arabic Manual. Comprising a condensed Grammar of both Classical and Modern Arabic; Reading Lessons and Exercises, with Analyses and a Vocabulary of useful Words. Fcap. 7s. 6d.

RICHARDSON, —.
Arabic, Persian, and English Dictionary. Edition of 1852. By F. Johnson. 4to., cloth. £4.

STEINGASS, Dr. F.
Students' Arabic-English Dictionary. Demy 8vo. 50s.
English-Arabic Dictionary. Demy 8vo. 28s.

TELOOGOO.

BROWN, —.
Dictionary, reversed; with a Dictionary of the Mixed Dialects used in Teloogoo. 3 vols. in 2. Roy. 8vo. £5.
Reader. 8vo. 2 vols. 14s.
Dialogues, Teloogoo and English. 8vo. 5s. 6d.

CAMPBELL, —.
Dictionary. Roy. 8vo. 30s
Pancha Tantra. 8s.

PERCIVAL, —.
English-Teloogoo Dictionary. 10s. 6d.

TAMIL.

BABINGTON, —
Grammar (High Dialect). 4to. 12s.
Gooroo Paramatan. Demy 4to. 8s.

PERCIVAL, —.
Tamil Dictionary. 2 vols. 10s. 6d.

POPE, Rev. G. U.
Tamil Handbook. In 3 Parts. 12s. 6d. each.

ROTTLER, —.
Dictionary, Tamil and English. 4to. 42s.

GUZRATTEE.

MAVOR, —.
Spelling, Guzrattee and English. 7s. 6d.

SHAPUAJI EDALJI.
Dictionary, Guzrattee and English. 21s.

MAHRATTA.

BALLANTYNE, JAMES R., of the Scottish Naval and Military Academy.
A Grammar of the Mahratta Language. For the use of the East India College at Hayleybury. 4to. 5s.

Æsop's Fables. 12mo. 2s. 6d.

MOLESWORTH, —.
Dictionary, Mahratta and English. 4to. 42s.
Dictionary, English and Mahratta. 4to. 42s.

MALAY.

BIKKERS, Dr. A. J. W.
Malay, Achinese, French, and English Vocabulary. Alphabetically arranged under each of the four languages. With a concise Malay Grammar. Post 8vo. 7s. 6d.

MARSDEN, —.
Grammar. 4to. £1 1s.

13 WATERLOO PLACE, PALL MALL. 41

CHINESE.
MARSHMAN, —.
Clavis Sinica. A Chinese Grammar. 4to. £2 2s.
MORRISON, —.
Dictionary. 6 vols., 4to.
View of China, for Philological Purposes. Containing a Sketch of Chinese Chronology, Geography, Government, Religion, and Customs, designed for those who study the Chinese language. 4to. 6s.

PUSHTO.
RAVERTY, Major H. G., Bombay Infantry (Retired), Author of the Pus'hto Grammar, Dictionary, Selections Prose and Poetical, Selections from the Poetry of the Afgháns (English Translation), Æsop's Fables, &c. &c.
The Pus'hto Manual. Comprising a Concise Grammar; Exercises and Dialogues; Familiar Phrases, Proverbs, and Vocabulary. Fcap. 5s.

MISCELLANEOUS.
COLLETT, —.
Malayalam Reader. 8vo. 12s. 6d.
Æsop's Fables in Carnatica. 8vo., bound. 12s. 6d.
MACKENZIE, Captain C. F., late of H.M.'s Consular Service.
A Turkish Manual. Comprising a Condensed Grammar with Idiomatic Phrases, Exercises and Dialogues, and Vocabulary. 6s.
REEVE, —.
English-Carnatica and Carnatica-English Dictionary. 2 vols. (Very slightly damaged.) £8.

W. H. ALLEN & Co.'s Oriental Manuals.

CLARKE, Captain H. W., R.E.
The Persian Manual. Containing a Concise Grammar, with Exercises, Useful Phrases, Dialogues, and Subjects for Translation into Persian; also a Vocabulary of Useful Words, English and Persian. 18mo. 7s. 6d.

GOUGH, A. E.
Key to the Exercises in Williams's Sanscrit Manual. 18mo. 4s.

MACKENZIE, Captain C. F.
A Turkish Manual. Comprising a Condensed Grammar with Idiomatic Phrases, Exercises and Dialogues, and Vocabulary. 6s.

PALMER, Professor E. H., M.A., &c., Author of "A Grammar of the Arabic Language."
The Arabic Manual. Comprising a Condensed Grammar of both Classical and Modern Arabic; Reading Lessons and Exercises, with Analyses and a Vocabulary of Useful Words. Fcap. 7s. 6d.

PINCOTT, FREDERIC, M.R.A.S., Corresponding Member of the Anjuman-i-Panjab, Editor and Annotator of the "S'akuntalá in Hindí," Editor of the Urdú "Alif Lailá," and Translator of the Sanskrit "Hitopadeś'a."
The Hindi Manual. Comprising a Grammar of the Hindi Language both Literary and Provincial; a Complete Syntax; Exercises in various styles of Hindi Composition; Dialogues on several subjects; and a Complete Vocabulary.

PLATTS, J. T.
Forbes's Hindustani Manual, Containing a Compendious Grammar, Exercises for Translation, Dialogues, and Vocabulary, in the Roman Character. New Edition, entirely revised. 18mo. 3s. 6d.

RAVERTY, Major H. G.
The Pushto Manual. Comprising a Concise Grammar Exercises and Dialogues; Familiar Phrases, Proverbs, and Vocabulary. Fcap. 5s.

SCHNURMANN, J. NESTOR.
The Russian Manual. Comprising a Condensed Grammar, Exercises with Analyses, Useful Dialogues, Reading Lessons, Tables of Coins, Weights and Measures, and a Collection of Idioms and Proverbs, alphabetically arranged.

TIEN, Rev. ANTON, Ph.D., M.R.A.S.
Egyptian, Syrian, and North-African Handbook. A Simple Phrase-Book in English and Arabic for the use of the British Forces, Civilians, and Residents in Egypt. Fcap. 4s.

WILLIAMS, MONIER.
Sanscrit Manual. To which is added a Vocabulary, by A. E. Gough. 18mo. 7s. 6d.

Oriental Works in the Press.

PINCOTT, FREDERIC, M.R.A.S.
An English-Hindi Dictionary.

Maps of India, &c.

Messrs. Allen & Co.'s Maps of India were revised and much improved during 1876, with especial reference to the existing Administrative Divisions, Railways, &c.

A General Map of India. Corrected to 1876. Compiled chiefly from Surveys executed by order of the Gevernment of India. On six sheets —size, 5ft. 3in. wide, 5ft. 4in. high, £2; or on loth, in case, £2 12s. 6d.; or rollers, varnished, £3 3s.

BRION, HENRY F.
A Relievo Map of India. In frame. 21s.

District Map of India. Corrected to 1876. Divided into Collectorates with the Telegraphs and Railways from Government Surveys. On six sheets—size, 5ft. 6in. high, 5ft. 8in. wide, £2; in a case, £2 12s. 6d.; or rollers, varnished, £3 3s.

Handbook of Reference to the Maps of India. Giving the Latitude and Longitude of places of note. 18mo. 3s. 6d.

Map of India. Corrected to 1876. From the most recent authorities. On two sheets—size, 2ft. 10in. wide, 3ft. 3in. high, 16s.; or on cloth, in a case, £1 1s.

Map of the Routes in India. Corrected to 1874. With Tables of Distances between the principal Towns and Military Stations. On one sheet—size, 2ft. 3in. wide, 2ft. 9in. high, 9s.; or on cloth, in a case, 12s.

Map of the Western Provinces of Hindoostan—the Punjab, Cabool, Scinde, Bhawulpore, &c.—including all the States between Candahar and Allahabad. On four sheets—size, 4ft. 4in. wide, 4ft. 2in. high, 30s.; or in case, £2; rollers, varnished, £2 10s.

Map of India and China, Burmah, Siam, the Malay Peninsula, and the Empire of Anam. On two sheets—size, 4ft. 3in. wide, 3ft. 4in. high, 16s.; or on cloth, in a case, £1 5s.

Map of the Steam Communication and Overland Routes between England, India, China, and Australia. In a case, 14s. on rollers, and varnished, 18s.

Map of China. From the most authentic sources of information. One large sheet—size, 2ft. 7in. wide, 2ft. 2in. high, 6s.; or on cloth, in case, 8s.

Map of the World. On Mercator's Projection, showing the Tracts of the Early Navigators, the Currents of the Ocean, the Principal Lines of great Circle Sailing, and the most recent discoveries. On four sheets— size, 6ft. 2in. wide, 4ft. 3in. high, £2; on cloth, in a case, £2 10s.; or with rollers, and varnished, £3.

Russian Official Map of Central Asia. Compiled in Accordance with the Discoveries and Surveys of Russian Staff Officers up to the close of the year 1877. In two sheets. 10s. 6d.; or in cloth case, 14s.

Works in the Press.

The Amphibion's Voyage.
By Parker Gillmore.

Where Chinesee Drive; or, English Student-Life at Peking.
By a Student Interpreter.

Men of Character.
By the late Douglas Jerrold. With 12 Original Illustrations by W. M. Thackeray. Edited by the late Blanchard Jerrold.

The Orders of Chivalry.
By Major Lawrence Archer. With an Illustration of Every Order. 4to.

Sporting Life in India.
By Colonel Heber Drury.

A Queen by Right Divine.
By Kathleen O'Meara.

A History of the Press.
By the late Blanchard Jerrold.

A Fly on the Wheel; or, How I helped to govern India.
By Colonel Lewin.

A History of Hindustan.
By H. G. Keene.

Soldiers' Tales.
By J. Menzies.

Linnæus, the Floral King.
Street Idylls.
Anomalous Tales.
By Albert Alberg.

The Victorian Era.
By Edward Walford, M.A.

Essays.
By W. Stigand.

A History of Gujerat.
By the late Professor Dowson.

Harrow School and its Surroundings. Compiled from the School Archives and other sources. By Percy M. Thornton. With Illustrations.

Poems.
By H. G. Keene.

A Dictionary of Mahommedanism
By the Rev. T. P. Hughes.

Persian Caligraphy.
By the late Professor Palmer.

Reiza, Queen of Delhi.
By Pierce Taylor.

NEW ORIENTAL WORKS.

A Dictionary of Urdu, Classical Hindi, and English. By JOHN T. PLATTS, M.A., Persian Teacher at the University of Oxford, late Inspector of Schools, Central Provinces, India. Imperial 8vo. 1,260 pp. £3 3s.

The Student's Arabic-English Dictionary. Companion Volume to the Author's English-Arabic Dictionary. By F. STEINGASS, Ph.D., of the University of Munich, &c. Royal 8vo. 1,242 pp. £2 10s.

English-Arabic Dictionary. For the Use of both Travellers and Students. By F. STEINGASS, Ph.D., of the University of Munich. Royal 8vo. 466 pp. 28s.

An English-Persian Dictionary. Compiled from Original Sources. By ARTHUR N. WOLLASTON, H.M.'s Indian (Home) Service, Translator of the " Anvar-i-Suhaili," &c. Demy 8vo. 462 pp. 25s.

A Tamil Handbook; or, Full Introduction to the Common Dialect of that Language, on the Plan of Ollendorf and Arnold. By the Rev. G. A. POPE, D.D. In Three Parts, 12s. 6d. each. Part I. Introduction—Grammatical Lessons—General Index. Part II. Appendices—Notes on the Study of the " Kurral "—Key to the Exercises. Part III. Dictionaries: I. Tamil-English—II. English-Tamil.

London :—
W. H. Allen & Co., 13 Waterloo Place. S.W.

In January and July of each year is published in 8vo., price 10s. 6d.,

THE INDIA LIST, CIVIL AND MILITARY.
BY PERMISSION OF THE SECRETARY OF STATE FOR INDIA IN COUNCIL

CONTENTS.

CIVIL.—Gradation Lists of Civil Service, Bengal, Madras, and Bombay. Civil Annuitants. Legislative Council, Ecclesiastical Establishments, Educational, Public Works, Judicial, Marine, Medical, Land Revenue, Political, Postal, Police, Customs and Salt, Forest, Registration and Railway and Telegraph Departments, Law Courts, Surveys, &c. &c.

MILITARY.—Gradation List of the General and Field Officers (British and Local) of the three Presidencies, Staff Corps, Adjutants-General's and Quartermasters-General's Offices, Army Commissariat Departments, British Troops serving in India (including Royal Artillery, Royal Engineers, Cavalry, Infantry, and Medical Department), List of Native Regiments, Commander-in-Chief and Staff, Garrison Instruction Staff, Indian Medical Department, Ordnance Departments, Punjab Frontier Force, Military Departments of the three Presidencies, Veterinary Departments, Tables showing the Distribution of the Army in India, Lists of Retired Officers of the three Presidencies.

HOME.—Departments of the Officer of the Secretary of State, Coopers Hill College, List of Selected Candidates for the Civil and Forest Services, Indian Troop Service.

MISCELLANEOUS.—Orders of the Bath, Star of India, and St. Michael and St. George. Order of Precedence in India. Regulations for Admission to Civil Service. Regulations for Admission of Chaplains. Civil Leave Code and Supplements. Civil Service Pension Code—relating to the Covenanted and Uncovenanted Services. Rules for the Indian Medical Service. Furlough and Retirement Regulations of the Indian Army. Family Pension Fund. Staff Corps Regulations. Salaries of Staff Officers. Regulations for Promotion. English Furlough Pay.

THE
ROYAL KALENDAR,
AND COURT AND CITY REGISTER,
FOR ENGLAND, IRELAND, SCOTLAND, AND THE COLONIES,

For the Year 1885.

CONTAINING A CORRECT LIST OF THE TWENTY-FIRST IMPERIAL PARLIAMENT, SUMMONED TO MEET FOR THEIR FIRST SESSION—MARCH 5TH, 1874.

House of Peers—House of Commons—Sovereigns and Rulers of States of Europe—Orders of Knighthood—Science and Art Department—Queen's Household—Government Offices—Mint—Customs—Inland Revenue—Post Office—Foreign Ministers and Consuls—Queen's Consuls Abroad - Naval Department—Navy List—Army Department—Army List—Law Courts—Police—Ecclesiastical Department—Clergy List—Foundation Schools—Literary Institutions—City of London—Banks—Railway Companies—Hospitals and Institutions—Charities—Miscellaneous Institutions—Scotland, Ireland, India, and the Colonies; and other useful information

Price with Index, 7s.; without Index, 5s.

Published on the arrival of each overland Mail from India. Subscription
26s. *per annum. Specimen copy,* 6d.

ALLEN'S INDIAN MAIL,
AND
Official Gazette
FROM
INDIA CHINA, AND ALL PARTS OF THE EAST.

ALLEN'S INDIAN MAIL contains the fullest and most authentic Reports of all important Occurrences in the Countries to which it is devoted, compiled chiefly from private and exclusive sources. It has been pronounced by the Press in general to be *indispensable* to all who have Friends or Relatives in the East, as affording the only *correct* information regarding the Services, Movements of Troops, Shipping, and all events of Domestic and individual interest.

The subjoined list of the usual Contents will show the importance and variety of the information concentrated in ALLEN'S INDIAN MAIL.

Summary and Review of Eastern News.

Precis of Public Intelligence	Shipping—Arrival of Ships
Selections from the Indian Press	,, ,, Passengers
Movements of Troops	,, Departure of Ships
The Government Gazette	,, ,, Passengers
Courts Martial	Commercial—State of the Markets
Domestic Intelligence—Births	,, Indian Securities
,, ,, Marriages	,, Freights
,, ,, Deaths	&c. &c. &c.

Home Intelligence relating to India, &c.

Original Articles	Arrivals reported in England
Miscellaneous Information	Departures ,, ,,
Appointments, Extensions of Furloughs, &c., &c.	Shipping—Arrival of Ships
,, Civil	,, ,, Passengers
,, Military	, Departure of Ships
,, Ecclesiastical and	,, ,, Passengers
,, Marine	,, Vessel spoken with
	&c. &c. &c.

Review of Works on the East, and Notices of all affairs connected with India and the Services.

Throughout the Paper one uniform system of arrangement prevails, and at the conclusion of each year an INDEX is furnished, to enable Subscribers to bind up the Volume, which forms a complete

ASIATIC ANNUAL REGISTER AND LIBRARY OF REFERENCE.

LONDON: W. H. ALLEN & Co., 13, WATERLOO PLACE, S.W
(PUBLISHERS TO THE INDIA OFFICE),
To whom Communications for the Editor, and Advertisements, are requested to be addressed.

EMINENT WOMEN SERIES.

Edited by JOHN H. INGRAM.

Crown 8vo. 3s. 6d. each. Already issued:—

George Eliot. By MATHILDE BLIND.

George Sand. By BERTHA THOMAS.

Maria Edgeworth. By HELEN ZIMMERN.

Emily Brontë. By A. MARY F. ROBINSON.

Mary Lamb. By ANNE GILCHRIST.

Margaret Fuller. By JULIA WARD HOWE.

Elizabeth Fry. By MRS. E. R. PITMAN.

Countess of Albany. By VERNON LEE.

Harriet Martineau. By MRS. FENWICK MILLER.

Volumes in Preparation:—

Madame Roland. By MATHILDE BLIND.

Susanna Wesley. By ELIZA CLARKE.

Madame de Stael. By BELLA DUFFY.

Margaret of Navarre. By MARY A. ROBINSON.

Vittoria Colonna. By MISS A. KENNARD.

London: **W. H. ALLEN & CO.**, 13 Waterloo Place. S.W.

www.ingramcontent.com/pod-product-compliance
Lightning Source LLC
Chambersburg PA
CBHW020318240426

43673CB00039B/846